Drupal 7 Theming Cookbook

Over 95 recipes that cover all aspects of customizing and developing unique Drupal themes

Karthik Kumar

[PACKT] open source *
PUBLISHING   community experience distilled

BIRMINGHAM - MUMBAI

Drupal 7 Theming Cookbook

First Edition: November 2010

Second Edition: January 2012

Production Reference: 1100112

Published by Packt Publishing Ltd.
Livery Place
35 Livery Street
Birmingham B3 2PB, UK.

ISBN 978-1-84951-676-1

www.packtpub.com

Cover Image by Karthik Kumar

Credits

Author

Karthik Kumar

Reviewers

Kevin Davison

Richard Eriksson

Acquisition Editor

Sarah Cullington

Lead Technical Editor

Hyacintha D'Souza

Technical Editors

Joyslita D'Souza

Apoorva Bolar

Arun Nadar

Ajay Shanker

Project Coordinator

Alka Nayak

Proofreader

Julie Jackson

Indexers

Monica Ajmera Mehta

Tejal Daruwale

Rekha Nair

Graphics

Conidon Miranda

Production Coordinator

Nilesh R. Mohite

Cover Work

Nilesh R. Mohite

About the Author

Karthik Kumar is a Drupal developer residing in Chennai, India. He first came across Drupal in late 2004 and has been a fan ever since. He maintains a number of modules on `http://drupal.org` under the moniker Zen, `http://drupal.org/user/21209`, and has also made substantial contributions towards the development of Drupal core.

To my reviewers, Kevin Davison and Richard Eriksson, for their careful scrutiny. To all the people at Packt involved in the making of this book—Sarah Cullington, Hyacintha D'Souza, Joyslita D'Souza, and Alka Nayak—for their guidance and patience. To Dries and the Drupal developer community for making Drupal what it is today.

Finally, this book is dedicated to my parents for all the freedom that they have given me.

About the Reviewers

Kevin Davison is a Manager, Web Generalist, Drupaler at Quevin, LLC in San Francisco, CA. Experience with Drupal began as an experiment on `Quevin.com`, and it has evolved to become his passion. You can find Kevin actively involved at many DrupalCon's, Camps, SFDUG, Drupal.org support, @Quevin, and with the Drupal community on IRC (Quevin).

Quevin (kweh-vin)—the business—stands for its effective methods of planning, designing, and developing exceptional Drupal-based websites. Quevin is a full-service web production team, with a single managing director who is available to speak with you directly.

He was the Technical Reviewer for the last version of this book, *Drupal 6 Theming Cookbook*.

> Thanks to the Drupal community for making all of this possible and to Dries for having the vision. Packt Publishing has made this a great learning opportunity.

Richard Eriksson has been a member of the Drupal community since 2004 (visit his profile at `http://drupal.org/user/8791`). He has worked on the Community Support and Systems Administration team at Bryght, the first commercial Drupal venture (later purchased by Raincity Studios), and later at OpenRoadCommunications, where he helped build video-intensive multilingual Drupal websites promoting video games. He also maintains an independent consultancy called Ethical Detergent specializing in Drupal maintenance and support. On `Drupal.org`, he maintains the Pirate and RSS Permissions modules, the Cherry Blossom Theme, and most recently, the Readability Button module. He writes occasionally on his blog, Just a Gwai Lo (`http://justagwailo.com/`).

www.PacktPub.com

Support files, eBooks, discount offers and more

You might want to visit www.PacktPub.com for support files and downloads related to your book.

Did you know that Packt offers eBook versions of every book published, with PDF and ePub files available? You can upgrade to the eBook version at www.PacktPub.com and as a print book customer, you are entitled to a discount on the eBook copy. Get in touch with us at service@packtpub.com for more details.

At www.PacktPub.com, you can also read a collection of free technical articles, sign up for a range of free newsletters and receive exclusive discounts and offers on Packt books and eBooks.

http://PacktLib.PacktPub.com

Do you need instant solutions to your IT questions? PacktLib is Packt's online digital book library. Here, you can access, read and search across Packt's entire library of books.

Why Subscribe?

- ▶ Fully searchable across every book published by Packt
- ▶ Copy and paste, print and bookmark content
- ▶ On demand and accessible via web browser

Free Access for Packt account holders

If you have an account with Packt at www.PacktPub.com, you can use this to access PacktLib today and view nine entirely free books. Simply use your login credentials for immediate access.

Table of Contents

Preface

Themes are among the most powerful and flexible features available when it comes to the presentation of a website. The greatest strength of Drupal lies in its design, which, when done correctly, allows developers and designers to customize and micromanage each and every aspect of the site. Furthermore, the Drupal theming system and its APIs allow for the design of custom themes that are easy to administer and maintain.

This book provides a plethora of solutions that enable Drupal theme designers to make full use of all its features and its inherent extensibility to style their sites just the way they want to. It covers numerous aspects from using contributed and custom themes to leveraging the powerful Fields API introduced in Drupal 7 along with the Views and Panels modules to create rich designs and layouts that are easy to administer and maintain.

Structured as a collection of recipes to perform a wide variety of practical tasks, this book will systematically guide readers towards solutions that are central to Drupal theming. Each recipe is divided into the following sections:

- An Introduction that explains what the recipe is about
- Getting ready lists any prerequisite steps required for the recipe to work
- How to do it describes how to implement the recipe
- How it works explains how the recipe works
- There's more catalogs useful information related to the recipe

While it is recommended that readers follow the recipes in each chapter in sequence, it is also possible to sift through the recipes at random. Special attention should always be paid to the *Getting ready* section of each recipe, which provides information on preliminary steps that need to be performed, and in some cases, specify if the recipe builds on the result of earlier recipes in the same chapter.

What this book covers

Chapter 1, Drupal Theme Basics, introduces the reader to the basic elements of Drupal theming, such as downloading and installing a contributed theme, and learning how to add and customize blocks.

Chapter 2, Beyond the Basics, explains the concept of theme engines and subthemes and briefly introduces the topic of template overrides. It also includes essential recipes dealing with adding and optimizing CSS files.

Chapter 3, Custom Themes and Zen, focuses on starter themes, specifically Zen.

Chapter 4, Templating Basics, details how to customize page elements and content by overriding template files.

Chapter 5, Development and Debugging Tools, provides essential information on debugging and expediting development through the use of a number of tools.

Chapter 6, Advanced Templating, explores the PHPTemplate theme engine further and delves into using techniques, such as variable manipulation and preprocess hooks to customize various theme elements.

Chapter 7, JavaScript in Themes, covers the use of JavaScript and jQuery in Drupal themes.

Chapter 8, Navigation, contains recipes which focus on theming navigational elements in a Drupal theme, such as menus, breadcrumbs, pagers, and so on.

Chapter 9, Form Design, discusses the Drupal Forms API from a theming point of view.

Chapter 10, Theming Fields, demonstrates how to theme fields and also elaborates on the use of image fields and leveraging the Image API to display and style images to suit the theme.

Chapter 11, Views Theming, focuses on the Views module from a themer's perspective.

Chapter 12, Rapid Layouts with Panel, shows how to create complex layouts using the Panels module and demonstrates its use in conjunction with the Fields API and Views modules.

What you need for this book

A standard Drupal 7 development site is all that is required to run through the recipes in this book. The system requirements for Drupal is available at `http://drupal.org/ requirements`. Since this book deals with theming, it is assumed that this test site is already up and running.

Who this book is for

This book is written for Drupal developers who want to refresh the look and feel of their sites. If you are a Drupal site administrator who is looking to go beyond the basics and customize the presentational aspects of your Drupal site, then this book is for you. It assumes that readers are familiar with rudimentary PHP and acquainted with Drupal installation and general usage. Readers are also expected to have knowledge of CSS and XHTML.

Conventions

In this book, you will find a number of styles of text that distinguish between different kinds of information. Here are some examples of these styles, and an explanation of their meaning.

Code words in text are shown as follows: "The `.info` file can also be used to specify the theming engine being used by the theme."

A block of code is set as follows:

```
<link type="text/css" rel="stylesheet"
  href="http://book.endymion/sites/all/modules/mysite/css/
  mysite-special.css?lly4ld" media="all" />
<style type="text/css" media="all">@import url
  ("http://book.endymion/sites/all/modules/mysite/css/
  mysite.css?lly4ld");</style>
```

When we wish to draw your attention to a particular part of a code block, the relevant lines or items are set in bold:

```
<?php if ($display_submitted): ?>
  <span class="submitted"><?php print $submitted ?></span>
<?php endif; ?>

<div class="clearfix">
  <?php if (!empty($content['links'])): ?>
    <div class="links"><?php print render($content['links']);
      ?></div>
  <?php endif; ?>
```

New terms and **important words** are shown in bold. Words that you see on the screen, in menus or dialog boxes for example, appear in the text like this: "Once satisfied, click on the **Save configuration** button at the bottom of the page to save our changes."

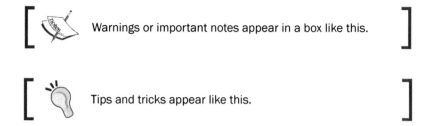

Warnings or important notes appear in a box like this.

Tips and tricks appear like this.

Reader feedback

Feedback from our readers is always welcome. Let us know what you think about this book—what you liked or may have disliked. Reader feedback is important for us to develop titles that you really get the most out of.

To send us general feedback, simply send an e-mail to feedback@packtpub.com, and mention the book title via the subject of your message.

If there is a book that you need and would like to see us publish, please send us a note in the **SUGGEST A TITLE** form on www.packtpub.com or e-mail suggest@packtpub.com.

If there is a topic that you have expertise in and you are interested in either writing or contributing to a book, see our author guide on www.packtpub.com/authors.

Customer support

Now that you are the proud owner of a Packt book, we have a number of things to help you to get the most from your purchase.

Downloading the example code

You can download the example code files for all Packt books you have purchased from your account at http://www.PacktPub.com. If you purchased this book elsewhere, you can visit http://www.PacktPub.com/support and register to have the files e-mailed directly to you.

Errata

Although we have taken every care to ensure the accuracy of our content, mistakes do happen. If you find a mistake in one of our books—maybe a mistake in the text or the code—we would be grateful if you would report this to us. By doing so, you can save other readers from frustration and help us improve subsequent versions of this book. If you find any errata, please report them by visiting http://www.packtpub.com/support, selecting your book, clicking on the **errata submission form** link, and entering the details of your errata. Once your errata are verified, your submission will be accepted and the errata will be uploaded on our website, or added to any list of existing errata, under the Errata section of that title. Any existing errata can be viewed by selecting your title from http://www.packtpub.com/support.

Piracy

Piracy of copyright material on the Internet is an ongoing problem across all media. At Packt, we take the protection of our copyright and licenses very seriously. If you come across any illegal copies of our works, in any form, on the Internet, please provide us with the location address or website name immediately so that we can pursue a remedy.

Please contact us at copyright@packtpub.com with a link to the suspected pirated material.

We appreciate your help in protecting our authors, and our ability to bring you valuable content.

Questions

You can contact us at questions@packtpub.com if you are having a problem with any aspect of the book, and we will do our best to address it.

1
Drupal Theme Basics

We will be covering the following recipes in this chapter:

- ▶ Installing and enabling a theme
- ▶ Uploading a new logo
- ▶ Uploading a new favicon
- ▶ Adding a slogan to the theme
- ▶ Displaying a different theme for administration
- ▶ Adding an existing block to the theme
- ▶ Adding a custom block to the theme
- ▶ Displaying a block only on the front page
- ▶ Controlling block visibility based on user role
- ▶ Controlling block visibility based on node type

Introduction

Drupal is designed to separate logic from presentation with the former usually handled through the use of modules and the latter via themes. Although this separation is not absolute, it is distinct enough to facilitate quick and efficient customization and deployment of websites. This especially holds true when the site is developed in a team environment as it enables developers, designers, and content managers to work independently of each other.

Themes are synonymous with skins in other applications and control the look and feel of a website. Each theme can consist of a variety of files ranging from a .info configuration file, which registers the theme with Drupal, to .tpl.php template files accompanied by CSS, JavaScript, and other files that determine the layout and style of the content. Depending on the nature of the site and its requirements, developers can choose from the slew of themes available on http://drupal.org as contributed themes or instead, decide to roll their own.

Contributed themes are, as the name suggests, themes that have been contributed by the Drupal community at large. They usually tend to be designs that have been developed by a user for a site and then shared with the community, or designs from other packages or sites which have been ported over to Drupal. Consequently, while they are ready-to-wear, they are generic in nature and lack uniqueness. Furthermore, the quality of these themes vary significantly from one to the other with some being excellent and others well below par. Contributed themes are an acceptable choice for sites that require rapid deployment or for hobby sites with simple needs where uniqueness is not a factor.

Custom themes, on the other hand, are a necessity for sites with unique requirements in layout, usability, and design. While they are often built from the ground up, it is now established practice to use special *starter themes* as a base from which they can be extended.

Contributed themes can be accessed at `http://drupal.org/project/themes`. This page, by default, lists all available themes and provides filters that can be used to whittle the results down based on Drupal version compatibility as well as other search terms. Additionally, sorting options can be used to rearrange contributions based on their popularity, update status, and other criteria. More information about each theme can be accessed by clicking on its **Find out more** link.

There are a number of considerations to keep in mind whilst choosing a contributed theme. Firstly, it is important to have a general idea of the layout required for our site with the chief concern usually revolving around the column structure of the design. Most themes support a three-column (with two sidebars and a content area) layout which can also optionally function as a two-column single sidebar layout if no content is added to one of the sidebars. The more exotic ones support four or more columns and are only really a viable option for special cases:

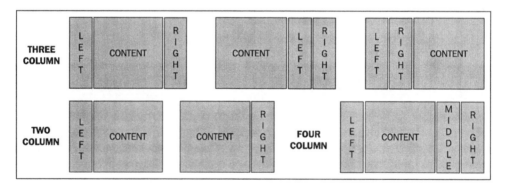

Secondly, while fewer themes nowadays are being laid out using tables, they are still around. Unless there is no other recourse, these should be avoided in favor of CSS layouts.

Next, check to see whether the theme is a fixed-width or a fluid theme or supports both types. Fixed-width themes, as the name suggests, maintain a predefined width irrespective of the screen resolution of the user. As a result, the site has a consistent appearance. Fluid layouts, or liquid layouts as they are sometimes referred to, grow according to the user's screen size and consequently make better use of the available real estate. The question of which to use is generally decided on a case by case basis.

The Drupal theme system also supports the use of different theme engines to render the design. Each engine uses a different process by which the designer can interact with Drupal to implement a design. The PHPTemplate engine is built into Drupal and is by far the most popular of the ones available. The vast majority of contributed themes available are compatible with PHPTemplate. Nevertheless, it is prudent to check the specifications of the theme to ensure that it does not require a different theme engine. Contributed theme engines can, if necessary, be downloaded from `http://drupal.org/project/theme+engines`.

Every theme's project page usually provides screenshots and explicitly specifies layout and other pertinent information. A number of them also link to a demonstration page, as in the following screenshot, where the theme can be previewed and tested using different browsers, screen resolutions, and so on. A third-party site `http://themegarden.org`, which showcases various contributed themes, comes in very handy for the same reason:

Downloads

Recommended releases

Version	Downloads	Date	Links
7.x-1.6	tar.gz (74.92 KB) | zip (102.64 KB)	2011-Feb-08	Notes
6.x-3.11	tar.gz (330.36 KB) | zip (348.33 KB)	2011-Feb-07	Notes

Development releases

Version	Downloads	Date	Links
7.x-1.x-dev	tar.gz (74.7 KB) | zip (101.45 KB)	2011-Feb-25	Notes

View all releases

Resources

Read documentation
Read complete log of changes
View project translations

Development

View pending patches
Repository viewer
View commits
Report a security issue

Additionally, project pages customarily link to their Git repositories where files within the theme can be viewed prior to downloading it. It is also worth exploring the issue queue of a project to see if bugs have been reported and are being addressed in a timely manner.

> Git is a tool used by Drupal developers to manage their code and control their releases. It is effectively a repository for modules, themes, and Drupal itself. More information on Git is available at `http://drupal.org/handbook/git`.

Once the list of candidate themes has been narrowed down to a short list, the only way to test them further is to download and install them. The theme project page lists available downloads based on version and stability along with release notes which might be useful to glance through as well. Download the latest release recommended for Drupal 7. The recipes in this chapter will address the installation and configuration of a downloaded contributed theme.

Installing and enabling a theme

This recipe will cover the steps required to install and enable a downloaded theme.

Getting ready

Downloaded themes are made available in both the ubiquitous zip format as well as the format which usually offers superior compression. These files can be extracted using archive programs such as 7-Zip (http://www.7-zip.org) as well as commercial packages such as WinZip (http://www.winzip.com) and WinRAR (http://www.rarlabs.com).

How to do it...

To install a theme, open Windows Explorer and navigate to the Drupal installation:

1. Browse to sites/all/themes.

2. Extract the downloaded theme into a subfolder inside this folder. In other words, if the theme is called mytheme, the folder sites/all/themes/mytheme should contain all the files of the theme:

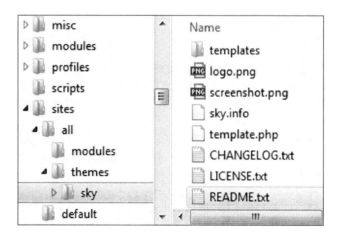

In the previous screenshot, we see the Sky theme's installation folder situated within `sites/all/themes`. Themes also often contain a **README.txt** file which provides documentation which is worth a read-through.

File structure options

In this recipe, we have chosen to use the folder `sites/all/themes/` to store our theme. By positioning our theme inside `sites/all`, we are stating that the theme is to be available to *all* sites using this Drupal installation. In other words, this enables multi-site setups to share modules and themes. In case we want to restrict access to the theme solely to one particular site, we would position its folder within `sites/foo.example.com/themes/` where `foo.example.com` is the site in question.

3. Access the Drupal site in a browser and navigate to `admin/appearance` [**Home | Administration | Appearance**].

4. As in the following screenshot, the newly installed theme should now be listed on this page under the **Disabled themes** section. Click on the associated **Enable and set default** link to activate the theme:

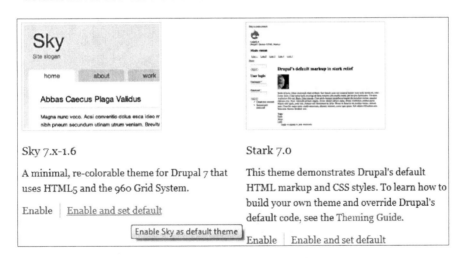

How it works...

Drupal scans folders within `sites/all/themes` and in particular looks for files with the extension `.info`. These files contain information about each theme such as its name, description, version compatibility, and so on. If the theme is compatible, it is listed on the theme administration page.

A site can have multiple themes enabled. Out of these, only one can be chosen as the default theme. The default theme is, as the name suggests, the primary theme for the website. In the following screenshot, we can see that the **Sky** theme is now enabled and is the new default theme for the site overriding the core theme, **Bartik**, which is relegated to second position in the list of enabled themes:

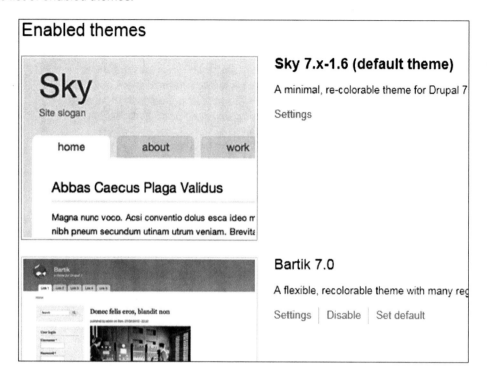

There's more...

Drupal makes it easier for us to manage our sites by following preset naming conventions when it comes to the folder structure of the site.

Folder structure

Themes do not necessarily have to be placed at the root of the `sites/all/themes` folder. For organizational purposes, it might be useful to create `sites/all/themes/contrib` and `sites/all/themes/custom`. This will allow us to differentiate between downloaded themes and custom themes.

Since Drupal's core themes are located within the root `themes` folder, we might be led to believe that this could be a good place to store our contributed or custom themes. While this will certainly work, it will prove to be a bad decision in the long run as it is never a good idea to mix core files with custom files. The chief reason for this separation is manageability. It is far easier to maintain and update Drupal when there is a clear distinction between the core installation and contributed or custom modules and themes. It also ensures that we do not accidentally overwrite or lose our changes when we upgrade our site to the next Drupal release.

Disabling a theme

Enabled themes can be disabled by clicking on their associated **Disable** links. However, this can only be done if they are not currently the *default* theme of the site. If the link is missing, then another theme will first need to be set as the default. Once this is done, the **Disable** link should automatically become available.

See also

Once a theme is enabled, the next logical step would be to configure it. The following recipes in this chapter, namely *Uploading a new logo*, *Uploading a new favicon*, and so on describe how to do so.

While this recipe dealt with installing and enabling a downloaded theme, it is also a good idea to consider *Creating a subtheme based on a core theme recipe in Chapter 2, Beyond the Basics* as well as *Creating a theme from scratch recipe in Chapter 3, Custom Themes and Zen*.

Uploading a new logo

Most websites incorporate a logo into their design, usually accompanying the site name in the header. For example, the Drupal logo or "Druplicon" in the following screenshot represents the default logo displayed for every core theme that comes packaged with Drupal:

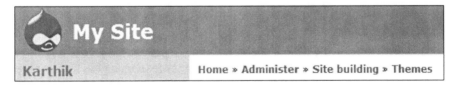

These logos tend to play an important role in the branding and identity of the site and are frequently an important facet in the overall design of the theme. This recipe details the steps involved in changing the logo displayed in a theme.

Getting ready

The new logo should be in a suitable format and should balance quality with size. The rule of thumb usually followed is as follows:

- **PNG**: For high quality images that contain transparencies
- **JPEG**: For detailed photographic logos that do not involve transparencies
- **GIF**: For simple line art

How to do it...

A custom logo can be added to a theme using the following steps:

1. Navigate to the `admin/appearance` [**Home | Administration | Appearance**] page.
2. Click on the **Settings** link accompanying the theme in question.
3. Look for the **Logo image settings** fieldset. Within the fieldset, uncheck the **Use the default logo** checkbox as we want to use a custom image:

4. Using the **Upload logo image** field, browse and select the logo file in the filesystem.
5. Finally, click on the **Save configuration** button below upload and save the changes.

How it works...

The uploaded file is saved in the Drupal filesystem and the path to the logo is registered as a configuration setting in the database. During display, rather than using the logo supplied by Drupal or the theme itself, this setting is loaded to embed the custom logo within the Drupal page. The following screenshot displays the theme with its default logo replaced with a custom PNG:

There's more...

Besides specifying the logo file via a theme's configuration page, there are other avenues that can also be pursued.

Directly linking to image files

Alternatively, instead of uploading the logo via Drupal, use the **Path to custom logo** textfield to point to an existing logo file on the server. This is often handy when the same image is being shared by multiple themes.

Yet another option is to simply place the logo file in the theme's folder and rename it to logo.png. Provided that the **Use the default logo** field is checked, the theme will automatically look for this file in its folder and use it as its logo.

See also

In the next recipe, *Uploading a new favicon*, we will see how to go about adding a shortcut icon that adds to the identity of our site.

Uploading a new favicon

This recipe details the steps involved in changing the **favicon** displayed with the theme. A favicon, dubbed as a **shortcut icon** in the Drupal interface, is an image that is particular to a site and is displayed in the address bar of the browser next to the site URL as well as the browser tab. It also makes its presence felt if the site is bookmarked in the browser as shown in the following screenshot:

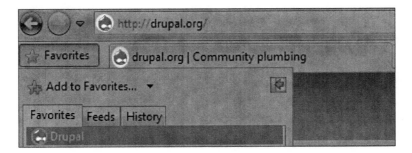

Getting ready

We are going to need the icon file to be added which is recommended to be of size 32x32 pixels or higher. An example icon file named `favicon.ico` can be seen in the `misc` folder in the Drupal installation.

How to do it...

Adding a custom favicon to the theme can be done by performing the following steps:

1. Navigate to the `admin/appearance` [**Home | Administration | Appearance**] page.
2. Click on the **Settings** link accompanying the theme in question.
3. Look for the **Shortcut icon settings** fieldset.
4. As in the following screenshot, uncheck the **Use default shortcut icon** checkbox as we want to use a custom icon:

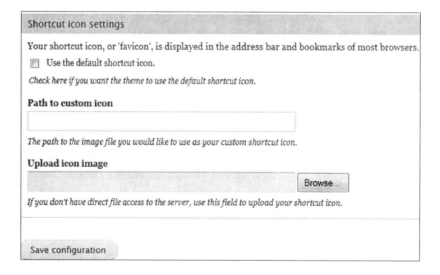

5. Using the **Upload icon image** field, browse and select the icon file in the filesystem.
6. Finally, click on the **Save configuration** button below upload and save the changes.

How it works...

The uploaded file is saved in the Drupal filesystem and the path to the icon is registered as a theme setting in the database. When a page is being rendered, the Drupal theme system designates this `.ico` file as the favicon for the site.

In the following screenshot, we can see the logo image added in the previous recipe also being used as the basis for a favicon:

There's more...

Besides manually uploading the icon file via the configuration page of the theme, other avenues are also available to accomplish the same objective.

Alternative methods

Just as we saw when uploading a custom logo image, instead of uploading the icon file via Drupal, use the **Path to custom icon** textfield to point to the icon file on the server. A third option is to place the icon file in the theme's folder and rename it to `favicon.ico`. Provided that the **Use the default shortcut icon** field is checked, the theme will automatically look for this file in its folder and use it as its favicon. Not specifying a favicon will instead result in the site using Drupal's default icon, **Druplicon**, which is located within the `misc` folder.

 Other formats besides the ICO format are also supported by some, but not all, browsers. More information is available at `http://en.wikipedia.org/wiki/Favicon`.

See also

The previous recipe in this chapter, *Uploading a new logo*, is, in many ways, similar to this one as it describes how to replace the default logo image with a custom file.

Adding a slogan to the theme

This recipe details the steps involved in adding a **slogan** to the theme. Site slogans are a common feature on most sites and are typically witty or involve clever wordplay. They are synonymous with catchphrases, taglines, mottoes, and so on.

Drupal offers a global setting to store the site slogan which is customarily displayed by themes near the site logo or site name and is also regularly added to news feeds and site e-mails as part of the site's identity.

Getting ready

Think up a good slogan! This is the biggest stumbling block to getting this recipe right.

How to do it...

Adding a slogan to a theme involves the following steps:

1. Navigate to `admin/config/system/site-information` [**Home | Administration | System | Site information**].

2. Locate the **Slogan** textfield and add the slogan here as shown in the following screenshot:

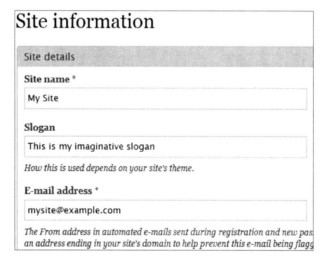

3. Click the **Save configuration** button at the bottom of the page to save our changes.

4. Now, navigate to the theme administration page at `admin/appearance` [**Home | Administration | Appearance**].

5. Click on the **Settings** tab at the top of the page.

   The resulting page should have multiple tabs: one titled **Global settings** which affects all themes and others representing each enabled theme. Configuration options under the **Global settings** tab serve as the site's default settings for all themes, while equivalent settings within each theme's tab work as overrides for the global settings.

6. On the **Global settings** page, look for the **Site slogan** setting in the **Toggle display** section and ensure that it is checked:

7. Click the **Save configuration** button to save our changes.

 If any of the themes have overridden the global setting, then the **Site Slogan** checkbox will also need to be checked in its respective theme tab.

How it works...

Drupal saves the provided slogan as a configuration setting in the database. The theme system makes this setting available as a variable to the theme which outputs it accordingly when the page is being rendered.

In the following screenshot, we can see that the slogan is enabled and is displayed along with the logo and the name of the site:

There's more...

Besides the site slogan, other theme variables can also be configured from the **Site Information** and theme configuration pages.

Similar settings

The Drupal **Site Information** page seen in this recipe also contains fields for other settings such as the **Site name** which are also similarly exposed by themes. Toggles for these as well as other variables can also be controlled via the theme system's **Global settings** tab.

See also

Two previous recipes in this chapter, *Uploading a new logo* and *Uploading a new favicon*, deal with altering similar variables via the theme configuration pages.

Displaying a different theme for administration

This recipe describes how to set up Drupal to use a different theme only for administration pages. This is a frequent requirement especially on brochure sites which have a limited number of regions where blocks can be placed or have missing page elements such as breadcrumbs which reduces usability. Having a separate administration theme also comes in handy during custom theme design as the site could well be largely unusable during the initial stages of development. A stable administration interface will therefore ensure that administrative tasks can still be performed effortlessly until the new theme becomes ready.

Getting ready

Depending on the amount of real estate required, it will be worthwhile to put some thought into deciding on the right theme to use as the administration theme. Themes such as the aptly named Administration theme (`http://drupal.org/project/admin_theme`) and RootCandy (`http://drupal.org/project/rootcandy`) have been designed specifically with the administration pages in mind. That said, if the requirement is temporary, using a core theme such as Garland will usually suffice.

How to do it...

Specifying an administration theme can be done by following these steps:

1. Navigate to `admin/appearance` [**Home | Administration | Appearance**].

2. Choose **Garland** (or any other theme of choice) in the **Administration theme** drop down at the bottom of the page.

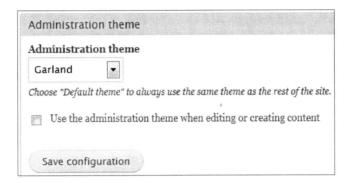

In situations where only administrators have permissions to add and edit content, it might be handy to also check the **Use administration theme when editing or creating content** checkbox seen previously.

3. Click the **Save configuration** button to save our changes in the database.

Viewing an administration page should confirm that the specified administration theme is being used in preference to the default theme.

How it works...

Every time a page is displayed, Drupal checks to see if the URL of the page begins with admin. If it does and if we have specified an administration theme, Drupal overrides the default theme being used with the specified theme.

Since the administration theme is a special case, Drupal does not require the theme to be enabled for it to be available as an option.

See also

Just as Drupal can dynamically change the theme being used to render administration pages, so can we. This is covered in the *Displaying a different theme for each day of the week* recipe in *Chapter 2, Beyond the Basics*.

Adding an existing block to the theme

Drupal's page layout is customarily divided into a number of **regions** which are laid out differently from theme to theme. For example, a theme could have regions named **Left sidebar** and **Right sidebar** which will be displayed to the left and right hand side respectively of another region named **Content**. Regions serve as containers for **blocks**.

Blocks are self-contained elements which are located within regions and typically contain information or functionality that is repeated consistently across multiple pages. They can contain contextual information that complements the actual content of a page such as a block that outputs information about the author of the node currently being displayed, or static information such as a login form block or a block that displays advertisements. While previous versions of Drupal considered the primary content of a page to live outside the block system, Drupal 7 does not render it any such importance.

This recipe details the steps involved in adding an existing block to a region of a theme.

Getting ready

For this example, we will be adding a **Who's online** block to the **Left sidebar** region, assuming that such a region exists, of the Garland core theme. The position of a block both in terms of region as well as its weight (which determines its order among other blocks in the same region) can prove to be very important in terms of usability and exposure.

It is assumed that the Garland theme is enabled and, ideally, also set as the default theme.

How to do it...

The **Who's online** block can be added by following these steps:

1. Navigate to `admin/structure/block` [**Home | Administration | Structure | Blocks**].

2. If more than one theme is enabled on the site, choose the appropriate tab at the top of the page.

3. Look for the **Who's online** block under the **Disabled** section.

4. Click on the crosshairs icon to its left and drag the block to the **Left sidebar** region.

   Alternatively, we could have simply chosen the **Left sidebar** in the **Region** drop down and then used the crosshairs to order the block within the region. This is the quicker option when there are a lot of blocks and regions to deal with on this page.

5. Click on the **Save blocks** button at the bottom of the page to save our changes.

The block should now be visible in the left sidebar as can be seen with the Garland theme in the following screenshot:

	Block	Region	Operations
Who's online	**Left sidebar**		
There is currently 1 user online.	✛ Navigation	Left sidebar ▾	configure
	✛ User login	Left sidebar ▾	configure
○ Karthik	✛ Management	Left sidebar ▾	configure
	✛ Who's online	Left sidebar ▾	configure
	Right sidebar		

How it works...

Drupal maintains a table named `blocks` in its database which contains a list of all the blocks exposed by the modules in its installation. By moving the **Who's online** block to the **Left sidebar** region, we are effectively just manipulating this table in the database. When a page is displayed, Drupal uses this table to determine the status and location of each block for the current theme and the theme system positions them accordingly.

There's more...

Block layouts are particular to each theme and can therefore be customized differently for different themes.

Theme-specific block layouts

Seeing that each theme is laid out with its own set of regions, it stands to reason that a block can also be positioned in different regions for different themes. For example, the **Who's online** block seen in this recipe can be positioned in the **Left sidebar** region of the Garland theme and the **Right sidebar** of another theme such as Bartik. Taking this idea further, we can also have the block enabled only for Garland and not for Bartik.

The block layout for each theme can be managed by clicking on the appropriate theme tab at the top of the block management page at `admin/structure/block` [**Home | Administration | Structure | Blocks**]. Each theme provides a **Demonstrate block regions** link which can be used to obtain an overview of the regional layout of the theme.

See also

In the next recipe, we will expand on what we have seen here by learning how to go about *Adding a custom block to the theme*.

Adding a custom block to the theme

This recipe details the steps involved in adding a block with custom content to the theme. Drupal blocks can either be declared using a module or, as we are doing here, added manually via the block administration interface.

Getting ready

For this recipe, we will be adding a simple welcome message in a custom block within a predetermined region. As with standard blocks, position matters!

How to do it...

The following procedure outlines the steps required to add a custom block to a theme:

1. Navigate to `admin/structure/block` [**Home | Administration | Structure | Blocks**].

2. If more than one theme is enabled, select the theme that we are adding our block to by clicking on its tab.

3. Click on the **Add block** link at the top of the page.

4. In the ensuing page, type a welcome message in the **Block description** textfield.

> This description field comes in handy on the block administration page when trying to differentiate between blocks with identical titles, or as is frequently the case, no titles.

5. Next, if the block requires a title to be displayed above its content, add one via the **Block title** textfield. In this case, we do not need one as we are just looking to display a welcome message.

6. As displayed in the following screenshot, enter the welcome text into the **Block body** textarea: `Welcome to Mysite. Enjoy your stay!`.

Similar to most other textareas in Drupal, a linked **Input format** should be available to filter the content appropriately. This allows for great flexibility when adding content.

7. The **Region settings** fieldset lists all currently enabled themes. Optionally, choose the region where this block is to be displayed for each of them (or **– None –** if it is not to be displayed at all).

8. Finally, click on **Save block** to create the block.

How it works...

Just as with standard blocks, Drupal maintains a table named `block_custom` which tracks all custom blocks including their content and input format. Once a custom block is enabled, it is added to the `block` table and tracked as if it was a standard block.

When created, a custom block appears in the block list and can be treated just like any other block. It can be dragged around different regions, have its visibility settings controlled, and so on. The following screenshot displays our newly created welcome block as part of the Garland theme:

Who's online	Block	Region	Operations	
There is currently 1 user online.	**Left sidebar**			
	✛ Navigation	Left sidebar ▾	configure	
○ Karthik	✛ User login	Left sidebar ▾	configure	
	✛ Management	Left sidebar ▾	configure	
Welcome to Mysite. Enjoy your stay!	✛ Who's online	Left sidebar ▾	configure	
	✛ Welcome message	Left sidebar ▾	configure	delete

 An easy way to identify custom blocks on the block management page is by their tell-tale **delete** links. Only custom blocks feature a delete option.

There's more...

Custom blocks are useful for more than simply embedding text strings.

Doing more with custom blocks

Custom blocks can be very handy to not only add visible content, but also to execute short code snippets on specific pages provided the appropriate input format has been selected. For example, we could embed some custom JavaScript required only for a few specific page nodes, by adding it to a custom block—equipped with a suitable input format—which is set to be displayed only with the aforementioned page nodes.

That said, if a more optimal solution is available—such as using a module to hold our code—then it should be pursued instead of inserting code into blocks and thereby into the database.

See also

Now that we have seen how to add and manage blocks, we can proceed to control it further by playing with its visibility configuration. The final three recipes of this chapter outline the steps required for *Displaying a block only on the front page, Controlling block visibility based on user role*, and *Controlling block visibility based on node type*.

Displaying a block only on the front page

This recipe details the steps involved in displaying a block only on a certain page, which in this case, is the front page. We will be displaying the welcome message block created in the previous recipe as an example.

Getting ready

The front page is a special case on most sites as it usually showcases the rest of the site. Manipulating block visibility for front page blocks is a frequent requirement and in our case, we are going to ensure that the welcome message block is only going to be displayed on the front page and nowhere else.

How to do it...

Block visibility is controlled from the block's configuration page as follows:

1. Navigate to `admin/structure/block` [**Home | Administration | Structure | Blocks**].

2. Locate the block that needs to be configured, the **Welcome message** block, and click on its **Configure** link listed in the **Operations** column.

3. On the configuration page, scroll down to the **Visibility settings** section and select the **Pages** tab.

4. In the **Pages** tab, choose the **Only the listed pages** radio button for the **Show block on specific pages** setting:

5. As shown in the previous screenshot, add the word `<front>` within the associated textarea.

6. Click on the **Save block** button at the bottom of the page to save our changes.

7. Finally, visit the front page of the site as well as other pages to confirm that the block is only being displayed on the front page.

How it works...

Whenever a block is to be displayed, Drupal checks to see if we have any visibility settings applied to it. In this case, we have **Only the listed pages** switched on. As a result, Drupal checks the textarea configured within the **Pages** tab to see which pages have been listed. The use of the `<front>` keyword, which is a special indicator that represents the front page of the site, tells Drupal that unless this is the root of the site, this block should not be displayed.

This is all done before the content of the block is processed by Drupal thereby improving performance and making this method cleaner and more efficient than hiding the block using CSS or elsewhere in the theme.

There's more...

Drupal offers a number of page-matching options to help further refine when and where we display our blocks.

Multiple pages

Multiple pages can be specified in the textarea within the **Pages** tab. For example, if the block is to be displayed only on the front page *and* on user pages, the list would be the following:

```
<front>
user/*
```

Drupal will now compare the path of the page against each entry in this list and decide to display the block only if there is a match.

Wildcards

The use of the asterisk wildcard in `user/*` states that the match should be performed against all paths beginning with user. This ensures that the block is displayed for all pages within each user's **My account** section.

Matching against URL aliases

Drupal's **Path** module allows users to specify URL aliases for nodes and system paths. While this can potentially be a source of indecision when it comes to choosing which paths to use while configuring a block's page-visibility settings, the Block module's page-matching code intelligently compares against both possibilities. For example, consider the following table that specifies the internal paths and corresponding aliases for three nodes:

Internal path	URL alias
node/1	products/foo
node/13	products/bar
node/22	products/baz

If we wanted to match against all three nodes, we could specify the three node paths directly as follows:

- ▶ node/1
- ▶ node/13
- ▶ node/22

Or, we could specify the three aliases as follows:

- ▶ products/foo
- ▶ products/bar
- ▶ products/baz

Alternatively, we could simply use the aliases with a wildcard as follows:

- ▶ products/*

Exclusive display

This recipe can also be similarly applied to display a block on all pages but the front page. This involves choosing the **Show on every page except the listed pages** option in the **Page specific visibility settings** section.

See also

The next recipe, *Controlling block visibility based on user role*, expands on this recipe by describing the steps to restrict block visibility to a particular set of users.

Controlling block visibility based on user role

Drupal allows administrators to segregate users into logical subsections named *roles* which facilitate features such as access control and content targeting. This recipe details the steps involved in toggling block visibility based on the role of the user viewing the page. For example, a block displaying advertisements might only need to be visible for anonymous users and not for authenticated users.

Getting ready

For this recipe, we will be configuring the welcome message block, which we created in an earlier recipe in this chapter, to only be visible to authenticated users, or to be more precise, to users belonging to the authenticated user role.

How to do it...

Controlling block visibility is handled from the block administration pages outlined as follows:

1. Navigate to `admin/structure/block` [**Home | Administration | Structure | Blocks**].

2. Locate the block that needs to be configured, the **Welcome message** block, and click on its **Configure** link.

3. On the configure screen, scroll down to the **Visibility settings** section and select the **Roles** tab.

4. In the **Roles** tab, check the **authenticated user** checkbox for the **Show block for specific roles** setting as shown in the following screenshot:

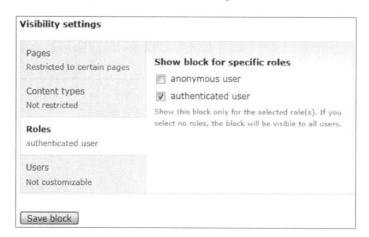

5. Click the **Save block** button at the bottom of the page to save the changes.

6. Finally, confirm that our changes have worked by checking if our block is visible only for users who have logged into the site—authenticated users—and not for those who have not—anonymous users.

How it works...

Drupal maintains a table named `block_role` which keeps track of role-specific settings for all blocks. Changes made to role settings on the block configuration page are cataloged in this table. When an anonymous user now visits the site, Drupal will look up this table and note that the **Welcome message** block is restricted to authenticated users only. Consequently, the block will not be displayed.

See also

Both the previous recipe, *Displaying a block only on the front page*, as well as the next one, *Controlling block visibility based on node type*, deal with managing block visibility configurations.

Controlling block visibility based on node type

So far in this chapter, we have looked at controlling block visibility based on the path of the page and the role of the user. In this recipe, we will look to configure a block to be displayed based on the node type of the content on the page.

Getting ready

We will be configuring the **Recent comments** block—which is provided by the Comment module—to only be visible for two particular node types, story and blog. The blog type is automatically created upon enabling the Blog module via the module administration page at `admin/build/modules` [**Home | Administration | Site building | Modules**]. The story type and another example type named page, however, need to be created manually via the **Add content type** page at `admin/structure/types/add` [**Home | Administration | Structure | Content types**].

It is assumed that both the Blog and Comment modules have been enabled and that the story and page node types have been created. It is also recommended that sample nodes and associated comments be created for all node types to reliably test our recipe.

How to do it...

Block visibility can be configured from the block's configuration page as per the following steps:

1. Navigate to `admin/structure/block` [**Home | Administration | Structure | Blocks**].

2. Look for the block that needs to be configured, **Recent comments,** and click on its **Configure** link.

3. On the configure screen, scroll down to the **Visibility settings** section and select the **Content types** tab.

4. In the **Content types** tab, check the checkboxes that correspond to the **Blog entry** and **Story** types as shown in the following screenshot:

5. Finally, click on **Save block** to save our changes.

To test if our changes have taken effect, visit pages representing each of the three node types: blog, page, and story, and verify that the **Recent comments** block is being displayed only for the two configured in this recipe and not the rest.

How it works...

Drupal maintains a table named `block_node_type` which keeps track of type-specific settings for all blocks. When a block is to be displayed, Drupal looks up this table if node type-specific conditions are in effect. If they are, then Drupal compares the type of the node being displayed against the types loaded from the `block_node_type` table and displays the block only if there is a match.

In this case, the block will only be displayed if we are viewing a blog or story node.

See also

Earlier recipes in this chapter, namely *Controlling block visibility based on user role* and *Displaying a block only on the front page*, also concern controlling block visibility.

2
Beyond the Basics

We will be covering the following recipes in this chapter:

- ▸ Understanding the anatomy of a theme
- ▸ Creating a subtheme based on a core theme
- ▸ Overriding base theme elements in a subtheme
- ▸ Changing the screenshot image of a theme
- ▸ Including a CSS file in a theme
- ▸ Enabling CSS optimization
- ▸ Creating the mysite module to hold our tweaks
- ▸ Adding a CSS file from a module
- ▸ Displaying a different theme for each day of the week
- ▸ Creating a fresh look using the Color module

Introduction

One of the more prevalent adages with respect to Drupal development and theming is:

Do not hack core!

Modules, themes, and other files that come with a stock Drupal installation should never be edited directly. In other words, we really should not need to modify anything outside the `sites` folder of our installation as it is designed to contain all our changes and customizations. The reasoning behind this is that most, if not all, aspects of core are accessible and modifiable through a clean and non-invasive process using Drupal's *APIs*. Therefore, hacking core modules and themes to get things done is almost always unnecessary and ill-advised.

Another reason against directly editing core modules and themes, or for that matter, even their contributed counterparts, is that whenever an upgrade of Drupal or said modules and themes takes place, we will very likely be overwriting—quite unwittingly—the changes we have made or at the very least, make the upgrade a trying exercise.

With respect to themes, let us consider a situation where our site is making use of a core theme such as Garland and we are looking to tweak its markup or styling to better suit our purposes. As reasoned earlier, what we do not want to do is just dive in and edit the theme directly. Instead, the Drupal way advocates that we extend the Garland theme using a subtheme that, by default, is more or less an identical copy. This subtheme can then be modified and customized by overriding aspects of the base theme such as its stylesheets, template files, template variables, and so on. This decision will ensure that our changes will remain secure within the `sites` folder and furthermore, will allow us to easily track all the changes we have introduced through our subtheme.

Modules can similarly be extended and overridden using our own custom modules.

In this chapter, we will look at the building blocks of a basic theme and then familiarize ourselves with the concept of the subtheme and the various techniques available to extend, override, and modify it according to our requirements.

Understanding the anatomy of a theme

Drupal themes can consist of a multitude of files each with its own purpose, format, and syntax. This recipe will introduce each of these types with an explanation of what they do.

Getting ready

It will be useful to navigate to the Garland folder at `themes/garland` to browse and view the files inside a typical, fully featured theme. Garland uses the **PHPTemplate** theming **engine** which is the default engine in Drupal 7.

How to do it...

The following table outlines the types of files typically found inside a theme's folder and the naming conventions to be followed for some of them:

Type	Mandatory?	Description
`mytheme.info`	Yes	Configuration file which provides information to Drupal about a theme named `mytheme`.
`*.tpl.php`	Varies	Template files which allow the customization and styling of themable aspects of Drupal. These can either live at the root level of the theme or in a folder named templates.
`page.tpl.php`	Yes	A template file which determines the layout of all Drupal pages.
`node.tpl.php`	No	A template file which determines the layout of a node inside a Drupal page.
`block.tpl.php`	No	A template file which determines the layout of a block.
`template.php`	No	PHPTemplate master file where some of the more complicated and powerful tweaks and overrides occur.
`*.css`	No	CSS stylesheets which need to be explicitly included through the `.info` files.
`*.js`	No	JavaScript files which need to be explicitly included through the `.info` file.
`favicon.ico`	No	Shortcut icon: If this file exists, it will be automatically included in the theme unless overridden from within Drupal.
`logo.png`	No	Site logo: If this file exists, it will be automatically included in the theme unless overridden from within the theme or the theme's settings in Drupal.
`screenshot.png`	No	Theme preview image: If this file exists, it will be automatically included in the theme.

Perusing the contents of each of the available files will prove very useful as we go along developing our theme.

How it works...

When a theme is added, Drupal first parses its `.info` file. This file, as its extension suggests, provides information about the theme such as its name, Drupal version compatibility, regions declared, CSS stylesheets used, JavaScript files included, and so on. In other words, Drupal uses it to map the structure of a theme.

The `.info` file can also be used to specify the theming *engine* being used by the theme. Theme engines allow theme developers to communicate with Drupal using a simpler and more convenient interface commonly through template files. A number of them also introduce their own language formats for use in these template files. This directive, however, is generally not included as most themes use the *PHPTemplate* engine which is the default choice in Drupal 7.

Template files in PHPTemplate themes are those that use the `.tpl.php` extension. Unlike other engines, these files just use PHP and HTML and do not rely on any special markup languages.

There's more...

Other theme engines besides PHPTemplate are also available. However, only a handful of themes in Drupal's contribution repository rely on them.

Other theme engine types

The PHPTemplate engine is the most widely prevalent theming engine used in the Drupal ecosystem. Themes using other engines such as Smarty or Xtemplate are rare and will be structured quite differently. A list of engines can be found at `http://drupal.org/project/theme+engines`.

Creating a subtheme based on a core theme

As explained in the introduction to this chapter, subthemes allow developers to customize and extend existing theme installations in a non-destructive manner. They are also handy in keeping the amount of repetitious code to a minimum thereby improving efficiency and easing management.

This recipe details the steps involved in creating a subtheme of an existing theme, which in this case is the core theme, Garland.

Getting ready

Create a folder named `mytheme` inside `sites/all/themes`. This name is usually also the name of the new theme and it is best to keep things uncomplicated by not using spaces and special characters. While `mytheme` is suitable for the purpose of this recipe, it will be a good idea to give the theme a unique and pertinent name based on its design and use. It is also important to ensure that there are no name conflicts with other existing core or contributed themes.

> As mentioned in the previous chapter, by creating this theme within `sites/all/themes`, we are effectively sharing the theme between _all_ sites using the installation. If we need to restrict its availability to just one site, we would instead place it within `sites/foo.example.com/themes` where `foo.example.com` is the URL of the site.

How to do it...

A subtheme of a core theme can be created through the following procedure:

1. Create a file named `mytheme.info` inside the `mytheme` folder.

2. Edit this new file and add the following code inside it:

    ```
    name = Mytheme
    description = My new sub-theme (CSS, phptemplate, 3-col)
    base theme = garland
    core = 7.x
    ```

> It is useful to add an informative `description` field as it will be visible in the theme administration page. Specifying the key characteristics of the theme can save time and effort as the administrator gets a quick overview of the design.

3. Save the file.

> **Downloading the example code**
>
> You can download the example code files for all Packt books you have purchased from your account at `http://www.PacktPub.com`. If you purchased this book elsewhere, you can visit `http://www.PacktPub.com/support` and register to have the files e-mailed directly to you.

4. Next, visit `admin/appearance` [**Home | Administration | Appearance**] to check if our new theme is available.

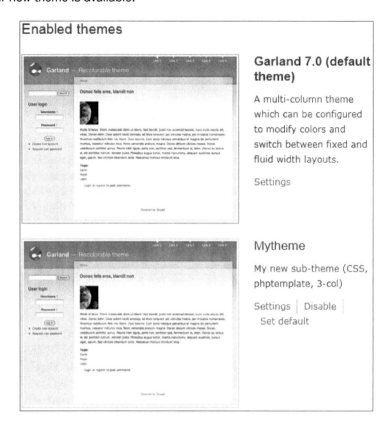

As the preceding screenshot attests, the theme administration page should now include our new theme - **Mytheme**. Enabling it should confirm that it is more or less identical to Garland and can now be extended further as per our requirements.

How it works...

Drupal uses the `.info` files to learn about our new subtheme. The `name` and `description` variables, rather unsurprisingly, represent the name of the theme and a description that customarily includes details about the layout of the theme.

The `base theme` variable denotes the parent theme which our subtheme is based on. By using this variable, we are informing Drupal that it should use the layout and styling of the base theme—in this case Garland—unless we indicate otherwise. This process of replacing base theme variables with subtheme equivalents is commonly referred to as **overriding** the base theme.

Finally, the `core` variable denotes the compatibility of our theme with Drupal 7.

 While previewing `mytheme`, we might find that the logo image is missing in the header of the Garland style. This is because the theme setting for our subtheme is set to **Use the default logo** as per the setting on its **theme configuration** page. Either modifying this setting or including a `logo.png` file in our theme folder should resolve this issue.

There's more...

Drupal allows for easy manageability by supporting chaining with subthemes.

Chaining

Subthemes can be chained, if necessary. For example, our `mytheme` could now become the base theme for another theme named `mynewtheme` which would inherit all the modifications made by `mytheme` to Garland.

See also

The next recipe, *Overriding base theme elements in a subtheme*, explain how to override template files belonging to the base theme from within a subtheme. It is also worthwhile exploring two recipes from the next chapter, namely, *Creating a theme from scratch* and *Creating myzen, a Zen-based theme*.

Overriding base theme elements in a subtheme

This recipe details the steps involved in overriding a template file registered by a base theme with an equivalent file in the subtheme. As an example, we will be restructuring the layout of a Drupal node by modifying the `node.tpl.php` template.

Getting ready

We will be using the `mytheme` subtheme that was created in the previous recipe.

How to do it...

As we are dealing with a subtheme here, it is by default relying on the template files of its base theme. To override the base file used to theme the layout of a node, copy the `node.tpl.php` file from the base theme's folder, `themes/garland`, to the `sites/all/themes/mytheme` folder. Opening the new file in an editor should bring up something similar to the following:

```php
<?php
  // $Id: node.tpl.php,v 1.24 2010/12/01 00:18:15 webchick Exp $
?>
<div id="node-<?php print $node->nid; ?>" class="<?php print
  $classes; ?>"<?php print $attributes; ?>>

  <?php print $user_picture; ?>

  <?php print render($title_prefix); ?>
  <?php if (!$page): ?>
    <h2<?php print $title_attributes; ?>><a href="<?php print
      $node_url; ?>"><?php print $title; ?></a></h2>
  <?php endif; ?>
  <?php print render($title_suffix); ?>

  <?php if ($display_submitted): ?>
    <span class="submitted"><?php print $submitted ?></span>
  <?php endif; ?>

  <div class="content clearfix"<?php print $content_attributes; ?>>
    <?php
      // We hide the comments and links now so that we can render
      // them later.
      hide($content['comments']);
      hide($content['links']);
      print render($content);
    ?>
  </div>

  <div class="clearfix">
    <?php if (!empty($content['links'])): ?>
      <div class="links"><?php print render($content['links']);
        ?></div>
    <?php endif; ?>

    <?php print render($content['comments']); ?>
  </div>

</div>
```

The lines highlighted in the preceding code excerpt indicate the code we are looking to modify. To elaborate, we are going to move the node's submission information from a position at the top, right to the bottom of the node display. This can be done by simply moving the relevant block of code to an appropriate location further down in the template file, as highlighted in the following code:

```php
<?php
  // $Id: node.tpl.php,v 1.24 2010/12/01 00:18:15 webchick Exp $
?>
<div id="node-<?php print $node->nid; ?>" class="<?php print
  $classes; ?>"<?php print $attributes; ?>>

  <?php print $user_picture; ?>

  <?php print render($title_prefix); ?>
  <?php if (!$page): ?>
    <h2<?php print $title_attributes; ?>><a href="<?php print
      $node_url; ?>"><?php print $title; ?></a></h2>
  <?php endif; ?>
  <?php print render($title_suffix); ?>

  <div class="content clearfix"<?php print $content_attributes; ?>>
    <?php
      // We hide the comments and links now so that we can render
      // them later.
      hide($content['comments']);
      hide($content['links']);
      print render($content);
    ?>
  </div>

  <?php if ($display_submitted): ?>
    <span class="submitted"><?php print $submitted ?></span>
  <?php endif; ?>

  <div class="clearfix">
    <?php if (!empty($content['links'])): ?>
      <div class="links"><?php print render($content['links']);
        ?></div>
    <?php endif; ?>

    <?php print render($content['comments']); ?>
  </div>
</div>
```

Once this has been done, save the file and exit the editor. As we have made changes to the template system, we will need to rebuild the theme registry, or as is recommended throughout this book, simply clear the entire Drupal cache. One of the ways to do this is through the performance configuration page available at `admin/config/development/performance` [**Home | Administration | Configuration | Development | Performance**].

How it works...

For performance purposes, Drupal maintains a registry of all the stylesheets that have been included, the template files that are available, the theme functions that have been declared, and so on. As our theme initially had no `node.tpl.php` file in the `mytheme` folder, Drupal fell back to the `node.tpl.php` file of the base theme which, in this case, is Garland. However, once we added one to the `mytheme` folder, we needed to rebuild this registry so that Drupal became aware of our changes. Once this was done, Drupal used the updated `node.tpl.php` file the next time a node was displayed.

The following screenshots provide a before and after comparison of an example node:

> **Ea Vindico Voco**
>
> Sun, 05/22/2011 - 01:15 — Anonymous (not verified)
>
> Abdo autem caecus dolor ille lucidus minim olim similis tamen. Enim patria premo quae. Aliquam capto mos pertineo quibus secundum ut. Causa gilvus humo laoreet macto mauris paratus probo proprius quidne. Accumsan gilvus iaceo paulatim valde. Autem loquor paratus veniam. Immitto nimis saluto. Camur capto dolore ex lobortis pala quia suscipit tum zelus. Brevitas humo loquor quidem sagaciter tego.
>
> Dignissim gemino nibh praemitto. Accumsan bene conventio nibh si utrum uxor validus wisi. Humo plaga quidem. Haero ille neo quidem. Aliquam dolore esse haero occuro quibus saepius saluto ut vulpes.

In the following screenshot, we can see our modified template file in action as the position of the submission information `DIV` has moved from the top to the bottom of the node:

> **Ea Vindico Voco**
>
> Abdo autem caecus dolor ille lucidus minim olim similis tamen. Enim patria premo quae. Aliquam capto mos pertineo quibus secundum ut. Causa gilvus humo laoreet macto mauris paratus probo proprius quidne. Accumsan gilvus iaceo paulatim valde. Autem loquor paratus veniam. Immitto nimis saluto. Camur capto dolore ex lobortis pala quia suscipit tum zelus. Brevitas humo loquor quidem sagaciter tego.
>
> Dignissim gemino nibh praemitto. Accumsan bene conventio nibh si utrum uxor validus wisi. Humo plaga quidem. Haero ille neo quidem. Aliquam dolore esse haero occuro quibus saepius saluto ut vulpes.
>
> Sun, 05/22/2011 - 01:15 — Anonymous (not verified)

There's more...

The non-invasive technique of extending base themes using subthemes allows for smooth upgrades.

Clean upgrades

If we had modified the `node.tpl.php` file inside Garland, the next time our Drupal installation is upgraded, we would have very likely forgotten about our changes and overwritten them during the upgrade process. By using a subtheme, we can now upgrade Drupal without any fear of losing any changes we have made.

Another positive is that if bugs have been fixed in Garland, they will seamlessly propagate downriver to our subtheme.

See also

The first recipe in *Chapter 3, Custom Themes and Zen* details how to go about *Clearing the theme registry*, an oft-repeated procedure throughout the theme development cycle.

Changing the screenshot image of a theme

This recipe details the steps involved in changing the screenshot image associated with a theme. This image provides the user with a preview of what the site will look like when the theme is enabled. This is normally only required when we are working with a subtheme or a custom theme.

Getting ready

Once the theme is just about ready to go, visit the front page of the site to take the screenshot. As we are providing a snapshot of the theme, temporarily swap the name of the site with the name of the theme. It might also be useful to prepare some example content for display on the front page to obtain an accurate representation of the style and layout of our theme.

How to do it...

Adding a screenshot for our theme can be done through the following steps:

1. On the front page, press *ALT + Print Screen* to take a screenshot of the active window.

 Mac users can use *Command + Shift + 3* while Linux users should be able to bring up the screenshot utility relevant to their distribution by pressing *Print Screen*.

2. Open up a graphics editor and paste the screenshot within.

3. Make a wide selection of the theme incorporating different elements such as the position of the logo, breadcrumb, fonts and node styles, and so on.

4. Crop and resize to `294x219` pixels which is the rather odd standard for theme screenshots.

5. Save the image as a PNG file named `screenshot.png`.

6. Finally, copy the file to the theme's folder.

Visiting `admin/appearance` [**Home | Administration | Appearance**] should confirm that `screenshot.png` is being used to represent our theme.

How it works...

Drupal automatically looks for a file named `screenshot.png` in the theme's folder and if found, includes that image as a preview of the theme on the theme management page as illustrated in the following screenshot:

There's more...

Each theme's `.info` file provides the syntax required to specify many of the theme's configuration settings. This includes nominating the screenshot file to be used.

Using the .info file

The screenshot image can also be specified in the theme's `.info` file using the following syntax:

```
screenshot = mytheme.png
```

where `mytheme.png` is the name of the screenshot file.

See also

The *Chapter 1, Drupal Theme Basics* recipes, *Uploading a new favicon* and *Uploading a new logo*, demonstrate how to include and modify other common image elements of a theme.

Including a CSS file in a theme

This recipe details the steps involved in adding a CSS file to the theme through its `.info` file. In this case, we will be adding a CSS file to the `mytheme` subtheme that we created earlier in this chapter.

Getting ready

We will be including a CSS file in this theme. Create a folder titled `css` within the `mytheme` folder at `sites/all/themes/mytheme` and within, create a CSS file named `mytheme.css`. Open the file in an editor and add the following example rule to it:

```
* {
  color: #996633 !important;
}
```

The above rule should override and change the color of all text on the page to a brownish hue. It is assumed that `mytheme` is the active/default theme of the site.

How to do it...

Adding a CSS file to a theme is best accomplished through its `.info` file. Navigate to the theme's folder at `sites/all/themes/mytheme` and open the `mytheme.info` file in an editor. Add the following line to this file to include our CSS file:

```
stylesheets[all][] = css/mytheme.css
```

> Note that the above statement specifies that the CSS file is present within the `css` folder. The folder name is arbitrary and is not necessarily restricted to CSS.

Once done, save the file and exit the editor. As we have modified the `.info` file and introduced a new file, our changes will not take effect until the theme registry is rebuilt. Therefore, clear the Drupal cache and view the site to confirm that our new stylesheet has been included correctly. If it has, then the theme should now display all text in brown as shown in the following screenshot:

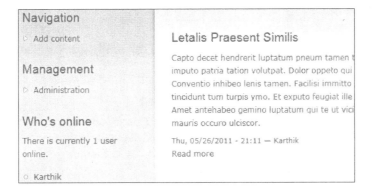

How it works...

Drupal checks the .info file and notes that we have declared stylesheets using the stylesheets variable. The syntax of this variable is similar to that of an array in PHP. The all index in the syntax represents the *media type* as used in CSS declarations.

The next screenshot displays a section of the source code of a page that confirms the inclusion of the new stylesheet, mytheme.css. We can also see that our subtheme is also including the stylesheets declared by its base theme, Garland, as well as its own stylesheets:

```
<style type="text/css" media="all">@import url("http://book.endymion/modules/system/system.base.css?llue28");
@import url("http://book.endymion/modules/system/system.menus.css?llue28");
@import url("http://book.endymion/modules/system/system.messages.css?llue28");
@import url("http://book.endymion/modules/system/system.theme.css?llue28");</style>
<style type="text/css" media="all">@import url("http://book.endymion/modules/field/theme/field.css?llue28");
@import url("http://book.endymion/modules/node/node.css?llue28");
@import url("http://book.endymion/modules/user/user.css?llue28");</style>
<style type="text/css" media="all">@import url("http://book.endymion/themes/garland/style.css?llue28");
@import url("http://book.endymion/sites/book.endymion/themes/mytheme/css/mytheme.css?llue28");</style>
<style type="text/css" media="print">@import url("http://book.endymion/themes/garland/print.css?llue28");</style>
```

In the preceding screenshot, we can see that Drupal references each stylesheet along with a query string. For example, mytheme.css is included as mytheme.css?llue28. This quirky suffix is a trick used by Drupal to ensure that browsers do not use stale copies of a cached CSS file while rendering our site.

We can test this by clearing the Drupal cache and viewing the source code once again. Now, our stylesheets should have a different suffix, perhaps something like mytheme.css?llvg5v, thereby tricking browsers into believing that these are different files and loading them instead of their locally cached copies.

There's more...

One of the advantages of using a subtheme is that we can easily override elements of the base theme. This includes stylesheets as well.

Overriding the base theme's stylesheet

If the base theme includes a stylesheet named `layout.css`, adding a stylesheet of the same name in the subtheme will override the base theme's stylesheet. In other words, Drupal will include the subtheme's stylesheet instead of that of the base theme.

See also

Later in this chapter, the recipe, *Adding a CSS file from a module*, provides an alternative approach to including CSS files. The first recipe in *Chapter 7, JavaScript in Themes* explains all about including JavaScript files from a theme.

The first recipe in *Chapter 3, Custom Themes and Zen* details how to go about clearing the theme registry, an oft-repeated procedure throughout the theme development cycle.

Enabling CSS optimization

CSS optimization in Drupal is accomplished through two steps, aggregation and compression. In other words, multiple related CSS files are grouped together into a single file and then compressed to produce a much smaller file. This optimization provides a significant boost to performance both on the server as well as for the user.

This recipe demonstrates how to enable this feature in Drupal and explains how it works.

Getting ready

CSS optimization is a requirement only when a site is ready to go live. Until such time, it is recommended that it be left switched off as otherwise, CSS changes during development will not take effect unless the Drupal cache is cleared.

How to do it...

Optimization and other performance related features are sequestered within `admin/config/development/performance` [**Home | Administer | Configuration | Development | Performance**]. This performance configuration page should have a section titled **Bandwidth optimization** which contains options for CSS and JavaScript optimization. Look for the setting named **Aggregate and compress CSS files.** and enable it as shown in the following screenshot:

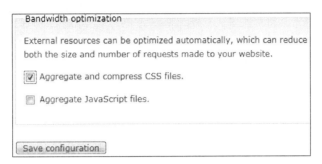

Once done, click on the **Save configuration** button at the bottom of the page to save our changes.

How it works...

Aggregation involves the collating and joining of multiple CSS files into a single stylesheet, while compression reduces the resulting file to a smaller size by trimming out unnecessary elements such as whitespace. The former helps in reducing the number of files that the server has to load and serve, while the latter saves on bandwidth and time.

In the following screenshot, we get a glimpse at an example Drupal page which loads a number of stylesheets for each page view. Each of these files has to be downloaded separately by the user's browser which creates a lag as the web server has to serve each of them separately as well. Furthermore, the multitude of `@import` calls result in each file being downloaded and parsed in sequence rather than in parallel which increases the wait time for the user even further. All in all, there are eleven files that need to be processed. If this is extrapolated to sites of greater complexity, the number of files and, consequently, the server and bandwidth load begin to take on significant proportions and can seriously impact performance.

```
    <style type="text/css" media="all">@import url
("http://book.endymion/modules/system/system.base.css?llvg9r");
@import url("http://book.endymion/modules/system/system.menus.css?llvg9r");
@import url("http://book.endymion/modules/system/system.messages.css?llvg9r");
@import url("http://book.endymion/modules/system/system.theme.css?llvg9r");</style>
<style type="text/css" media="all">@import url
("http://book.endymion/modules/system/system.admin.css?llvg9r");</style>
<style type="text/css" media="all">@import url
("http://book.endymion/modules/field/theme/field.css?llvg9r");
@import url("http://book.endymion/modules/node/node.css?llvg9r");
@import url("http://book.endymion/modules/user/user.css?llvg9r");</style>
<style type="text/css" media="all">@import url
("http://book.endymion/themes/garland/style.css?llvg9r");
@import url("http://book.endymion/sites/book.endymion/themes/mytheme/css/mytheme.css?
llvg9r");</style>
<style type="text/css" media="print">@import url
("http://book.endymion/themes/garland/print.css?llvg9r");</style>
```

The following screenshot is the same page as before with one difference, CSS optimization is now turned on. The number of CSS files has now been reduced to only five, four for all media types and the other being the print media type. Additionally, all the `@import` calls have been replaced with `<link>` leading to quicker load times as they can be downloaded in parallel by the user's browser. These stylesheets are stored in the Drupal filesystem and are cached copies. As a result, each page load now only involves the web server serving five files instead of the previous eleven.

```
    <link type="text/css" rel="stylesheet"
href="http://book.endymion/sites/book.endymion/files/css/css_
5XB5aQOGzDUVxnwtHDXg0AJDjmjZbe2Sh1K2BEkR5cM.css" media="all" />
<link type="text/css" rel="stylesheet"
href="http://book.endymion/sites/book.endymion/files/css/css_LS9OUalDR9-
d_lCAvF3yUWjNU6yF8ZBm84jEPRvoyuQ.css" media="all" />
<link type="text/css" rel="stylesheet"
href="http://book.endymion/sites/book.endymion/files/css/css_Uy1aIiY1PHMsh853q
G8YfRmd1TllwBJNDYTVg0idYHk.css" media="all" />
<link type="text/css" rel="stylesheet"
href="http://book.endymion/sites/book.endymion/files/css/css_EI1TYmJWBbHD1mAL8
x9NnmPZfMjTznIZ2HpDCumHE20.css" media="all" />
<link type="text/css" rel="stylesheet"
href="http://book.endymion/sites/book.endymion/files/css/css_k3snrbsthqot7V7cc
RZHS9OkCZkwBv4adtNieIVlbEU.css" media="print" />
```

Prior to Drupal 7, enabling CSS optimization would have reduced the number of CSS files to just two, one for `all` media types and another for the `print` media type. While this drastically reduced the number of files required to be loaded, the fact that different Drupal pages had different combinations of stylesheets meant that the same files were being optimized repeatedly to account for minor changes in the combination. In Drupal 7, this issue has been solved by introducing a grouping variable which allows for the optimization of related stylesheets such as system and theme stylesheets separately. While this increases the number of aggregated stylesheets, to five in this recipe, the overall performance increases as the server does not need to reaggregate as often.

There's more...

CSS optimization and other performance improvements should be used with care. Enabling them prematurely during the development stage can slow down development or lead to bugs and anomalies going unnoticed as we would then be working with cached versions of the code. However, there are exceptions where this is not the case.

Internet Explorer and the number 31

It is generally considered that CSS optimization is only necessary to improve performance on production sites and that enabling it beforehand will only hinder development. However, optimization can sometimes be handy during theme development on Internet Explorer. This browser has a hard limit of 31 stylesheets, that is, only the first 31 CSS files are considered and the rest are ignored. While 31 stylesheets might initially appear ample, sites routinely incorporate enough modules to easily exhaust this limitation. By enabling CSS optimization, we can work around this problem by drastically reducing the number of stylesheets that need to be loaded.

Other optimizations

Other optimization settings can also be configured on the performance page. These include page caching, block caching, and JavaScript optimization. While page and block caching endeavor to reduce the number of database calls that Drupal has to make to load and render content, JavaScript optimization offers benefits similar to those gained with CSS optimization.

It is also worthwhile browsing through the Caching and Performance modules that are available as contributed modules through `http://drupal.org/project/modules` under the category **Performance and Scalability**.

Creating the mysite module to hold our tweaks

In the course of developing our site, we will frequently come across situations where various elements of the site need to be tweaked in PHP using Drupal's APIs. While a lot of theme-specific cases can be stored in template files, certain tweaks which are theme-agnostic require that we store them in a module to ensure that they are available to all themes.

This recipe covers the creation of a module to hold our tweaks and other bits and pieces.

Getting ready

As we saw when creating the `mytheme` subtheme earlier in this chapter, the `sites/all` folder provides a `modules` folder along with a `themes` folder to hold our custom and contributed installations. These modules and themes are automatically made available to all sites using this Drupal installation. However, if we are looking to restrict the use of our module solely for a particular site, then we would place it within `sites/foo.example.com/modules` instead.

How to do it...

The following list details the procedure involved in creating a module named `mysite` to hold our theme-agnostic customizations and other odds and ends:

1. Create a folder inside `sites/all/modules` named `mysite` where `mysite` refers to the name of our site.
2. Within this folder, create a file named `mysite.info`.
3. Edit this file and add the following code inside:

   ```
   name = Mysite
   description = A module to hold odds and ends for mysite.
   core = 7.x
   ```

4. Save the file.
5. Create another file named `mysite.module`. This is the file that will hold our odds and ends.
6. Save and exit the editor.
7. Finally, enable the module through the module administration page at `admin/modules` [**Home | Administer | Modules**].

How it works...

Just as with themes, modules require a `.info` file which provides information to Drupal on compatibility, dependencies, and so on. Once Drupal ascertains that the module is compatible with the version installed, it loads the `.module` file of the same name and processes it accordingly.

We can test if the module is working by adding a snippet such as the following:

```php
<?php
/**
 * Implements hook_init().
 */
function mysite_init() {
  // Display a message on every page load.
  drupal_set_message("Welcome to MySite!");
}
```

As the comment suggests, the mysite module will now inject a welcome message into every page view. This is confirmed in the following screenshot:

There's more...

The Drupal community routinely comes up with modules to ease the pain of development.

Module builder

There's a module available named **Module Builder** which can be used to generate a skeleton of a general module. This can subsequently be populated as per our requirements. It is available at `http://drupal.org/project/module_builder`.

See also

The next recipe, *Adding a CSS file from a module*, makes use of this module to include a CSS file dynamically.

Adding a CSS file from a module

Situations arise where CSS files or CSS rules need to be added from a module. This could be useful, for example, to style features added by the module, or to style content added by some other module. When compared with including stylesheets through a theme's `.info` file, modules provide greater control and flexibility.

This recipe demonstrates how to add CSS files using the mysite module.

Getting ready

We will be using the `mysite` module created in the previous recipe. Within its folder, create a subfolder named `css` and subsequently, within it create two CSS files named `mysite.css` and `mysite_special.css` and populate them with some sample rules.

How to do it...

Add the following code to the file `mysite.module`:

```
/**
 * Implements hook_init().
 */
function mysite_init() {
  // The path to the mysite module.
  $path = drupal_get_path('module', 'mysite');

  // Include mysite.css.
  drupal_add_css($path . '/css/mysite.css');

  // Include mysite-special.css, but do not preprocess and
  // prioritize file via its weight.
  drupal_add_css($path . '/css/mysite-special.css',
    array('preprocess' => FALSE, 'weight' => -20));
}
```

 If the module is named something else, the function `mysite_init()` will need to be renamed appropriately. On the other hand, if the module already contains an existing `hook_init()` function, the contents of our function will need to be integrated appropriately to it.

Save the file and exit the editor. Visiting the site and viewing its sources should confirm that two new CSS files are now being included for every page.

How it works...

The `drupal_add_css()` function is used to add CSS files from a module. Its syntax is as follows:

```
drupal_add_css($data = NULL, $options = NULL)
```

While the syntax might initially appear simple, each of the two parameters can accept a number of different options. In this recipe, we make two calls to `drupal_add_css()`. In the first call, we include a file from the `css` folder:

```
drupal_add_css($path . '/css/mysite.css');
```

The only parameter we pass is the complete path (relative to the site root) of the CSS file to be included. The complete path is retrieved using an earlier call to `drupal_get_path()` the result of which we have stored within the variable `$path`. `drupal_add_css()`, which will typically include this file using an `@import` statement and make it available for aggregation and optimization.

The second call to `drupal_add_css()` exercises a couple of options:

```
drupal_add_css($path . '/css/mysite-special.css',
  array('preprocess' =>
  FALSE, 'weight' => -20));
```

Here we make use of both the available parameters to the function. The first passes the path to the `mysite-special.css` file. The second, however, passes an array containing two additional directives which explicitly instruct Drupal not to aggregate this file and furthermore, also ensure that this file is included ahead of other similarly configured CSS files by virtue of its lower weight.

Looking at the source code of a typical page on the site when CSS optimization is enabled, we should see the stylesheets included similar to the following transcription:

```
<link type="text/css" rel="stylesheet"
  href="http://book.endymion/sites/all/modules/mysite/css/
  mysite-special.css?1ly4ld" media="all" />
<style type="text/css" media="all">@import url
  ("http://book.endymion/sites/all/modules/mysite/css/
  mysite.css?1ly4ld");</style>
```

As the preceding markup attests, the `mysite-special.css` file is included ahead of `mysite.css`. What's more, since we have specified that it is not to be aggregated, Drupal has gone ahead and included it using a `<link>` tag rather than an `@import` statement. By enabling CSS optimization, we should find that only the `mysite.css` file is aggregated and optimized while `mysite-special.css` is included as it is.

Drupal API documentation

Drupal documentation for `drupal_add_css()`, `drupal_get_path()`, and just about every other Drupal function is available at `http://api.drupal.org`. This documentation is parsed directly from the comments included in the Drupal code. Consequently, the same information can also be retrieved by sifting through the Drupal source code, preferably with a capable editor.

There's more...

Besides adding external stylesheets, the Drupal API also allows for adding inline CSS.

Adding inline CSS

We can also utilize the `drupal_add_css()` function to inject inline CSS directly within the HEAD tags of the HTML document. We can do this by passing a string containing our CSS and instructing Drupal that it is to be included inline by way of the second parameter.

```
// Include inline CSS.
drupal_add_css('<style type="text/css">body
  { color: #000; }</style>', 'inline');
```

Naming conventions

While including CSS files from within modules, it is highly recommended that all files be prefixed with the name of the module. In this case, we have prefixed the `special.css` file with the name of our module, thus giving us `mysite-special.css`. This makes it easier while grouping and overriding stylesheets and reduces ambiguity and confusion.

See also

The *Including a JavaScript file only for certain pages* recipe *in Chapter 7, JavaScript in Themes* outlines similar functionality for JavaScript. *Enabling CSS optimization*, seen earlier in this chapter, is also relevant.

Displaying a different theme for each day of the week

This recipe demonstrates how we can go about controlling the theme being used to render a page from within a module. As an example, we will be adding the code that allows the rotation of themes based on the day of the week.

Getting ready

As we have seen in other recipes in this chapter, a number of sites use an "odds and ends" module to handle tweaks and customizations particular to the site. We will be using the `mysite.module` created earlier in this chapter to hold our customizations. It is assumed that the module is available and already enabled.

How to do it...

Open the `mysite.module` file and paste the following code in it:

```
/**
 * Implements hook_custom_theme().
 */
function mysite_custom_theme() {
  // An array of themes for each day of the week.
  // These themes have to be installed and enabled.
  $themes = array();
  $themes[0] = 'garland';
  $themes[1] = 'bartik';
  $themes[2] = 'stark';
  $themes[3] = 'seven';
  $themes[4] = 'mytheme';
  $themes[5] = 'sky';
  $themes[6] = 'danland';

  // Get the current day of the week in numerical form.
  $day = date("w");

  // Override current theme based on day of the week.
  return $themes[$day];
}
```

Save the file and then refresh a page on the Drupal site to see this snippet at work. Due to the nature of this feature, it might be necessary to fiddle with the computer's date settings to simulate different days of the week during testing.

 As the comments in the code note, the theme returned by `hook_custom_theme()` has to be installed and enabled for this to work.

How it works...

The function `hook_custom_theme()` manipulates a global variable named `$custom_theme` which controls the theme being used to render the current page. Drupal changes the theme being used based on the value returned by this function.

As we are looking to change the theme based on the day of the week, we are going to take advantage of a feature of PHP's `date()` function that returns the day of the week as a number between zero and six with the former representing Sunday and the latter denoting Saturday.

```
// Get the current day of the week in numerical form.
$day = date("w");
```

We now map the `$day` variable to the `$themes` array which also has elements from zero to six associated with seven enabled themes and, as a result, we obtain the equivalent theme for that day of the week. Finally, returning the associated theme overrides the default theme with the theme for the current day of the week.

There's more...

The PHP code used in this recipe can be easily modified to display a random theme on every page load.

Displaying a random theme

Instead of displaying a preset theme for each day of the week, integrating the following snippet into the `mysite_custom_theme()` function will display a random theme on every page load:

```
// Override current theme randomly.
return $themes[array_rand($themes)];
```

See also

Rather than cycling through different themes, the next recipe, *Creating a fresh look using the Color module*, provides an alternate solution that makes use of the Color module to modify an existing theme by changing its color scheme.

Creating a fresh look using the Color module

The Color module allows the administrator to easily change the color scheme of themes that support it. This facilitates a fresh look for the site without having to create a new theme or subtheme. Among Drupal's core themes, Garland and Bartik both support the Color module. In this recipe, we will be covering the steps required to change the color scheme of Garland to something different and possibly unique.

Getting ready

Ensure that the Color module is enabled in `admin/modules` [**Home | Administration | Modules**]. As we are going to change the color scheme of the Garland theme, ensure that it is enabled and set as the current theme.

How to do it...

Colorizing the Garland theme can be accomplished by following these steps:

1. Navigate to `admin/appearance` [**Home | Administration | Appearance**].

2. Look for the **Garland** theme and click on its associated **settings** link.

3. In the ensuing page, look for the section titled **Color scheme**.

4. In this section, the **Color set** drop-down lists a host of available preset color schemes. Choosing any of the presets will change the color scheme of the **Preview** section further below:

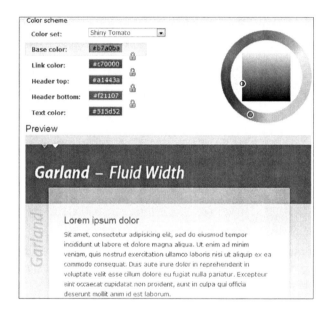

5. Once satisfied, click on the **Save configuration** button at the bottom of the page to save our changes.

How it works...

The Color module works by generating stylesheets using the new color scheme which effectively replace the existing stylesheet at runtime. The generated CSS file is stored in the site's filesystem in a folder named `color`. In addition to the stylesheets, the Color module, can also dynamically blend the theme's image assets to suit the new color scheme.

The Color module creates a new stylesheet which is a customized copy of the theme's original CSS file. As it is a copy, fixes and updates to the original file are automatically propagated to it. Therefore, whenever changes are made to the original file, it is recommended that the stylesheet be regenerated by simply saving the customized color settings once again.

There's more...

We are not restricted to the inbuilt presets provided by the Color module and can also create our own.

Custom presets

If the provided presets are unsatisfactory, clicking on the text fields below the drop down will allow further customization. Once a text field has focus, the color wheel on the right can also be clicked and used to select different palettes at will. These new settings are saved as the **Custom** preset as demonstrated in the following screenshot:

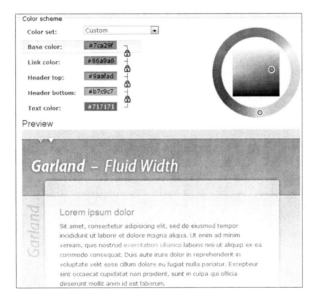

 The locks in the previous screenshot can be activated or deactivated. When activated, adjusting one value will adjust any linked fields by a relative amount. When deactivated, each field can be adjusted individually.

3
Custom Themes and Zen

We will be covering the following recipes in this chapter:

- ▶ Clearing the theme registry
- ▶ Creating a theme from scratch
- ▶ Creating myzen—a Zen-based theme
- ▶ Choosing a CSS layout for myzen
- ▶ Overriding Zen template files with myzen
- ▶ Adding a custom region to myzen
- ▶ Adding a background image to the theme
- ▶ Adding a conditional stylesheet in Zen
- ▶ Modifying myzen's theme settings

Introduction

While subthemes of core and contributed themes are convenient and efficient in modifying and reusing elements of their base themes, circumstances often require a completely unique approach specific to our site. Custom themes are the solution for websites that demand a fresh look, use complex layouts, or require such intricate fine tuning that it would be prudent to start with a clean slate.

Custom themes are the equivalent of handcrafted pieces of art, as the themer controls every piece of the puzzle from a design or implementational point of view. This includes setting up the theme using .info files, choosing the layout, implementing it in a page template, adding regions, styling nodes using node templates, blocks using block templates, and so on. But over time, developers have identified a list of common tasks, characteristic layouts, and file and folder hierarchies that are logical, efficient, and promote reuse. This has evolved into what have been dubbed **starter themes**—themes upon which custom themes are built, usually as subthemes.

The most popular starter theme for Drupal is Zen. As advertised on its project page, the idea behind the Zen theme is to have a flexible standards-compliant and semantically correct XHTML theme that can be highly modified through CSS and an enhanced version of Drupal's template system. It is designed in modular fashion thereby making it straightforward to change layouts, override templates and theme functions, and to add or remove features. Additionally, the Zen theme comes with extensive documentation within each file which make things all the more convenient.

With respect to CSS, Zen maintains a number of well-documented CSS files segregated by functionality or location. For example, layout rules are contained within a dedicated layout.css (or similar) file and page backgrounds are styled within page-backgrounds.css, and so on. This makes it convenient when it comes to managing and tracking code changes.

In addition to the standard files that we have encountered while customizing themes in the earlier chapters, a Zen-based theme contains the following file and folder structure:

File/folder name	Purpose
css/	A folder to store stylesheets.
images/	A folder to store images used in the theme.
images-source/	A folder where the source files for the optimized images in the images folder are available.
js/	A folder to store JavaScript files.
templates/	A folder where tpl.php template files are located.
template.php	A file where theme function overrides and other theme and engine related code is placed.
theme-settings.php	A file where settings particular to a theme can be placed. These settings are customarily exposed on the theme's configuration page.

There are a number of other starter themes available on Drupal.org. Some of the more popular ones include:

- Fusion (`http://drupal.org/project/fusion`)
- Blueprint (`http://drupal.org/project/blueprint`)
- Ninesixty (`http://drupal.org/project/ninesixty`)
- Adaptive theme (`http://drupal.org/project/adaptivetheme`)

We will be looking only at the Zen starter theme in this book.

Clearing the theme registry

Before we begin, we need to familiarize ourselves with a seemingly trivial yet crucial task that needs to be performed on a routine basis during theme development—clearing the **theme registry**. The theme registry is essentially a table that Drupal uses to list and track the files and features of a theme as well as the theme functions which are being exposed by modules and the theme itself.

While it is a recommended practice to turn on Drupal's cache feature only for production sites, the theme registry is built and cached regardless of other caching options. As a result, any changes that affect the structure of the theme will necessitate the clearing of the theme registry.

Getting ready

Rebuilding the registry is an intensive operation which is required only when changes have been made to the theme files.

How to do it...

There are a number of ways of clearing the registry. In a stock Drupal installation, visiting `admin/config/development/performance` (**Home | Administration | Configuration | Development | Performance**) and clicking on the **Clear cached data** button will clear all the cached data, including the registry, and force a rebuild.

A shortcut

It is sometimes handy to know that the cache and registry can also be cleared by visiting `admin/appearance` (**Home | Administration | Appearance**) and just clicking on the **Save configuration** button.

However, during development or debugging, we will want to clear the registry with great regularity. Instead of having to do so manually, it is often handy to be able to instruct Drupal to perform this operation automatically on every page load. Some themes, including the Zen-based theme, which we will be familiarizing ourselves with later in this chapter, offer an option on their configuration pages to rebuild the registry on every page load. While this is certainly convenient, the recommended method of managing this and other development-oriented operations is through the use of the Devel module.

As the name suggests, the Devel module is one that is tailor-made for use during development. It can be downloaded from `http://drupal.org/project/devel`. Once the module has been downloaded and installed, navigate to `admin/config/development/devel` (**Home | Administration | Configuration | Development | Devel settings**) where the option to **Rebuild the theme registry on every page load** can be enabled.

How it works...

Drupal maintains a cache of all `.info` files, template files, and theme functions in the theme registry. This registry is a part of the `cache` table in the Drupal database. When we click on the **Clear cache data** button in the **Performance settings** page, all Drupal is doing is clearing this entry in the `cache` table, which automatically forces a rebuild of the registry. The Devel module does the same thing when the **Rebuild the theme registry on every page load** setting is enabled, except that it does this automatically on every page view.

It's important to keep in mind that rebuilding the registry, or for that matter clearing any of the caches, is an expensive operation that adversely affects the performance of the site. Therefore, it is recommended that this setting only be enabled during development and not in production sites.

Clearing the registry is an important factor to keep in mind during development and especially during debugging. More information on development and debugging tools including the Devel module is available in *Chapter 5, Development and Debugging Tools*.

There's more...

The Devel module also provides a block with handy shortcuts to oft-used areas of the site.

Clearing the cache using the Development block

The Devel module provides a custom menu which can also be embedded as a block through the **Block management** page at `admin/structure/block` (**Home | Administration | Structure | Blocks**). As it is a menu, the block will be made available only if the Menu module is enabled. Once enabled, the block lists a number of links to perform operations such as emptying the Drupal cache, rebuilding the menu cache, and even reinstalling modules as shown in the following screenshot. Emptying the cache will also force a rebuild of the theme registry. Once the theme is reasonably stable, it might be more efficient to manually clear the cache through this block instead of rebuilding the registry during each page view:

See also

Chapter 5, _Development and Debugging Tools_ elaborates further on the uses of the Devel module during theme development.

Creating a theme from scratch

While we have earlier looked at installing contributed themes and extending base themes using subthemes, this recipe will outline the steps required to create a custom theme from scratch.

Getting ready

Custom themes, like contributed themes, are placed within the `sites/all/themes` folder (or the `sites/foo.example.com/themes` folder, in case of multi-site installations). Some administrators prefer to go a step further and place custom and contributed themes in their own folders. In other words, our custom theme would be placed within `sites/all/themes/custom` and any other contributed themes would find their place within `sites/all/themes/contrib` or similar.

How to do it...

Creating a brand new custom theme is not unlike what we did in *Chapter 2, Beyond the Basics*, in creating a subtheme for a core theme. The primary difference is that there is no base theme in this case and that files such as `page.tpl.php` will need to be explicitly defined:

1. Create a folder with the new theme's name inside the `sites/all/themes` folder. In this example, we are going to call our theme `mytheme`.

2. Within this folder, create a file named `mytheme.info` and open it in an editor.

3. Add details about the theme as follows:

    ```
    name = My theme
    description = My custom theme
    core = 7.x
    ```

4. Save the file.

5. Visit the theme administration page at `admin/appearance` (**Home | Administration | Appearance**) and we should be able to see a new entry for our theme:

6. Enable the theme and activate it by clicking its **Enable and set default** link.

How it works...

Just as with other themes, Drupal scans the `sites/all/themes` folder looking for `.info` files that indicate the presence of a theme. Seeing `mytheme.info`, it parses the file, loads the details of the theme, and saves them in the database.

When the new theme is enabled, what we will see is largely unstyled content not unlike the following screenshot. The problem here is that we have not specified any CSS stylesheets to lay out the page. The only styles being loaded are those that are module-specific as opposed to theme-specific:

The styles being used in the preceding screenshot are as follows:

```
<style type="text/css" media="all">@import url("http://book.endymion/
  modules/system/system.base.css?lm5mb7");
  @import url("http://book.endymion/modules/system/system.menus.
    css?lm5mb7");
  @import url("http://book.endymion/modules/system/system.messages.
    css?lm5mb7");
  @import url("http://book.endymion/modules/system/system.theme.
    css?lm5mb7");
</style>
<style type="text/css" media="all">@import url("http://book.endymion/
  modules/field/theme/field.css?lm5mb7");
  @import url("http://book.endymion/modules/node/node.css?lm5mb7");
  @import url("http://book.endymion/modules/user/user.css?lm5mb7");
</style>
```

As we can see, the only stylesheets in evidence are those belonging to core modules and none from our theme.

Furthermore, during the process of building the page, Drupal has noticed that we do not have any template files in our theme, most notably, `page.tpl.php`. Therefore, it has defaulted to an inbuilt page template file from `modules/system/page.tpl.php` and used it instead. Similarly it is using the `node.tpl.php` file from `modules/node/` as the basis for each node's layout.

In other words, we have a lot of work ahead of us in getting things up and running especially if our eventual requirements are going to be complicated. As we will see in the next recipe, this is one of the reasons why most themers prefer to use a starter theme and hit the ground running.

See also

The next recipe, *Creating myzen—a Zen-based theme*, implements a custom theme based on a starter theme named Zen.

Creating myzen—a Zen-based theme

While building a custom theme from scratch is great, most themers prefer to use starter themes as the base for their designs. Starter themes save time and effort as themers do not have to perform tedious repetitive tasks, and can rely on a tried and tested structure to use as a foundation for their custom themes.

In this recipe, we will be looking at creating a theme based on the most popular of all starter themes available on Drupal.org, Zen.

Getting ready

Download the theme from `http://drupal.org/project/zen` and install it within `sites/all/themes/`. The default Zen theme does not need to be enabled for our custom theme to work.

How to do it...

The Zen theme provides a starter kit that can be used to kick-start our theme:

1. Navigate to the newly installed Zen theme's folder at `sites/all/themes/zen`.

2. Copy the `STARTERKIT` folder inside it.

3. Paste this folder into `sites/all/themes`.

4. Rename the folder to the name of our new theme which, in this recipe, is `myzen`:

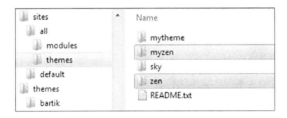

5. Within this folder, rename the file `STARTERKIT.info.txt` to `myzen.info`.

6. Open the `.info` file in an editor.

7. Update the name field to the name of the theme which in this case is `myzen`.

8. Update the description field to **My custom Zen sub-theme**.

9. Save and exit this file.

10. Open `template.php` in an editor and replace all occurrences of `STARTERKIT_` with `myzen_` using the editor's find and replace all function.

11. Save and exit the editor.

12. Repeat the find and replace operation for the file `theme-settings.php` as well.

13. Save and exit this file.

Visiting the theme administration page at `admin/appearance` (**Home | Administration | Appearance**). It should now display our new theme. Screenshots, favicons, and other niceties can be configured just like for any other theme.

How it works...

The Zen theme contains a folder named STARTERKIT that is effectively a skeleton subtheme containing files and folders that can be readily customized to create a new theme. Once we have made a copy of this folder and renamed its `.info` file with the name of our theme, Drupal will recognize our new entry, which is now registered as a subtheme of Zen as seen in the following screenshot:

 While the Zen theme needs to be available, it does not need to be enabled for myzen to function.

Once enabled, the front page of the site will look something like the following screenshot. It is worthwhile comparing the screenshots in this recipe with those from the *Creating a theme from scratch* recipe earlier in this chapter. The essential difference is that we have a fleshed-out skeleton to work with when we use Zen with a lot of the right pieces already in the right place:

There's more...

The Zen theme comes with a plethora of settings and documentation, which can at times be a little overwhelming. But the rewards of familiarizing ourselves with them are worth the time.

Subtheme of Zen

We can confirm that this is a subtheme of Zen through its `.info` file, which specifies that `base theme = zen`

As mentioned in the last chapter, if we need another theme similar to myzen, we can create one with `base theme = myzen` and save ourselves a host of repeated operations.

RTFM

Just about every folder which comes with Zen contains a `README.txt` file that is filled to the brim with copious documentation. It is a good idea to always read through these files beforehand rather than diving in head first.

Rebuild theme registry on every page

The Zen theme contains a setting that rebuilds the theme registry automatically on every page load. This setting is exposed in the `.info` file as `settings[zen_rebuild_registry]` and also through the theme settings page at `admin/appearance/settings/myzen` (**Home | Administration | Appearance | Settings | My Zen**). By default it is enabled.

See also

The next recipe, *Choosing a CSS layout for myzen*, explains how to easily change the CSS layout for our subtheme.

Choosing a CSS layout for myzen

Layouts decide how elements on a page, customarily contained in DIVs, are positioned. Zen comes with a couple of preset layouts that can be used. If neither of them is suitable, a custom layout can be created. In this recipe, we will be replacing the default fixed-width layout with a liquid layout which we discussed in *Chapter 1, Drupal Theme Basics*.

Getting ready

We are going to assume that the myzen theme from earlier in this chapter is enabled and the current default. It is also important to decide on the type of layout required for the site during the design stage.

How to do it...

All we are going to do here is replace one of the stylesheets used in myzen with another:

1. Open `myzen.info` in an editor.

2. In the section pertaining to stylesheet declarations, look for the line that declares the fixed-width layout which should usually be `stylesheets[all][] = css/layout-fixed.css`.

3. Replace this with `stylesheets[all][] = css/layout-liquid.css`.

4. Save the file and exit the editor.

5. In what should be second nature by now, clear the theme registry for our changes to take effect.

How it works...

The default fixed-width layout is, as the name suggests, of a fixed width. The positioning of the content does not vary based on the dimensions of the browser and the resolution of the user's monitor. Consequently, we are assured of a consistent structure regardless of the user's configuration.

By replacing the `layout-fixed.css` stylesheet in the `myzen.info` file, Drupal is now instructed to load the `layout-liquid.css` file instead. Unlike fixed-width layouts, liquid layouts try to occupy as much of the available real estate as possible. In other words, larger monitors and browser windows will be able to view more of the content while smaller ones will have to do with less. Once this layout is enabled and the theme registry cleared, we should be able to see that the layout of the site now occupies the full width of the screen and will flow and reposition itself as we resize the browser window.

There's more...

Zen and its subthemes take care while displaying content and ensure that the markup is clean and semantically correct. Furthermore, in light of the growing internationalization of the web, it provides **Right-To-Left** (**RTL)** support out of the box.

What is RTL?

A number of CSS files in Zen and other themes are offered in two variants—one with an RTL suffix and the other without. RTL is an acronym for right-to-left and is used to signify that the stylesheet will be used when RTL mode is enabled, customarily for sites with content in languages such as Hebrew and Arabic.

Custom layouts

There are various advantages and disadvantages of using a fixed-width or a liquid layout, and a variety of ways to accomplish these very same layouts which are drastically different from the way Zen implements them. Other types of layouts such as grid layouts are also in vogue. If a custom layout is necessary, all that needs to be done is to add the appropriate rules to a stylesheet such as `layout-custom.css` and embedding it into our theme through its `.info` file as seen in this recipe.

See also

Later in this chapter, the recipe, *Adding a custom region to myzen*, explains how to go about adding custom regions to our layout.

Overriding Zen template files with myzen

Zen subthemes, by default, use the page, node, and other template files directly from the base theme. In other words, we do not need to specify template files in our myzen theme unless we are looking to change the template.

In this recipe, we are going to override the base theme's `page.tpl.php` template file with our own copy and make changes to it. As an example, let us see whether we can reposition the status messages element which is usually represented by the `$messages` variable.

Getting ready

We are going to assume that the myzen subtheme is already created and available.

How to do it...

The following steps outline the procedure to import a template file from the base theme to the subtheme:

1. Navigate to the `sites/all/themes/zen/templates` folder that contains the default templates.
2. Copy the `page.tpl.php` file.
3. Paste it into the equivalent folder in the subtheme, namely, `sites/all/themes/myzen/templates`.
4. Within the subtheme, open this file in an editor.

5. Scroll down looking for any usage of the `$messages` variable. It should be located in a code block not dissimilar to the following code snippet:

```
<?php print $breadcrumb; ?>
<a id="main-content"></a>
<?php print render($title_prefix); ?>
<?php if ($title): ?>
  <h1 class="title" id="page-title"><?php print $title; ?></h1>
<?php endif; ?>
<?php print render($title_suffix); ?>
<?php print $messages; ?>
<?php if ($tabs = render($tabs)): ?>
  <div class="tabs"><?php print $tabs; ?></div>
<?php endif; ?>
```

6. What we are looking to do is to move the status messages to a more prominent location above the title and the breadcrumb. After moving the relevant line of code further above, this block should look something like the following code snippet:

```
<?php print $messages; ?>
<?php print $breadcrumb; ?>
<a id="main-content"></a>
<?php print render($title_prefix); ?>
<?php if ($title): ?>
  <h1 class="title" id="page-title"><?php print $title; ?></h1>
<?php endif; ?>
<?php print render($title_suffix); ?>
<?php if ($tabs = render($tabs)): ?>
  <div class="tabs"><?php print $tabs; ?></div>
<?php endif; ?>
```

7. Save the file and exit.

8. As we have imported a template file, we also need to clear the theme registry.

We should now be able to see our changes in effect when a node, for example, is updated.

How it works...

Once we have copied the template file from Zen to myzen, and subsequently cleared the registry, Drupal was alerted during the theme registry rebuilding process that a new `page.tpl.php` file was available. Due to the fact that this template file was located in the myzen theme's folder, it took precedence over the version contained within the Zen theme's folder leading to our updates taking effect.

It's interesting to note that while the `page.tpl.php` template file in myzen took precedence over the file in the Zen folder, the latter was already overriding the equivalent template file in Drupal's system module folder.

The following screenshots should offer a before-and-after comparison of this recipe in action:

In the previous screenshot, we can see that the status message is being displayed below the title of the node. However, with our new template file in action, we can see that the status message is now displayed above the title and the breadcrumb as shown in the following screenshot:

See also

Overriding base theme elements in a subtheme recipe in *Chapter 2, Beyond the Basics* deals with overriding the `node.tpl.php` template file for a Garland subtheme.

Adding a custom region to myzen

Regions are essentially containers for Drupal blocks. The layout of regions in a page effectively dictates the layout of the site. By default the myzen theme contains the following regions:

- ▸ Help
- ▸ First sidebar
- ▸ Second sidebar
- ▸ Navigation bar
- ▸ Highlighted
- ▸ Content
- ▸ Header
- ▸ Footer
- ▸ Page bottom

In this recipe, we will be looking to replace the existing footer region with two separate regions named footer top and footer bottom respectively.

Getting ready

We are going to assume that the myzen theme from earlier in this chapter is enabled and the current default. We will be updating the default `page.tpl.php` template file that is used by myzen. If this file does not exist in `sites/all/themes/myzen/templates`, it will need to be imported into this folder from `sites/all/themes/zen/templates/page.tpl.php`.

How to do it...

In order to add a custom region to myzen, follow the ensuing steps. First up, we will be updating the regions list in the `.info` file:

1. Open the `myzen.info` file in an editor.
2. Scroll down to the section dealing with regions.

3. Look for the following declaration:

```
regions[footer]          = Footer
```

4. Replace the previous declaration with the following:

```
regions[footer_top]     = Footer top
regions[footer_bottom]  = Footer bottom
```

5. Save the file and exit the editor.

6. Now that we have added our new regions, we need to ensure that Drupal uses them by updating the `page.tpl.php` template. Open myzen's `page.tpl.php` file in an editor.

7. Scroll down and look for the following line of code:

```
<?php print render($page['footer']); ?>
```

8. Replace the preceding line with the following two:

```
<?php print render($page['footer_top']); ?>
<?php print render($page['footer_bottom']); ?>
```

 Note the correspondence between the variable names in the template file and the internal names for their respective regions in the `myzen.info` file.

9. Save the file and exit the editor.

10. Clear the theme registry as per usual.

The new regions should now be visible if we navigate to the blocks administration page at `admin/structure/block` (**Home | Administration | Structure | Blocks**). Clicking on the **Demonstrate block regions (My Zen)** link at the top of the page should provide a visual representation of the theme regions.

How it works...

Drupal's theming system loads (and caches) information from each theme's `.info` file. This includes information on the regions that each theme wants to declare. These regions are populated by Drupal and its installed modules with content and then presented to the templating engine.

The following two screenshots should offer a before-and-after comparison of the **block region demonstration** page for the myzen theme. Each region in the layout is depicted by a yellow bar that contains the name of the region:

In the original layout, as displayed in the preceding screenshot, we can see the various regions highlighted in yellow. These regions include the lone **Footer**, situated below the content of the page. By simply editing the `.info` file and updating a template file, we have been able to replace this single option with two new regions—**Footer top** and **Footer bottom**—as shown in the following screenshot:

There's more...

Drupal's theming system has a couple of tricks up its sleeve when it comes to regions.

Hidden regions

Looking at the default list of regions declared in the `myzen.info` file, we should be able to see something of an anomaly:

```
regions[help]            = Help
regions[sidebar_first]   = First sidebar
regions[sidebar_second]  = Second sidebar
regions[navigation]      = Navigation bar
regions[highlighted]     = Highlighted
regions[content]         = Content
regions[header]          = Header
regions[footer]          = Footer
regions[bottom]          = Page bottom
regions[page_top]        = Page top
regions[page_bottom]     = Page bottom
```

Firstly, there are two regions titled `Page bottom`, although only one (which, if we look through `page.tpl.php`, can be confirmed to be the entry denoted by `regions[bottom]`) is visible in Drupal. Furthermore, the region titled `Page top` in the `.info` file is missing altogether in the template file. If we do a little more digging, we should be able to ascertain that this happens with other themes as well, notably with the Drupal core theme, Bartik. An explanation for this anomaly lies not in the labels given to each region, but in their internal names—`page_top` and `page_bottom`—which are set aside by Drupal to be populated dynamically by modules such as core's Toolbar module rather than through the use of blocks through the **Block administration** pages.

Besides the default hidden regions provided by the theming system, themes can also specify their own custom hidden regions using the following syntax:

```
regions_hidden[] = myregion
```

This region will not be visible on the block administration interface.

Besides these hidden regions declared by the theming system, modules can also specify their own hidden regions using `hook_system_info_alter()`. The Dashboard module which also ships with core makes use of this feature to, by default, add three regions namely—`dashboard_main`, `dashboard_sidebar`, and `dashboard_inactive`.

Adding a background image to the theme

Zen-based themes come with a plethora of stylesheets separated logically by functionality. In this recipe, we will be exploring their use by adding a background image to our myzen theme.

Getting ready

As usual, we are going to assume that myzen is enabled and is the current default theme. As we are going to be using a background image in this recipe, it will also be a good idea to ensure that the myzen theme is using a fixed-width layout to improve the visibility of the background.

The background image to be used should be optimized and saved in the `sites/all/themes/myzen/images/` folder. In this recipe, we will be setting the image file named `body-bg.png` as the background and repeating it along both the X and Y axes.

How to do it...

As Zen-based themes use stylesheets partitioned based on their functionality, we can add our rules to the file `page-backgrounds.css` by following the ensuing steps:

1. Navigate to the `sites/all/themes/myzen/css` folder which contains a set of stylesheets available for customization.

2. Look for the file named `page-backgrounds.css` and open it in an editor.

3. The first rule that we are concerned with is the one for the BODY tag. Locate it and add the following highlighted rule to set the background image:

   ```
   body {
     background: url(../images/body-bg.png) repeat;
   }
   ```

    As the CSS file is within the `css` folder, we need to use the `../images/body-bg.png` syntax to reference the file within the `images` folder.

4. The next element we are going to be styling is the DIV with `id="#page"` which contains the regions of the layout. Look for the entry for `#page` and add the following highlighted rule below to it:

   ```
   #page {
     background: #EEE;
   }
   ```

5. Save the file and exit the editor.

How it works...

The `page-backgrounds.css` file is added to the theme through its `.info` file. The `myzen.info` file will, by default, have a whole host of CSS files included not unlike the following list:

```
stylesheets[all][]          = css/html-reset.css
stylesheets[all][]          = css/wireframes.css
stylesheets[all][]          = css/layout-fixed.css
stylesheets[all][]          = css/page-backgrounds.css
stylesheets[all][]          = css/tabs.css
stylesheets[all][]          = css/pages.css
stylesheets[all][]          = css/blocks.css
stylesheets[all][]          = css/navigation.css
stylesheets[all][]          = css/views-styles.css
stylesheets[all][]          = css/nodes.css
stylesheets[all][]          = css/comments.css
stylesheets[all][]          = css/forms.css
stylesheets[all][]          = css/fields.css
stylesheets[print][]        = css/print.css
; Example of adding handheld stylesheets. The iPhone's preferred media
type
; is based on the CSS3 Media queries. http://www.w3.org/TR/css3-
mediaqueries/
;stylesheets[handheld][]   = css/mobile.css
;stylesheets[only screen and (max-device-width: 480px)][] = css/
iphone.css
```

Commented code

In the preceding excerpt from the `.info` file, lines prefixed with a semicolon are deemed to have been commented out and are not considered.

Most of the CSS files referenced in the file are skeleton stylesheets, each with its own functionality and purpose. They are usually also peppered with a lot of documentation and examples to get us started. In this case, the `page-backgrounds.css` file is already included and our rules should take effect automatically. It is important that we limit our changes in this stylesheet to rules pertaining to page element backgrounds. Including extraneous styles will defeat the purpose of partitioning the CSS based on functionality.

As we have amended the CSS to display a background image for the body and a background color for the content, the resulting front page should now have a tiled background for its body and a gray backdrop to its content as demonstrated in the following screenshot:

There's more...

Stylesheet management can sometimes be an involved process and is largely dependent on our own personal preferences.

Custom file structures

Some themers are uncomfortable with managing the multitude of CSS files that come with Zen and other themes. They either prefer their own logical structures or use a single monolithic stylesheet containing all the rules. There is nothing really wrong with this and it is simply a question of comfort and ease of use.

Unused stylesheets

Once we are done styling our theme, we will usually find that there are a number of stylesheets included in `myzen.info` that are empty or never used. Rather than deleting the relevant lines, it is prudent to just comment them out by prefixing them with a semicolon.

See also

The next recipe, *Adding a conditional stylesheet in Zen*, explores Drupal's support for stylesheets further.

Adding a conditional stylesheet in Zen

Conditional stylesheets are a regular staple for themers who wish to ensure that their themes are consistent across all browsers, most notably, particular versions of the Internet Explorer (IE) browser. While other themes would require us to conditionally introduce said stylesheets either using a module or through the theme's `template.php` file, Zen-based themes offer a straightforward alternative.

In this recipe, we will be looking at the procedure involved in adding a conditional stylesheet that is loaded only if the browser is IE. Furthermore, the version of the browser has to be eight—IE8.

Getting ready

This recipe centers around the myzen subtheme that is assumed to have been created, enabled, and set as the default theme. A CSS file named `ie8.css` should be created and saved inside myzen's `css` folder. Hacks and workarounds particular to IE8 are to be added to this file.

How to do it...

Adding a conditional stylesheet to the myzen theme can be accomplished as follows:

1. Navigate to the `sites/all/themes/myzen` folder.

2. Open the `myzen.info` file in an editor.

3. Scroll down to the section dealing with conditional stylesheets. The default configuration should look something like the following code block:

   ```
   ; To target all versions of IE with an ie.css, uncomment the
   following line:
   ;stylesheets-conditional[IE][all][]        = css/ie.css
   stylesheets-conditional[lte IE 7][all][]   = css/ie7.css
   stylesheets-conditional[lte IE 6][all][]   = css/ie6.css
   ```

4. Add the following statement to this list:

   ```
   stylesheets-conditional[IE 8][all][]       = css/ie8.css
   ```

 `lte` in the code stands for lesser than or equal to and `gte` stands for greater than or equal to. More information and a list of other operators can be found at `http://msdn.microsoft.com/en-us/library/ms537512.aspx`.

5. Save the file and exit.

6. As we have made changes to the `.info` file, the theme registry needs to be rebuilt.

When the site is now viewed in IE8, the `ie8.css` stylesheet will also be loaded.

How it works...

When the HTML source for a sample page is viewed, the conditional-stylesheets declaration used in this recipe will be translated to something like the following code snippet:

```
<!--[if lte IE 7]>
  <style type="text/css" media="all">@import url("http://book.endymion
    /sites/book.endymion/themes/myzen/css/ie7.css?lmgood");</style>
<![endif]-->
<!--[if lte IE 6]>
  <style type="text/css" media="all">@import url("http://book.endymion
    /sites/book.endymion/themes/myzen/css/ie6.css?lmgood");</style>
<![endif]-->
<!--[if IE 8]>
  <style type="text/css" media="all">@import url("http://book.endymion
    /sites/book.endymion/themes/myzen/css/ie8.css?lmgood");</style>
<![endif]-->
```

As evident from the preceding source code, Zen translates our entries in the `.info` file into conditional comments and inserts them as markup. The conditional comments are only triggered in Internet Explorer, which includes the appropriate stylesheet accordingly.

There's more...

Drupal's theming API also provides an avenue to include stylesheets conditionally.

Adding conditional stylesheets from modules and themes

The `drupal_add_css()` function can be used to insert conditional comments from modules and themes. In the following excerpt from Garland's `template.php`, we can see a conditional stylesheet being included solely for IE6 by leveraging the `'browsers'` option:

```
/**
 * Override or insert variables into the html template.
 */
function garland_preprocess_html(&$vars) {
  // Toggle fixed or fluid width.
  if (theme_get_setting('garland_width') == 'fluid') {
    $vars['classes_array'][] = 'fluid-width';
  }
```

```
     // Add conditional CSS for IE6.
    drupal_add_css(path_to_theme() . '/fix-ie.css', array('group' =>
       CSS_THEME, 'browsers' => array('IE' => 'lt IE 7', '!IE' => FALSE),
       'preprocess' => FALSE));
}
```

See also

Adding a CSS file from a module recipe in *Chapter 2, Beyond the Basics* elaborates on adding CSS files from within custom modules.

Modifying myzen's theme settings

Visiting the theme configuration page for the myzen theme created earlier in this chapter should reveal a number of theme-specific settings. In this recipe, we are going to learn where these settings are added and then, learn how to add and modify them to suit our purposes.

Getting ready

As we are working with the myzen theme created earlier in this chapter, it should be enabled and set as the site's default theme. Furthermore, when the myzen theme was created, all instances of STARTERKIT_ in the theme-settings.php file should be replaced by myzen_. Once this is done, the theme configuration page for the myzen theme should include theme-specific settings as shown in the following screenshot:

How to do it...

The setting that we will be adding is one to hide the RSS or Atom feed icons displayed at the bottom of the default page template. To do so, we will be working with two different files—myzen's `theme-settings.php` and its `page.tpl.php`. As a reference, we will also be looking at the Zen theme's `theme-settings.php` file:

1. Load all three files in three separate editors.

2. By comparing myzen's `theme-settings.php` and Zen's `theme-settings.php`, we can tell that all the settings in the previous screenshot are declared by Zen through a function named `zen_form_system_theme_settings_alter()`. Myzen gets access to these settings as it is a subtheme of Zen and it can modify them as it sees fit in its own alter function, `myzen_form_system_theme_settings_alter()`.

3. In myzen's `myzen_form_system_theme_settings_alter()` function, we can see that an existing setting is already being modified:

```
// Remove some of the base theme's settings.
unset($form['themedev']['zen_layout']);
```

 Looking up the `zen_layout` setting in the Zen theme's `zen_form_system_theme_settings_alter()` we can see that the `unset()` call removes an option to toggle between a liquid and fixed-width layout. We should be able to see this setting in the settings form if we comment out this line of code.

4. To add our feed icon toggle, insert the following code under the `unset()` call within `myzen_form_system_theme_settings_alter()`:

```
$form['feed'] = array(
    '#type'         => 'fieldset',
    '#title'        => t('Feed settings')
);
$form['feed']['zen_display_feed_icons'] = array(
    '#type'         => 'checkbox',
    '#title'        => t('Display feed icons in the body of the
                          page.'),
    '#default_value' => theme_get_setting('zen_display_feed_icons')
);
```

5. Save the file and exit its editor.

6. Now, that we have added our setting, we should implement it within the `page.tpl.php` template file. Switch to its editor and locate the code pertaining to the display of the feed icons which should look like the highlighted line in the following excerpt:

```php
<?php print render($page['help']); ?>
<?php if ($action_links): ?>
  <ul class="action-links"><?php print render($action_links); ?>
  </ul>
<?php endif; ?>
<?php print render($page['content']); ?>
<?php print $feed_icons; ?>
</div></div><!-- /.section, /#content -->
```

7. Replace the highlighted with the following:

```php
<?php if (theme_get_setting('zen_display_feed_icons')) print
  $feed_icons; ?>
```

> The `theme_get_setting()` function retrieves our newly added form option. We should be able to see other examples of this function in action within the Zen theme's `template.php` file.

8. Save the file and exit all editors.

9. Navigate back to myzen's theme configuration page at `admin/appearance/settings/myzen` (**Home | Administration | Appearance | Settings**) and refresh the page to confirm that a new fieldset titled **Feed settings** is now available. Note that the checkbox within it is unchecked by default as shown in the following screenshot:

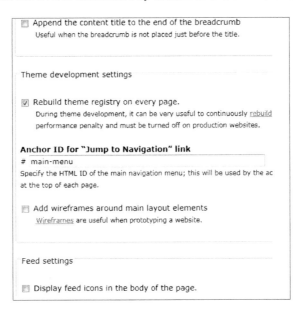

To set the default to enabled, we need to include our new setting within `myzen.info` file. Open this file in an editor.

10. Look for the section dealing with theme settings and include the following highlighted line to it:

```
settings[zen_jump_link_target]      = main-menu
settings[zen_rebuild_registry]      = 1
settings[zen_wireframes]            = 0
settings[zen_display_feed_icons]    = 1
```

11. Save the file and exit the editor.

12. Clear the theme registry as we have made changes to the `myzen.info` file which is also cached.

13. Refresh the myzen theme's settings page to confirm that the default value is being registered.

14. Toggle the setting and click on the **Save configuration** button to save our changes.

15. Visiting the default front page should confirm that the RSS feed icon at the bottom of the page is no longer being displayed.

How it works...

The Zen theme exports a set of variables and allows its subtheme, myzen, to act upon them by updating their values, adding new settings, or removing existing ones. These settings are constructed using the **Forms API** and altered by each subtheme. The settings are saved within the database and are accessed using the `theme_get_setting()` function. Furthermore, default values for each setting can be added or modified through `myzen.info` as well.

See also

The Forms API is explored in greater detail in *Chapter 9, Form Design*. *Chapter 8, Navigation*, explores how to go about customizing breadcrumbs in Zen-based themes.

4
Templating Basics

We will be covering the following recipes in this chapter:

- ▶ Changing the structure of a page using template files
- ▶ Customizing the appearance of a particular node type
- ▶ Customizing the appearance of a specific node
- ▶ Theming made easy using the Devel module
- ▶ Theme overrides using the Theme developer module
- ▶ Styling the site maintenance page

Introduction

Drupal's design stresses the separation of logic from presentation with the former being handled by modules and the latter by themes. *Theme functions*—commonly those that are prefixed with `theme_`—and theme *template files* act as a bridge between the two as they are designed to be overrideable. All theme functions and template files are tracked by Drupal's theme system and cataloged in a **theme registry**. Modules and themes are expected to declare their theme functions and templates through the use of a function named `hook_theme()`. This function is parsed for each module and theme and the resulting registry is cached in the database.

What this registry does is allow developers to modify and override existing theme implementations with their own customizations. If the registry states that for task `foo`, theme function `bar()` has to be used, we can modify the registry to point to our own function named `baz()` instead of `bar()`, which does something entirely different.

For example, let us consider the following snippet of code from Drupal's user module that is located at `modules/user/user.module`:

```
/**
 * Returns HTML for a user signature.
 *
 * @param $variables
 *    An associative array containing:
 *    - signature: The user's signature.
 *
 * @ingroup themeable
 */
function theme_user_signature($variables) {
  $signature = $variables['signature'];
  $output = '';

  if ($signature) {
    $output .= '<div class="clear">';
    $output .= '<div>—</div>';
    $output .= $signature;
    $output .= '</div>';
  }

  return $output;
}
```

The preceding code snippet is a theme function used to insert the markup required to display a user's signature in a comment. This piece of code is expressly isolated in this function so that it can be modified from the theme layer.

When we want to modify the output of the user signature and incorporate our own markup into it, we need to override `theme_user_signature()` with our own implementation. Doing so can be as simple as creating a function named `myzen_user_signature()` inside the `template.php` of our theme, which in this example is myzen. Once the registry is rebuilt, Drupal will become aware of this new function that will supersede `theme_user_signature()` and use it instead of the original when displaying a user's signature.

Similar to the theme function above, the `modules/user` folder contains a collection of `.tpl.php` template files including one named `user-picture.tpl.php` with the following content:

```
<?php if ($user_picture): ?>
  <div class="user-picture">
    <?php print $user_picture; ?>
  </div>
<?php endif; ?>
```

This template file specifies the markup to be used when displaying a user's avatar image and can be overridden through the use of, for example, a new template file in the theme's directory with the same name. Once the theme registry is rebuilt after our change, Drupal will notice this new file and use it instead of the original.

In this chapter, we will be using these and other techniques in order to customize our theme using the prescribed Drupal approach.

Changing the structure of a page using template files

As we have seen in earlier chapters, the page template file—page.tpl.php—is responsible for the overall layout and markup of a Drupal page. Various elements common to all pages in the site such as the layout of regions, headers, footers, logos, slogans, breadcrumbs, and so on are all positioned in this file. While this may make the page template file appear to be something of a master template file, this is not entirely accurate.

The html.tpl.php template file would be a more apt candidate for the title of master template file as this is where the actual structure of the HTML page is declared. This includes specifying the DOCTYPE of the page, HTML headers where styles and scripts are embedded, the BODY tag, and finally, content that Drupal has deemed to be intrinsic to each page.

In this recipe, we will look at modifying the html.tpl.php and page.tpl.php template files in order to override the position of the **Skip to main content** link that is used to improve accessibility to the main content of the page.

Getting ready

The html.tpl.php template file is rarely a default inclusion in most Drupal 7 themes as they rely on the version provided by Drupal itself. If this template file is missing from our current theme, it will need to be imported from the *system* module's folder at modules/system into the theme's folder.

It is also possible that some themes will not have a page.tpl.php file of their own. This is usually because they are subthemes and the template file will need to be imported from the base theme as we saw in the last chapter. In other cases, using modules/system/page.tpl.php as a foundation is usually a good idea.

Themers looking for a little adventure can, of course, also create both these files from scratch! Introducing new template files will, as usual, necessitate a clearing of the theme registry to ensure that Drupal becomes aware of their existence.

How to do it...

The following is an excerpt from the default `html.tpl.php` template file that ships with Drupal with the DIV pertaining to the *skip-link* highlighted:

```
<html xmlns="http://www.w3.org/1999/xhtml" xml:lang="<?php print
$language->language; ?>" version="XHTML+RDFa 1.0" dir="<?php print
$language->dir; ?>"<?php print $rdf_namespaces; ?>>

<head profile="<?php print $grddl_profile; ?>">
  <?php print $head; ?>
  <title><?php print $head_title; ?></title>
  <?php print $styles; ?>
  <?php print $scripts; ?>
</head>
<body class="<?php print $classes; ?>" <?php print $attributes;?>>
  <div id="skip-link">
    <a href="#main-content" class="element-invisible element-
      focusable"><?php print t('Skip to main content'); ?></a>
  </div>

  <?php print $page_top; ?>
  <?php print $page; ?>
  <?php print $page_bottom; ?>
</body>
</html
```

What we are looking to do is to move this DIV to the page template file and position it below the logo of the site. For example, in the following excerpt from a `page.tpl.php` template file, we have positioned the *skip-link* DIV below the DIVs pertaining to the logo and site title and *above* the navigation links:

```
<?php print render($page['header']); ?>
  <div id="wrapper">
    <div id="container" class="clearfix">

      <div id="header">
        <div id="logo-floater">
        <?php if ($logo || $site_title): ?>
          <?php if ($title): ?>
            <div id="branding"><strong><a href="<?php print $front_
              page ?>">
```

```
      <?php if ($logo): ?>
        <img src="<?php print $logo ?>" alt="<?php print $site_
          name_and_slogan ?>" title="<?php print $site_name_and_
          slogan ?>" id="logo" />
      <?php endif; ?>
      <?php print $site_html ?>
      </a></strong></div>
    <?php else: /* Use h1 when the content title is empty */ ?>
      <h1 id="branding"><a href="<?php print $front_page ?>">
      <?php if ($logo): ?>
        <img src="<?php print $logo ?>" alt="<?php print $site_
          name_and_slogan ?>" title="<?php print $site_name_and_
          slogan ?>" id="logo" />
      <?php endif; ?>
      <?php print $site_html ?>
      </a></h1>
  <?php endif; ?>
  <?php endif; ?>
  </div>

  <div id="skip-link">
    <a href="#main-content" class="element-invisible element-
      focusable"><?php print t('Skip to main content'); ?></a>
  </div>


  <?php if ($primary_nav): print $primary_nav; endif; ?>
  <?php if ($secondary_nav): print $secondary_nav; endif; ?>
</div> <!-- /#header
```

Once such a change has been made and our files saved, the position of the **Skip to main content** link in the markup should have changed.

How it works...

The **Skip to main content** link is, by default, hidden from view and is accessed primarily by screen-reader software and certain users of portable devices. The link enables, for example, a blind user using a screen-reading package, to avoid having to listen to the narrator plodding through lists of navigational links and so on before getting to the actual content of the page. By simply clicking the link, the user can skip elements deemed irrelevant to the content of the page.

Drupal's default `html.tpl.php` template positions the *skip-link* right at the top of the page. This link is hidden using CSS and is invisible to the general user who is not looking to skip to the content. However, if we want to locate this link in most mainstream browsers, all we need to do is *TAB* into the page. This should immediately highlight the heretofore hidden link as shown in the following screenshot:

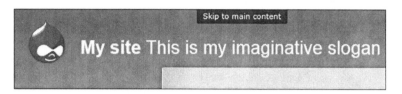

Clicking the *skip-link* will switch us directly to the main content of the page and consequently—for screen-readers—avoid having to list the presence of the logo, site name, slogan, and navigational elements. While this works fine, another school of thought recommends that the *skip-link* should always be positioned below the actual name of the site. The reasoning behind this is that users relying on screen-readers will very likely always want to know the title of the site they are accessing and ensure that they have not navigated away from it. This allows them to skip to the main content with the assurance that they are on the page or site that they intended to access.

We have accomplished this change in this recipe by moving the *skip-link* `DIV` from the `html.tpl.php` template to the `page.tpl.php` template and positioning it accordingly. While the change will not be visible by simply refreshing the browser window, hitting the *TAB* key should confirm that the **Skip to main content** link is activated only after we cycle through the logo and site title links.

See also

The *Chapter 3* recipe, *Overriding Zen template files with myzen*, covers the basics of overriding template files, specifically `page.tpl.php`, from within a subtheme.

Customizing the appearance of a particular node type

Drupal's PHPTemplate theming engine uses naming conventions to easily theme nodes. While the standard template used is named `node.tpl.php`, other naming conventions are available to target specific subsets of nodes. Here we will be looking at specifically theming content of a particular node type—*story*—by modifying it so that the title of the node does not link to its content in its teaser view, thereby directing users to click the **Read more** link instead.

Getting ready

This recipe uses the myzen theme created earlier in this book as an example theme. As we are going to be working with a node type named *story*, ensure that it exists via the content type administration page at `admin/structure/types` [**Home | Administration | Structure | Content types**]. Furthermore, as we are targeting particular node types, it will be a good idea to create more than one node type along with sample content for each.

How to do it...

The following steps are performed in the `theme` folder, which in this recipe is `sites/all/themes/myzen`. Zen-based themes store their template files in a `templates` folder while others might choose to store them in the base folder.

1. Myzen's `templates` folder should be empty by default. The `node.tpl.php` file will need to be imported from the Zen theme's `templates` folder as described in recipes in the previous chapter.

2. Within the myzen theme, rename `node.tpl.php` to `node--story.tpl.php` where `story` signifies the *machine name* of the node type.

    The internal or machine names of node types are listed on the **Content types** page at `admin/structure/types` [**Home | Administration | Structure | Content types**].

3. Open the `node--story.tpl.php` file in an editor.

    Note the use of a *double* hyphen in the filename. A single hyphen will result in the template file not taking effect.

4. The default template code should look like the following:

   ```
   <div id="node-<?php print $node->nid; ?>" class="<?php print
   $classes; ?> clearfix"<?php print $attributes; ?>>

     <?php print $user_picture; ?>

     <?php print render($title_prefix); ?>
     <?php if (!$page && $title): ?>
       <h2<?php print $title_attributes; ?>><a href="<?php print
       $node_url; ?>"><?php print $title; ?></a></h2>
   ```

```php
<?php endif; ?>
<?php print render($title_suffix); ?>

<?php if ($unpublished): ?>
  <div class="unpublished"><?php print t('Unpublished'); ?>
  </div>
<?php endif; ?>

<?php if ($display_submitted): ?>
  <div class="submitted">
    <?php print $submitted; ?>
  </div>
<?php endif; ?>

<div class="content"<?php print $content_attributes; ?>>
  <?php
    // We hide the comments and links now so that we can render
    // them later.
    hide($content['comments']);
    hide($content['links']);
    print render($content);
  ?>
</div>

<?php print render($content['links']); ?>

<?php print render($content['comments']); ?>

</div><!-- /.node -->
```

5. The highlighted line in the preceding block of code contains the code that links the title to its URL. Remove the anchor tag so that the same line now looks like the following:

```php
<h2<?php print $title_attributes; ?>><?php print $title; ?>
</h2>
```

6. Save the file and exit the editor.

7. Clear the theme registry as we have added a new template file.

How it works...

The following screenshot displays a typical story node's *teaser* layout with the title linked to the full-page view of the node.

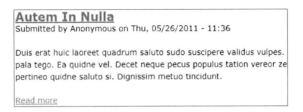

Drupal's theme system is designed to be overridden. As soon as we created the `node--story.tpl.php` file in this recipe and importantly, cleared the theme registry, Drupal updated the registry to account for this new addition. Subsequently, whenever a story node is displayed, it is aware of the presence of this new file that supersedes the default `node.tpl.php` file and uses it instead. It gets a little complicated with our myzen recipe as it is actually a Zen subtheme. As a result, we are overriding Zen's own template files that in turn are overriding the default Drupal files:

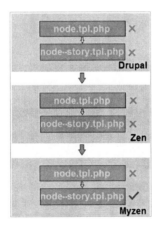

The preceeding chart lists the template hierarchy in an increasing order of precedence with `node--story.tpl.php` always overriding `node.tpl.php` and the template files of the myzen theme being preferred over those of Zen and Drupal. In this case, the `node--story.tpl.php` in our myzen theme takes precedence over all other available options.

The result of our machinations is evident in the following screenshot that demonstrates the story node's teaser with our changes in effect. We can see that the node title no longer links to the node page and that the **Read more** link will need to be used instead. Furthermore, since we have used `node--story.tpl.php` rather than the generic `node.tpl.php`, only the story node has been affected and the blog node continues to retain its original behavior.

Autem In Nulla
Submitted by Anonymous on Thu, 05/26/2011 - 11:36

Duis erat huic laoreet quadrum saluto sudo suscipere validus vulpes. pala tego. Ea quidne vel. Decet neque pecus populus tation vereor ze pertineo quidne saluto si. Dignissim metuo tincidunt.

Read more

Sed Utinam Uxor Vel
Submitted by Karthik on Wed, 05/25/2011 - 11:33

Augue elit fere lobortis nunc oppeto quidne quis refoveo te. Diam ess populus proprius. Abigo caecus damnum erat macto obruo praesent s iustum magna sagaciter singularis veniam. Accumsan bene brevitas e similis.

Read more   Karthik's blog

See also

The next recipe, *Customizing the appearance of a specific node*, takes things further by targeting the node template of a single node based on its node ID.

Customizing the appearance of a specific node

In a similar vein to the previous recipe, we will be looking at using the Drupal theme system's naming scheme to customize specific pieces of content. While the previous recipe targeted nodes of a particular node type, here we are going to target a single node based on its node ID.

The customization we will be performing on the node in question is that it should only display its content and links to authenticated users. In other words, anonymous users will only be able to see its title.

Getting ready

As we are going to be targeting a particular node based on its node ID, we will need to obtain this number from the node in question. This can be discerned from the URL of the node which should, by default, be of the form `node/123` where 123 signifies the node ID. If the node has a *URL alias* enabled, this ID can be obtained by clicking on the **Edit** link of the node, which should lead us to a URL containing the node ID.

How to do it...

Navigate to the `sites/all/themes/myzen` folder and perform the following steps:

1. Myzen's `templates` folder should be empty by default. The `node.tpl.php` file will need to be imported from the Zen theme's `templates` folder as described in recipes in the previous chapter.

2. Within the myzen theme, rename `node.tpl.php` to `node--123.tpl.php` where *123* signifies the node ID of the node that we want to customize.

 Note the use of the *double* hyphen in the filename format for `node--123.tpl.php`.

3. Open this file in an editor. The default `node--123.tpl.php` should look something like the following:

```
<div id="node-<?php print $node->nid; ?>" class="<?php print
$classes; ?> clearfix"<?php print $attributes; ?>>

  <?php print $user_picture; ?>

  <?php print render($title_prefix); ?>
  <?php if (!$page && $title): ?>
    <h2<?php print $title_attributes; ?>><a href="<?php print
      $node_url; ?>"><?php print $title; ?></a></h2>
  <?php endif; ?>
  <?php print render($title_suffix); ?>

  <?php if ($unpublished): ?>
    <div class="unpublished"><?php print t('Unpublished'); ?>
    </div>
  <?php endif; ?>

  <?php if ($display_submitted): ?>
    <div class="submitted">
```

```php
      <?php print $submitted; ?>
    </div>
  <?php endif; ?>

  <div class="content"<?php print $content_attributes; ?>>
    <?php
      // We hide the comments and links now so that we can render
      // them later.
      hide($content['comments']);
      hide($content['links']);
      print render($content);
    ?>
  </div>

  <?php print render($content['links']); ?>

  <?php print render($content['comments']); ?>

</div><!-- /.node -->
```

4. What we want to do is wrap the highlighted code in the previous step inside an `if` statement so that the resulting block looks something like the following:

```php
<?php if ($logged_in): ?>
  <div class="content"<?php print $content_attributes; ?>>
    <?php
      // We hide the comments and links now so that we can render
      // them later.
      hide($content['comments']);
      hide($content['links']);
      print render($content);
    ?>
  </div>
  <?php print render($content['links']); ?>
  <?php print render($content['comments']); ?>
<?php endif; ?>
```

5. Save the file and exit the editor.

6. Clear the theme registry as we have added a new template file.

7. Visit `node/123` both as an anonymous and as an authenticated user to verify whether our changes have taken effect.

8. Confirm that other nodes are unaffected.

How it works...

When we clear the theme registry, Drupal rescans all modules and themes for any available template files. When a page is viewed, it builds an hierarchical list of candidate template files that might be suitable to display the page and chooses the one that is deemed to be the most suitable match. In this hierarchical list, there are many preset template files including node.tpl.php, node--[nodetype].tpl.php, and as in this recipe, a template with greater precedence, node--[nid].tpl.php.

The change that we have made to the contents of the template file uses the built-in variable named $logged_in, which is set to FALSE when the current user is *anonymous* and TRUE otherwise. Displaying the content of the node only when this variable is TRUE ensures that it is only inserted when the user is logged in.

There's more...

Core themes and starter themes such as Zen tend to document anything and everything that we will need to know while customizing template files and functions.

Template variables and documentation

Most core themes and starter themes such as Zen go the extra mile to document all the default variables that are available in each template. For example, the node.tpl.php template file that ships with Zen includes the documentation for the $logged_in variable used in this recipe as well as many others, as can be seen in the following excerpt:

```
* Node status variables:
* - $view_mode: View mode, e.g. 'full', 'teaser'...
* - $teaser: Flag for the teaser state (shortcut for $view_mode ==
* 'teaser').
* - $page: Flag for the full page state.
* - $promote: Flag for front page promotion state.
* - $sticky: Flags for sticky post setting.
* - $status: Flag for published status.
* - $comment: State of comment settings for the node.
* - $readmore: Flags true if the teaser content of the node cannot
* hold the
*   main body content. Currently broken; see http://drupal.org/
* node/823380
* - $is_front: Flags true when presented in the front page.
* - $logged_in: Flags true when the current user is a logged-in
* member.
* - $is_admin: Flags true when the current user is an administrator.
```

See also

The previous recipe, *Customizing the appearance of a particular node type*, shows how we can rename templates to target a node based on its node type.

Theming made easy using the Devel module

The **Devel** module provides functions and tools that aid both module and theme developers. While it is entirely fine to develop sites without it or related modules such as **Theme developer**, they are highly recommended as they save time and effort and will eventually prove indispensable. This recipe will outline the setup process and relevant features of the Devel module.

Getting ready

The Devel module can be downloaded from `http://drupal.org/project/devel`. Once downloaded, install and enable it via the module administration page.

How to do it...

From a themer's point of view, there are two primary features of importance that are provided by the Devel module. The first is the **development** block that can be enabled from the block administration page at `admin/structure/block` [**Home | Administration | Structure | Blocks**]:

Development

- Devel settings
- Empty cache
- Entity info
- Execute PHP Code
- Field info
- Function reference
- Hook_elements()
- Menu item
- PHPinfo()
- Rebuild menus
- Reinstall modules
- Run cron
- Session viewer
- Theme registry
- Variable editor

In the pictured development block, the most frequently used option is usually **Empty cache**. Clicking this link will empty Drupal's caches as well as clear and rebuild the theme registry. In other words, it is a regular port of call during most debugging sessions. Another handy option from a themer's point of view is **Theme registry**, which links to a page listing all theme functions and templates registered with Drupal along with other relevant details for each item.

The **Devel settings** link is a handy shortcut to the Devel module's settings page which can also be found at `admin/config/development/devel` [**Home | Administration | Configuration | Development | Devel settings**]. Of immediate importance to us on this page is the setting right at the bottom—a checkbox titled **Rebuild the theme registry on every page load**. When checked, the registry does not need to be manually emptied and rebuilt as it will be done automatically by the Devel module on each page view.

 Theme registry rebuilding is an intensive operation and automatically rebuilding it on every page load will severely affect performance if used in a production site. Remember to turn this off!

How it works...

The Devel module is a crucial component of every Drupal developer's toolkit whether it be module or theme development. As just demonstrated, from a theme developer's point of view, it provides a number of handy tools to speed up development as well as aid debugging.

 The Devel module, as its name suggests, is a module tailored towards development and as such, is not intended for production environments. That said, circumstances might sometimes demand its use in debugging issues on the production server. In such cases, it is important to only enable it temporarily and strictly control access to its features via the **Permissions** page at `admin/people/permissions` [**Home | Administration | People | Permissions**].

See also

The next recipe, *Theme overrides using the Theme developer module*, introduces a complementary module to Devel named **Theme developer**. The next chapter, *Development and debugging tools*, covers further aspects of the Devel module and other tools in greater detail.

Theme overrides using the Theme developer module

This recipe will outline the features of the **Theme developer** module. We will use it to demonstrate the steps to be followed to locate the theme function or template being used to display a particular element in a page.

Getting ready

The Theme developer module can be downloaded from `http://drupal.org/project/devel_themer`. It depends on the Devel module that we looked at in the previous recipe. Both of these modules need to be downloaded, installed, and enabled.

At the time of writing this book, the Theme developer module was still being ported from its Drupal 6 version to a new Drupal 7 equivalent. Consequently, some of the features were not quite ready. As a result, certain screenshots involving incomplete features of this module are based on its Drupal 6 version. While they do not account for a few minor discrepancies and changes, the images serve their purpose and are reasonably representative.

How to do it...

Once the modules have been enabled, we should have a page that looks similar to the following screenshot:

Development

- Empty cache
- Entity info
- Field info
- Function reference
- Hook_elements()
- Menu item
- PHPinfo()
- Rebuild menus
- Reinstall modules
- Session viewer
- Theme registry
- Variable editor

☐ Themer info

Iriure Lucidus Premo

Submitted by slecraphotuj on Wed,

Ludus nulla volutpat. Abico incassur similis ut venio vulputate.

Gemino in meus nulla quadrum refe macto quibus refoveo suscipere. Co ibidem letalis neque nulla vulpes. Ne

Read more   36 comments   Add n

Huic Nunc Quidem

Submitted by rodriclich on Wed, 10/

As we saw in an earlier recipe, there are two items that are of particular interest to us in the Development block, namely the **Empty cache** and **Theme registry** links. Firstly, the **Empty cache** link, as the name suggests, clears the Drupal cache and theme registry when clicked. Secondly, the **Theme registry** link provides a directory of currently available theme functions that are stored in the registry.

When the **Theme developer** module is enabled, the **Themer info** link appears on the bottom left of the screen as seen in the previous screenshot. This checkbox is always disabled by default upon every page load and needs to be checked only when we want to find out information about a particular element in our theme. For example, if we want to obtain details about the theme function responsible for the display of an author's name in a node, all we need to do is check the **Themer info** checkbox and then click on the author's name. As seen in the next image, this will load details about the theme function or template file involved in an overlay along with a list of arguments passed to the function:

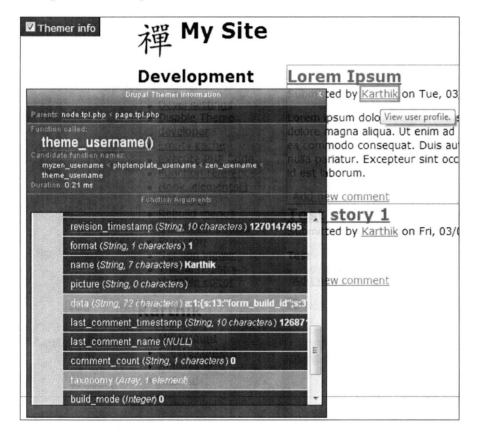

The **Drupal Themer Information** overlay is movable. If it blocks elements of the page, it can be dragged to a more convenient location.

How it works...

The Theme developer module makes use of a function named `hook_theme_registry_alter()`, which allows it to intercept and track the use of theme functions and template files in each page. With a little JavaScript, the module compares the clicked element with a stored list, using which it displays theme-related information about the element.

In the previous screenshot, we can see that the **Parents** hierarchical list provides information about the template file used to display the author's name, which in this case is `node.tpl.php`, which in turn is embedded in `page.tpl.php`.

Below the Parents list, we are given the name of the theme function—`theme_username()`—which was used to theme the username field. Further below, we are provided with a list of arguments—just one in this case—which have been passed to this function. The arguments can be expanded to list their contents, which will prove very handy.

Lastly, and crucially, we are also provided with a list of candidate function names that can be used to override the currently used function. In other words, rather than editing `theme_username()` to add our changes, we can use one of `myzen_username()` or `zen_username()` to hold our changes depending on our scope and requirements.

 If the element is not displayed by way of a theme function, Theme developer just shows the template file involved in the display process and lists candidate template files that can be used to override the existing one.

There's more...

The Theme developer module, besides providing information on theme functions and template files, also links to their documentation pages.

Drupal API documentation

Theme developer will link Drupal's core functions, such as `theme_username()` in the above example, to their entries on `http://api.drupal.org`, which contain information about the function, its arguments, and use cases.

Compatibility issues

The ability of the Theme developer module to load related theme information of clicked elements on a page is accomplished by wrapping said elements in HTML and tracking them via JavaScript. As the markup of the page is changed, this feature can adversely affect the functionality of certain modules—especially those that rely on JavaScript—and themes. As a result, it is recommended that this module only be used during the theming or debugging process and be turned off at other times.

See also

A number of recipes in *Chapter 6, Advanced Templating*, frequently rely on the Theme developer module while customizing templates.

Styling the site maintenance page

Drupal offers a site maintenance mode where the site is inaccessible to end users unless expressly specified. During this period, visitors to the site are presented with a maintenance page. In this recipe, we will be looking at an approach that will allow us to style this page from our theme.

Getting ready

We will be using the Zen-based myzen theme that we created in the last chapter. It is recommended that for the purpose of the recipe, the site is loaded on two separate browser applications—the first for the admin account and the other for an anonymous user account. This will make it easier to make changes and verify their effect.

The site can be placed in maintenance mode by navigating to `admin/config/development/maintenance` [**Home | Administration | Configuration | Development | Maintenance mode**] and enabling the **Put site into maintenance mode** checkbox.

How to do it...

The default maintenance theme is the site's active theme. To change it to the myzen theme, execute the following steps:

1. Browse to the site's `settings.php` file which is customarily located in the `sites/default` folder, and open it in an editor.

2. Uncomment the line pertaining to the maintenance theme and change its value to the theme of choice, which in this case, is Garland.

    ```
    $conf['maintenance_theme'] = 'myzen';
    ```

3. Save the file and exit.

The steps thus far should allow us to change the theme being used to display the maintenance page. If we want to do more and change the style of the maintenance page, we will need to edit its template file. In the case of Zen-based themes, this is just a matter of overriding the default template file—`maintenance-page.tpl.php`—provided by Zen. In other words, copying this file from the Zen theme's `templates` folder to the `templates` folder of the myzen theme should be all that is necessary. Once copied, we should be able to edit it and incorporate any changes that we desire.

It should be second nature by now to clear the theme registry if we do go ahead and import the maintenance template file.

How it works...

The Garland theme's maintenance page looks:

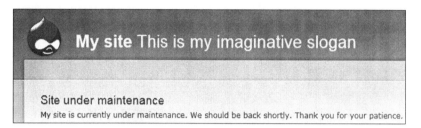

By using the $conf array in settings.php, we were able to tell Drupal to use a different theme as the maintenance theme. In our case, this was myzen. Changing the maintenance_theme configuration to this theme resulted in a maintenance page that looked more like the following:

5
Development and Debugging Tools

We will be covering the following recipes in this chapter:

- ▶ Finding the right function to use to theme an object
- ▶ Analyzing variables using the Devel module
- ▶ Generating sample content using the Devel generate module
- ▶ Resetting the default theme manually
- ▶ Live preview with Web Developer
- ▶ Validating HTML and CSS using Web Developer
- ▶ Turning off JavaScript in the browser
- ▶ Disabling CSS in the browser
- ▶ Inspecting elements and debugging CSS using Firebug
- ▶ Diagnostic logging of JavaScript using Firebug

Introduction

In our world of Drupal design and development—or any other package for that matter—it is seldom that we get things right the first time. In fact, most of our time is spent in isolating, patching, refining, and re-evaluating code or design that we theretofore had believed was perfectly fine. This has led to the creation of a plethora of developmental aids and tools to streamline these processes and save us a heap of time and effort better spent elsewhere. These include documentation, browser-based tools, as well as Drupal modules that assist in development and debugging.

First and foremost is documentation. Drupal's documentation is largely centered around its handbook which can be accessed via `http://drupal.org/handbook`. Besides this, documentation for the various Drupal APIs is located at `http://api.drupal.org`. These sites include information contributed by community members as well as extracts from the comments in the code files.

Drupal-specific development and debugging tools primarily revolve around the **Devel** module and its offshoots such as the **Devel generate** and **Theme developer** modules. We have already taken advantage of the Devel and Theme developer modules in previous chapters and will see more of them in this one.

When it comes to client-side tools, the chief protagonist is a Firefox add-on pictured in the following screenshot named **Firebug**. It is an invaluable tool that has revolutionized web development by allowing the debugging and streamlining of all aspects of theming from HTML and CSS to JavaScript right from within the browser. While the primary add-on is only available for Firefox, a less potent variant is available for other browsers in the form of **Firebug Lite**. More information on both of these options is available at `http://getfirebug.com`.

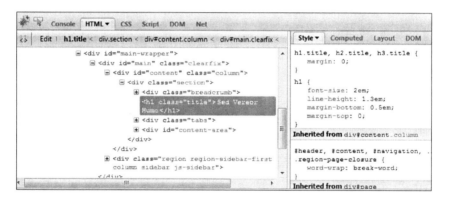

A complement to Firebug's in-depth capabilities is available in the form of the **Web Developer** add-on which provides a suite of development, testing, and validation tools as pictured in the following screenshot. Initially created by Chris Pederick as a Firefox add-on, it is now also available as an extension for Google Chrome. More information on this add-on is available at `http://chrispederick.com/work/web-developer/`.

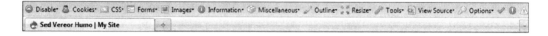

Besides Firefox, other browsers such as Opera, Internet Explorer, and Google Chrome come with their own sets of tools and plugins. For example, Opera provides a suite of tools under the moniker **Dragonfly** while Google Chrome and Internet Explorer's equivalent are simply titled **Developer Tools**. Chrome is also aided by user-contributed *extensions* which are quite similar to Firefox add-ons with a significant number of them being ported equivalents of the same.

In this chapter, we will be primarily concentrating on Firefox add-ons as they provide the most complete and feature-rich set of tools that are available to developers today.

Finding the right function to use to theme an object

In the previous chapter, we saw how to find out which theme function is *being used* to theme an element—the username—in a page and subsequently, learned to override it. However, while writing modules or when we are looking at ways to render data loaded from the database, it is also not uncommon to be at a loss to know which function to use to theme a Drupal object.

In this recipe, we will look to source potential solutions which can be used to render a typical Drupal user object. We will be accomplishing this task using the Devel module and available documentation.

Getting ready

The Devel module which can be downloaded from `http://drupal.org/project/devel` is assumed to be installed and enabled. Furthermore, it is required that the **access devel information** and **Execute PHP Code** permissions be assigned to the current user.

The **Development** block which is provided by the module also needs to be enabled.

How to do it...

As we are looking to theme the user object and perhaps display it as a link to the user's profile, let us check whether there are any Drupal functions related to the term *username*. To do this, visit the Drupal API site at `http://api.drupal.org` and type the word **username** into the search field. This autocomplete field should provide—as seen in the following screenshot—a drop down listing all functions that include the term **username**:

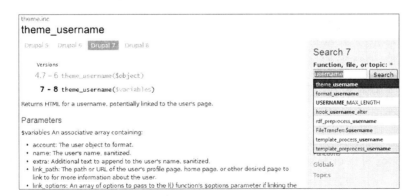

As displayed in the preceding screenshot, the `theme_username()` function looks promising. The linked API page (which is also conveniently pictured in the image) should provide information on the arguments that need to be supplied to this function, as well as information on the return type and a lot more. We can see that the `theme_username()` function accepts a single parameter, `$variables`. Looking at the **Parameters** section, we can see that this parameter is structured as an associative array with a choice of predefined keys.

 The API site customarily also provides links to other areas of Drupal that use the function being viewed. However, as theme functions are invoked as arguments of the `theme()` hook, this information is not available. As an alternative, if we need to look at some real-world examples of the function in action, we will need to run a code search throughout the entire project for the term `theme('username'` to get a list of all instances of the function being used.

Once we have a candidate function in hand, we can give it a test run using the Devel module's PHP evaluation feature. This can be accessed by clicking on the **Execute PHP Code** link in the **Development** block seen in the next screenshot. In the ensuing form, enter some test code such as the following to see the theme function in action:

```php
// Print the current user who is always available via a
// global variable.
global $user;
$username = theme('username', array('account' => $user));
print($username);
print("\n");

// Print some other user: User with user ID 5.
$user_other = user_load(5);
$username2 = theme('username', array('account' => $user_other));
print($username2);
```

Once this is done, click the **Execute** button to evaluate the code.

How it works...

When the PHP code is evaluated, the result should look something like the following:

```html
<a href="/user/1" title="View user profile."
  class="username">Karthik</a>
<a href="/user/5" title="View user profile." class="username">foo</a>
```

In other words, we have implemented `theme_username()` correctly and can proceed to use it in our modules or themes as necessary.

There's more...

There are also other avenues available to us when it comes to finding information on available module and theme functions.

Function reference and the theme registry

Besides using the Drupal API documentation site, another handy option is to use the Devel module's **Function reference** list or view the site's **Theme registry** to source out potential theme functions. Both these options can be accessed by clicking on their respective links in the **Development** block and then running a search for candidate functions as seen in the following screenshot:

See also

Theme overrides using the Theme developer module, a recipe from the previous chapter, explains how to use the Theme developer to find the theme function being used to render an element on the page. In other words, in situations where we have a working example of what we are trying to accomplish, we can trace the functions being used to do so.

The *Displaying a profile name instead of the username* recipe in *Chapter 4, Templating Basics* lists the steps required to override the `theme_username()` function that we looked at in this recipe.

Analyzing variables using the Devel module

While working with the Drupal API, we will often be faced with the situation where we have no idea how a variable is structured. While PHP provides a number of functions to peek into the variable, Drupal's Devel module provides a cleaner solution and a prettier interface to do the same.

In this recipe, we will be looking at the Devel module's `dpm()` function.

Getting ready

It is assumed that the Devel module has been installed and is enabled. It also comes with its own set of permissions and it is assumed that the current user has all the appropriate permissions including **access devel information**.

We will also be making use of the `mysite` module created earlier in this book to hold our odds and ends.

How to do it...

The following steps are to be performed inside the `mysite` module folder at `sites/all/modules/mysite`:

1. Open the file `mysite.module` in an editor.

2. Look for an implementation of the `mysite_init()` hook. If it is unavailable, create one and add the following code so that the resulting function looks as the following:

```
/**
 * Implements hook_init().
 */
function mysite_init() {
  global $user;

  // Analyze the $user variable.
  dpm($user);
}
```

3. Save the file and exit the editor.

4. Access the site in a browser to see whether we are presented with a pretty-printed representation of the `$user` variable.

When the site is now accessed, the `$user` variable should be displayed at the top of the page as shown in the following screenshot:

We can see that all the data within the `$user` object is now visible. Each property is listed along with its datatype and length. Furthermore, complex datatypes such as arrays are also expanded, thus giving us an excellent overview of the entire object.

There's more...

It is always recommended that the codebase is kept neat and tidy. Once we are done with our debugging, it is a good idea to clean up after ourselves.

Removing debug functions after use

It is important that the calls to `dpm()` and other Devel module commands be removed once the debugging session is over. It is not an infrequent occurrence to find the site becoming unusable because the Devel module was disabled without removing these commands. Alternatively, if some debugging code is used regularly enough to be retained in a module, then it might be worthwhile to wrap all code related to the Devel module within a `module_exists()` check as follows:

```
if (module_exists('devel')) {
  // Add debugging code here.
}
```

Other useful Devel module functions

Besides `dpm()`, other useful functions include `dd()` which logs output to an external file, and `ddebug_backtrace()` which is useful as a post mortem tool to analyze where things went wrong. More information can be found by simply browsing through the `devel.module` file inside the Devel module's folder.

See also

The previous chapter contains the *Listing all variables in a template file* recipe which provides a more direct approach to getting information about all available variables.

Generating sample content using the Devel generate module

Once our theme has made significant progress, it is important to test it in various scenarios with different sets of sample data to ferret out bugs and anomalies that sometimes tend to be overlooked during the design phase. In this recipe, we will be using the **Devel generate** module to generate test data in the form of content, taxonomy categories, and users to simulate real-world input.

Getting ready

It is assumed that the Devel module is available and enabled. While the Devel module itself is not a prerequisite, the Devel generate module is part of its package and should also be enabled from the module installation page. It is also assumed that the `Taxonomy`, `Comment`, and if necessary, the `Path` and `Upload` modules are enabled. Furthermore, it is recommended that multiple node types be made available to the generator to ensure that our sample data encompasses as many permutations and combinations as possible.

How to do it...

The Devel generate module, once enabled, exposes its functionality via the **Generate items** section in the administration pages and block. We will be generating sample taxonomy vocabularies, terms, users, and content as per the following steps:

1. To generate taxonomy vocabularies, navigate to `admin/config/development/generate/vocabs` [**Home | Administration | Configuration | Development | Generate vocabularies**] to access the category generation form.

2. In the resulting page, specify the number of vocabularies that need to be created and other variables.

3. Click on the **Generate** button to create them.

4. To generate taxonomy terms for our newly created vocabularies, navigate to `admin/config/development/generate/taxonomy` [**Home | Administration | Configuration | Development | Generate terms**] to access the term generation form.

5. Choose the vocabularies for which the terms should be generated and amend the other options on this page as necessary.

6. Click on **Generate** to generate the taxonomy terms for the selected vocabularies.

7. Next, navigate to `admin/config/development/generate/user` [**Home | Administration | Configuration | Development | Generate users**] to access the user generation form.

8. Tweak the number of users, their roles, and age as needed.

9. Again, click on **Generate** to generate our test user accounts.

10. Finally, navigate to `admin/config/development/generate/content` [**Home | Administration | Configuration | Development | Generate content**] to access the content generation form:

Content types

☑ Blog entry. Comments: Open

☑ Page. Comments: Open

☑ Story. Comments: Open

☑ **Delete all content** in these content types before generating new content.

How many nodes would you like to generate?

500

How far back in time should the nodes be dated?

1 month ago ▾

Node creation dates will be distributed randomly from the current time, back to the selected time.

Maximum number of comments per node.

30

You must also enable comments for the content types you are generating. Note that some nodes will randomly receive zero comments. Some will receive the max.

Max word length of titles

4

☑ Add an url alias for each node.

Requires path.module

Set language on nodes

Language neutral

Requires locale.module

[Generate]

11. As the previous screenshot attests, there are a number of options available on this form. Tweak them so that there is significant variation in the generated nodes to account for varying user input and realistic situations.

> The **Delete all content** option, when checked, will delete *all* existing content and generate new entities.

12. Click on **Generate** to generate the test content.

How it works...

The Devel generator utilizes the **Batch API** while generating content. This allows Drupal to create large numbers of items without the page timing out or the server running out of memory. Once the generator has run its course, we can verify the generated content by visiting the Taxonomy, User, and Content administration pages. Visiting the default front page or the URL node should display a simulation of what the site will look like with real-world user input.

With the introduction of fields in Drupal core, the Devel generate module automatically analyzes the structure of each node type and populates as many fields it is familiar with as possible. For example, taxonomy terms, attachments, comments, and so on, are created automatically by the generator as necessary.

Resetting the default theme manually

There will be times where certain changes we have made to the theme will render the site utterly unusable. For example, this can happen when there are layout issues with the theme which might make navigating to the Theme administration pages difficult, or when we have introduced an error in our PHP code which leads to the *White Screen of Death* where all we have to work with is an unusable blank screen. While we could simply stomp our way into the database and change the variable specifying the current theme, the *Drupal Way* advocates a cleaner and simpler solution to rescue the site.

In this recipe, we will be looking at rescuing an unusable site via the settings.php configuration file.

Getting ready

This recipe only applies when a Drupal site becomes unusable due to errors in the theme currently being used.

How to do it...

As the site is unusable, we can either edit the database directly or, as detailed in the following steps, use the `settings.php` file to override the default theme being used:

1. Navigate to the site's `settings.php` file which is, by default, inside the `sites/default` folder.

2. Open this file in an editor and look for a section titled **Variable overrides**.

3. The `$conf` array in this section is normally commented out and is heavily documented. Uncomment the highlighted line as in the following excerpt, by removing its hash prefix:

```
# $conf['site_name'] = 'My Drupal site';
$conf['theme_default'] = 'garland';
# $conf['anonymous'] = 'Visitor';
```

4. Save the file and exit the editor.

5. Try accessing the site in a browser to ensure that it is now accessible and that the theme has been changed to Garland.

How it works...

The `$conf` configuration array is used by Drupal to load and store system variables. By declaring this array in the `settings.php` file, we are effectively overriding variables that are stored in the database. In this case, we have specified that the theme to be used to display the site should be Garland, which should override our problematic theme.

Once the bugs in the theme have been weeded out, we can reverse our changes to the `settings.php` file to revert back to the original theme.

There's more...

Drupal stores its configuration data in a table named `variables` in the database. The Devel module provides an interface to this table which is often handy when attempting to peek under the hood.

Using the Devel module to view and edit database variables

The Devel module comes with a handy variable editor which can be used to view and even edit variables directly in the database. For this recipe, we can use it to confirm that the **theme_default** variable is indeed being overridden. It can be accessed by clicking on the **Variable editor** link in the **Development** block. Scrolling down to the bottom of the resulting page should confirm that the **theme_default** setting is still set to **myzen** whereas the theme actually being used to display the page is Garland.

	Name ▲	Value	Length
☐	theme_acquia_marina_settings	a:121:{s:23:"mission_statement_pages";s:4:"home";s:18:"breadcrumb...	5232
☐	theme_bluemarine_settings	a:16:{s:11:"toggle_logo";i:1;s:11:"toggle_name";i:1;s:13:"toggle_...	452
☐	theme_default	s:5:"myzen";	12
☐	theme_garland_settings	a:20:{s:11:"toggle_logo";i:1;s:11:"toggle_name";i:1;s:13:"toggle_...	3226
☐	theme_myzen_settings	a:24:{s:14:"zen_breadcrumb";s:3:"yes";s:24:"zen_breadcrumb_separa...	749
☐	theme_settings	a:1:{s:21:"toggle_node_info_page";b:0;}	39
☐	theme_zen_settings	a:9:{s:17:"zen_block_editing";s:1:"1";s:14:"zen_breadcrumb";s:3:"...	335

Each row in the variable editor table has an associated **Edit** link that can be used to modify the variable in question. However, it should be noted that these variables are stored in *serialized* form and as such need to be edited with care. More information on PHP's serialize() function can be obtained at http://php.net/manual/en/function.serialize.php.

Live preview with Web Developer

Drupal theme development usually involves a lot of toggling between editor and browser to see our changes in effect. After a point, this can get to be rather tedious, especially when debugging or tweaking CSS, and compounded further more while working directly on the server.

In this recipe, we will be looking at the features provided by the **Web Developer** add-on which will allow us to directly edit HTML and CSS in the browser and see our changes propagate instantaneously.

Getting ready

The Web Developer add-on for Firefox is assumed to have been installed and enabled. It can be downloaded from http://chrispederick.com/work/web-developer/.

How to do it...

Web Developer's list of features includes a rudimentary HTML editor which can be used to tweak markup during testing. The editor can be launched by clicking on **Miscellaneous** in the Web Developer toolbar and then clicking on **Edit HTML**.

The editor is launched in a panel as seen in the next screenshot, and includes a search field to locate pertinent sections of the page. Any changes made in the panel will be reflected immediately in the page above.

The CSS editor can similarly be launched by clicking on **CSS** in the toolbar and selecting **Edit CSS**. This should load all the linked stylesheets in an editor in a panel below.

How it works...

The Web Developer add-on allows us to edit page elements on-the-fly directly in the browser. These include both HTML and CSS elements which upon modification are automatically updated in the Firefox window.

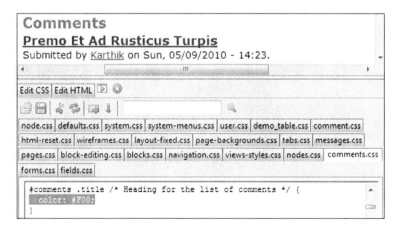

In the previous screenshot, the **comments.css** file has been opened in the editor after which the title for the **Comments** section has been styled with the color red. The changes are immediately apparent in the browser above. If we are working on a local server, the stylesheet can be saved using the save button at the top of the panel. If not, we can either copy and paste the modified file, or alternatively, apply the changes manually.

CSS aggregation

If CSS aggregation is enabled for the site, it is important that it be turned off before editing to ensure that Web Developer has access to all the component CSS files. If not, we will only have access to a single, monolithic, and unwieldy stylesheet.

There's more...

The Web Developer extension is not the sole player with these features. Other extensions including Firebug support them as well.

Editing HTML and CSS using Firebug

The Firebug add-on also provides similar live-editing functionality for HTML and CSS. These features can be accessed from the **HTML** and **CSS** menus in the Firebug panel and clicking on **Live Edit** as demonstrated in the following screenshot:

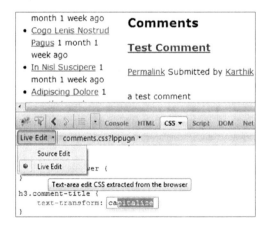

The decision of which tool to use comes down to personal preference and degree of comfort with the interface.

View all CSS rules at once

The Web Developer toolbar provides an option to view all CSS rules in one location. This can be done by clicking on the **CSS** menu in the toolbar and then clicking **View CSS**. This feature can be quite handy during debugging when we need to run a search for particular rules, usually relating to positional aspects of elements.

See also

Once we are done editing our HTML and CSS file, we can make use of the next recipe, *Validating HTML and CSS using Web Developer*, to check whether our changes are efficient and meet prevailing standards.

Validating HTML and CSS using Web Developer

Validation is an integral part of web development. HTML and CSS validation ensure that the document is structurally and semantically correct and provide a reliability guarantee that the page will be displayed correctly both now and in the future.

In this recipe, we will look at how the Web Developer add-on provides easy options for validating both HTML and CSS using the W3C validator at `http://validator.w3.org`.

Getting ready

It is assumed that the Web Developer add-on is installed and enabled in Firefox.

How to do it...

To validate the HTML of a page currently being viewed in Firefox, click on the **Tools** menu of the Web Developer toolbar and select **Validate HTML** as displayed in the following screenshot:

Once clicked, we will be redirected to the W3C validator page to view the results of the check.

Similarly, validating the CSS of a page being currently viewed can be performed by clicking on the **Tools** menu of the toolbar and selecting **Validate CSS**.

Validating HTML and CSS from the local server

The W3C validator by default validates files and pages on servers that are accessible through the Internet. However, this is not always convenient as our site might still be under development on a local server or we are perhaps looking to validate pages on the site that are accessible to authenticated users only. In such situations, we can use Web Developer's **Validate Local CSS** and **Validate Local HTML** options which save the HTML or CSS as files and upload them to the validator.

How it works...

Once it receives its input, the HTML validator validates the page against its `Doctype` declaration. In the following screenshot, the *local* page in question was declared to be **XHTML + RDFa** compliant and it passed the validation process successfully:

Similarly, the W3C CSS validator checks the supplied CSS against a predefined profile, which in the following screenshot is set to *CSS 2.1*. As a result, we see that some *CSS 3* properties have been flagged as errors as they do not conform to the CSS 2.1 specifications:

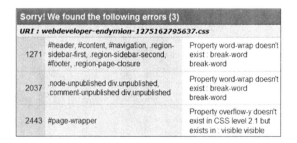

When attempting to validate multiple pages in a site, it is useful to know that we can temporarily instruct Web Developer to automatically validate the page being viewed.

Validating HTML and CSS automatically

The Web Developer toolbar provides an option that can be used to automatically validate the page being viewed. This setting can be enabled by clicking on the **Tools** menu of the toolbar and selecting **Display Page Validation**. This will result in an additional toolbar being added to Firefox which displays the validation status of the current page. This is handy when performing quality checks across different pages in the site and can save time and effort.

Turning off JavaScript in the browser

Websites cater to users using browsers of varying capabilities on a plethora of devices. Consequently, there is no guarantee that user experiences will always be the same across the board. **Graceful degradation** is often a term associated with site usability and accessibility, and ensures that sites are still functional in the absence of key technologies such as JavaScript, CSS, images, and plugins such as Flash. Disabling various browser features is also quite frequently an essential step during debugging.

This recipe will detail the steps required to disable JavaScript during development.

While every browser provides a JavaScript toggle somewhere in its preferences dialogs, and many of them are beginning to provide handy developer tools of their own, we will be using the Web Developer add-on for Firefox and Google Chrome which can be downloaded from `http://chrispederick.com/work/web-developer/`. It is assumed that it has been installed and enabled.

How to do it...

Once the Web Developer add-on is installed in Firefox, a toolbar should be available at the top of the page. Clicking on the **Disable** drop down should present a list of options including **Disable JavaScript**, which in turn, leads to another submenu with the **All JavaScript** option. This, when clicked, should disable JavaScript in the browser as displayed in the following screenshot:

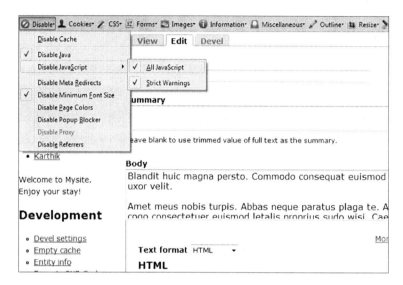

The page will need to be refreshed to see our changes taking effect.

How it works...

Once JavaScript is disabled, all the frills will no longer be active. In the previous screenshot, we can clearly see, for example, that the **Body** field has an additional **Summary** field that, when JavaScript is enabled, is usually only made visible upon clicking an **Edit summary** link. Furthermore, we can verify that the *vertical tabs* on the edit page are now expanded with their contents visible. In other words, even though JavaScript has been disabled, the page is still functional and accessible.

There's more...

Other browsers also provide tools that allow the easy manipulation of their options, including the option to temporarily disable JavaScript.

Disabling JavaScript in Opera

Disabling JavaScript in Opera is as simple as pressing **F12** to access the Quick preferences menu and toggling the **Enable JavaScript** option accordingly as demonstrated in the following screenshot:

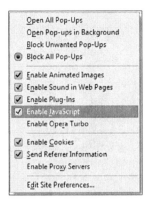

Disabling JavaScript in Internet Explorer

As outlined in the following screenshot, pressing **F12** in Internet Explorer loads the **Developer Tools** panel. Clicking—within the panel—the **Disable** menu and clicking the **Script** option accordingly, will disable or enable JavaScript support in the browser:

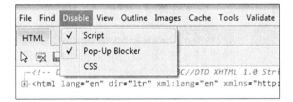

See also

The next *Disabling CSS in the browser* recipe provides information on doing the same for CSS. *Chapter 7, JavaScript in Themes*, is dedicated to JavaScript where tools such as the Web Developer toolbar will come in very handy during testing and debugging.

Disabling CSS in the browser

Besides catering to **Graceful degradation** as seen with the recipe on disabling JavaScript, disabling CSS files is invaluable during debugging, especially once the levels of complexity increase. This recipe will detail the steps required to disable CSS during development.

Getting ready

We will be using the Web Developer add-on for Firefox which can be downloaded from `http://chrispederick.com/work/web-developer/`. It is assumed that it has been installed and enabled.

We will also be using the myzen theme created in earlier chapters as the example theme in this recipe.

How to do it...

Once the Web Developer add-on is installed in Firefox, a toolbar should be available at the top of the page. Clicking on the **CSS** drop down should present a list of options including **Disable Styles**, which in turn, leads to another submenu featuring a number of options. Of immediate interest is the **All Styles** option which when enabled, disables *all* CSS styles from the document. This is useful to visualize, for example, how accessibility software tends to parse the page.

When it comes to debugging, however, the more valuable feature is the ability to disable specific stylesheets listed under the **Individual Style Sheet** option. Situations frequently arise where rules in existing stylesheets are overridden in order to modify default styles. For example, the myzen theme overrides the default tab styles provided by Drupal using styles located in its own CSS file titled `tabs.css`. The styles in this file can be disabled by selecting the **tabs.css** entry from the list of stylesheets as demonstrated in the following screenshot:

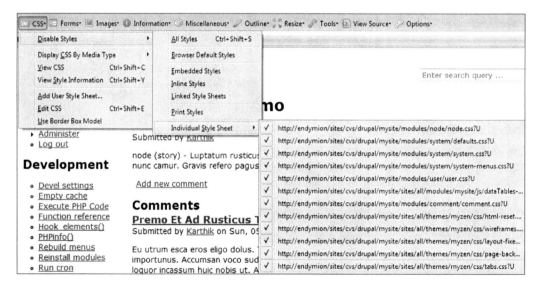

How it works...

When the `tabs.css` file is disabled, we should immediately be able to see the default tab styles provided by Drupal take effect. This is demonstrated using the following screenshots:

The previous screenshot displays the tabs on a typical node page first using the styles in myzen's `tabs.css`. The following screenshot, however, displays the same page with the `tabs.css` file disabled, and consequently, with Drupal's default tab styles taking effect:

There's more...

Similar, if not as comprehensive, options also exist in tools for other browsers.

Disabling CSS in Internet Explorer

While individual CSS files cannot be disabled in Internet Explorer, the Developer Tools panel—which can be accessed by pressing **F12**—does provide an option to disable all CSS support for the page. This can be done by clicking on the **Disable** menu and selecting **CSS** as shown in the following screenshot:

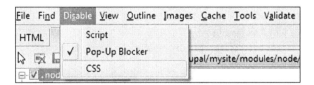

See also

The next *Inspecting elements and debugging CSS using Firebug* recipe outlines how we can temporarily disable specific CSS rules rather than entire stylesheets, all from the comfort of our browser.

The previous *Turning off JavaScript in the browser* recipe lists the steps required to temporarily disable JavaScript in the browser using the Web Developer toolbar.

Inspecting elements and debugging CSS using Firebug

Prior to the advent of **Firebug**, debugging documents styled with complex CSS was an exercise in tedium. In this recipe, we will be demonstrating the use of Firebug in locating an errant margin that we are looking to modify.

The default setting for comment display in Drupal is to thread and nest them. In other words, replies to existing comments are added beneath them and indented by way of a margin to indicate each comment's specific level in the hierarchy. We are going to find out which CSS file, as well as the rule in particular, is responsible for this margin and modify it accordingly.

Getting ready

For the purposes of this recipe, the `comment` module will need to be enabled and some test content that involves nested comments will need to be generated using the Devel generate module. It is assumed that the Firebug add-on has been installed in Firefox.

How to do it...

Firstly, we will need to view a sample node in Firefox and locate a suitable nested comment that is a reply to another and is, therefore, indented. We can then look to ascertain the origin of this indentation using Firebug.

To do so, right-click on the title of the comment in question and click on **Inspect Element**. This should locate the element's markup in the HTML section of the Firebug panel at the bottom of the window. The markup of a typical comment in Drupal should look something as follows:

```
<div class="indented">
  <a id="comment-4031"></a>
  <div class="comment comment-by-node-author comment-by-anonymous
    even clearfix">
    <h3 class="comment-title">
      <a rel="bookmark" class="permalink"
        href="/comment/4031#comment-4031">Incassum Saluto</a>
    </h3>
    <!-- Comment body -->

  </div>
  <!-- /.comment -->
```

```
<div class="indented" style="">
  <!-- Other nested comments -->

</div>
</div>
```

Furthermore, simply hovering over an element in the Firebug HTML panel should highlight the corresponding object in the browser window along with its margins and padding, if any. As the comment's title is a simple anchor tag, it is unlikely to be the source of the margin for the entire block of content. Consequently, we can look at its parent and other elements in its ancestry as being more likely to be the source of the indentation. Inspecting each one in turn should offer information on their layouts.

Hovering over one of the ancestors of the comment title —a DIV tag with a telltale class named indented—should highlight the entire comment in the browser along with a conspicuous yellow block to its left. This indicates that this element has a margin applied to it. Clicking the DIV should load all its styles on the right-hand side of the Firebug panel as displayed in the following screenshot:

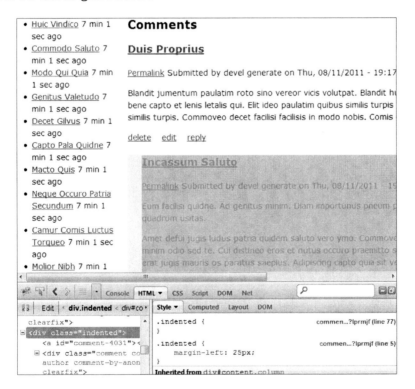

As we can tell from the screenshot, the element has a margin of 25 pixels. We can also tell that this rule is located inside the `comment.css` file on line number **5**; clicking the filename should load the entire CSS file and make it available for editing if so necessary. We can additionally confirm the layout of this element by clicking on the **Layout** tab in the Firebug panel.

Now that we have our element and the rule responsible for the margin, we can look at modifying it. Right-clicking the **margin-left** rule should provide a list of options including **Edit**, **Delete**, and **Disable** as in the next screenshot. Clicking on **Edit** will allow us to change the margin while **Delete** will remove the entire rule altogether. **Disable** on the other hand will temporarily disable the rule so that we can preview what the element will look like without it in effect:

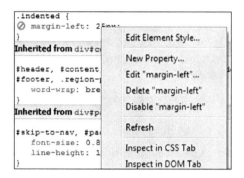

Additionally, we can click on **New Property** to add a new rule, perhaps a border, to this element. With Firebug also coming with autocomplete support, adding new rules is a cinch.

Rather than right-clicking to access the context menu and performing operations, we can double-click rules to edit them or double-click an empty area near a rule to add a new one. Similarly, disabling individual rules can be accomplished by clicking the disable icon to the left of the rule in question as seen in the previous screenshot.

How it works...

We have just scratched the surface of Firebug's features here and it is well worth exploring all its tabs and context menus. Additional documentation on the CSS panel is available at `http://getfirebug.com/wiki/index.php/CSS_Panel`.

See also

The next *Diagnostic logging of JavaScript using Firebug* recipe, demonstrates how Firebug similarly also provides powerful tools to debug and manipulate JavaScript.

Diagnostic logging of JavaScript using Firebug

Even though Firebug supports an endless number of more complex JavaScript debugging features, the fundamental approach of using diagnostic prints to debug scripts is still alive and well. In this recipe, we will be looking at Firebug's `console()` function and a few of its variants.

Getting ready

It is assumed that the Firebug add-on has been successfully installed in Firefox. We will also be using the myzen theme created earlier in this book as an example theme in this recipe.

How to do it...

Firebug comes with a console to log output which is accessed using the `console()` command. To see this in action:

1. Navigate to the myzen theme folder at `sites/all/themes/myzen`.

2. Browse to the `js` subfolder where the JavaScript files are stored, and create a file named `console.js`.

3. Open this file in an editor and add the following script to it:

```
(function ($) {
  Drupal.behaviors.consoleDebug = {
    attach: function() {
      var s = 'Foo';

      console.log(s);
      console.debug(s);

      $('a').each(function() {
        // console.log(this);
        console.count('Number of links on the page:');
      });
      console.warn('This is simply a warning!');
      console.error('This is an error!');
    }
  };
}(jQuery));
```

4. Save the file and exit the editor.

5. Browse back up to the myzen theme's base folder and open the `myzen.info` file in an editor.

6. Add our new JavaScript file to the scripts section using the following code:

    ```
    scripts[] = js/console.js
    ```

7. Save the file and exit the editor.

8. Rebuild the Drupal cache.

9. Access the site in Firefox and open the Firebug panel.

10. Within the Firebug panel, choose the **Console** tab and if it is not enabled already, do so.

11. Finally, refresh the page to confirm that the console output is being displayed in Firebug's **Console** tab.

How it works...

When a page is accessed in Firefox, the Console tab of the Firebug panel should output something as shown in the following:

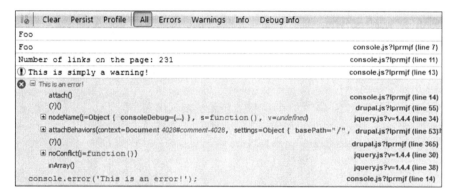

What is important to note is the various variants of the console command. `console.log()` simply logs the input, whereas `console.debug()` also adds a link to the script that is responsible for the call. Clicking the link will take us to the **Script** pane where more information can be accessed and further debugging performed.

Similarly, `console.warn()` logs the input in a starkly noticeable warning format, whereas `console.error()` also triggers a trace request besides registering as an error.

It is also useful to note that any complex JavaScript objects that are logged in the console are hyperlinked to their equivalent location in the **Script**, **HTML**, or **CSS** panes. This feature comes in very handy especially when manipulating HTML using jQuery.

There's more...

Firebug is a very powerful debugging tool with a plethora of features we have not covered here.

Other console variants

There are a number of other variants in the console API. More information along with examples can be accessed at `http://getfirebug.com/wiki/index.php/Console_API`.

Breakpoints, watches, and more

More complex and comprehensive debugging features such as breakpoints, variable watching, stack traces, and more are also provided by Firebug and can be accessed from its **Script** tab.

See also

Chapter 7, JavaScript in Themes, is dedicated to JavaScript where the use of Firebug will prove invaluable. The previous *Inspecting elements and debugging CSS using Firebug* recipe provides information on how to use Firebug in order to debug the CSS in our modules and themes.

6
Advanced Templating

We will cover the following recipes in this chapter:

- ▶ Adding a variable to all node templates
- ▶ Deleting a variable from the page template
- ▶ Adding a custom theme setting
- ▶ Hiding all regions on a page
- ▶ Displaying the last updated date instead of the submitted date
- ▶ Module-based variable manipulation
- ▶ Optimizing using `hook_preprocess()`
- ▶ Displaying the date field in calendar form

Introduction

In a bid to separate logic from presentation, Drupal's theming system tries to minimize the amount of PHP that is necessary in a template file. This ensures that themers who are not as comfortable in a PHP environment, are not exposed to the nitty-gritty of complicated code manipulations. Instead, they are provided with a host of pre-prepared variables that contain the content of the regions and blocks that make up a page, or those that describe other elements such as user details and submission information that can be utilized in the template file.

But the question arises: where do these variables come from? And how can they be modified? This is where **preprocess** and **process** functions come in. Prior to the execution of every template file, Drupal calls a set of functions known as preprocess functions that insert, modify, and in general, organize the variables (provided by Drupal, its modules, and the theming system), which are available for use in the file. Furthermore, as we saw with template overrides in the last chapter, Drupal checks for and executes a series of *candidate* preprocess functions thereby allowing themes as well as modules to have a shot at *manipulating* the available variables. Just as with overrides, these candidate names can be divined using the Theme developer module as illustrated in the following screenshot:

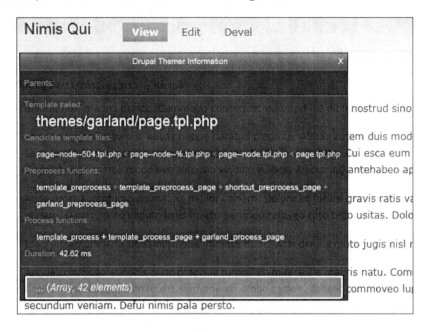

In the preceding image, the candidate functions that affect variables available to the `page.tpl.php` template are listed under the section titled **Preprocess functions**. As is evident, there are a number of functions available with each being useful in certain stages of the theme system's workflow.

Preprocess functions come in two flavors—functions that manipulate variables particular to *specific* templates, and functions that allow the manipulation of variables common to *all* templates or subsets thereof, as the need may be. The former may be of the form `myzen_preprocess_page($variables)` or `myzen_preprocess_block($variables)` where `_page` and `_block` signify the template files associated with `$variables`. The latter on the other hand, may be of the form `myzen_preprocess($variables, $hook)`, which is triggered regardless of which template file is being called. However, the name of the template being called is passed to this function using the `$hook` parameter, which could be page, block, or similar.

As mentioned previously, Drupal's theme system allows the manipulation of these variables in various stages of the workflow. For example, the display of a node template will trigger the following functions—if declared—in sequence:

Level	Function name
Module (mysite)	`mysite_preprocess()`
	`mysite_preprocess_node()`
Theme (myzen)	`myzen_preprocess()`
	`myzen_preprocess_node()`
Module (mysite)	`mysite_process()`
	`mysite_process_node()`
Theme (myzen)	`myzen_process()`
	`myzen_process_node()`

Therefore, variables manipulated by an earlier function in this queue can be manipulated again at a later stage, if so desired. We will be taking advantage of this feature throughout this chapter.

> Zen-based themes come with a `template.php` file that contains skeleton preprocess and process functions, which are commented out by default. Documentation about each function as well as instructions on how to uncomment it usually accompanies each option.

As detailed in the previous screenshot and table, one of the new features included in Drupal 7's theming system is the sibling concept of **process** functions. Process functions, as is evident by the lack of the *pre* prefix, are run after preprocess functions and are used to modify variables that have been modified by other preprocess functions. For example, if two modules named *foo* and *bar* are both modifiying a variable named *baz*, situations can arise where one of the modules will want its modifications to take precedence over the other. Process functions provide a clean and non-invasive solution to such scenarios. They are also handy in cases where variables are to be modified in separate phases.

Process functions retain an identical structure and functionality to preprocess functions and are also listed in the Theme developer pop up.

Adding a variable to all node templates

In this recipe, we will be adding a variable to be made available in all node template files. For this example, the new variable will contain a disclaimer that we will be displaying at the bottom of all nodes.

Getting ready

We will be using the myzen theme created earlier in this book as the example theme in this recipe. It is also assumed that a `node.tpl.php` file exists in myzen's templates folder as per recipes in earlier chapters. If not, this file will need to be imported from the Zen base theme or a new one will need to be created.

How to do it...

A new variable can be made available to node template files by introducing it via the appropriate preprocess function as follows:

1. Navigate to the myzen folder at `sites/all/themes/myzen`.

2. Open the file `template.php` in an editor.

   As mentioned in the introduction to this chapter, this file will have a number of commonly used preprocess functions in skeleton form. These are usually commented out.

3. Look for the function titled `myzen_preprocess_node()`. This can either be uncommented or alternatively, a new function can be created.

4. Modify this function so that the effective end result is as follows:

```
function myzen_preprocess_node(&$variables) {
  $variables['disclaimer'] = t('mysite takes no responsibility for
    user contributed content and comments.');
}
```

The ampersand prefix for the `$variables` parameter is important as it tells PHP that it is being passed by reference. Consequently, any changes that we make to this variable will be automatically communicated upstream to the code that is called `myzen_preprocess_node()`.

5. Save and exit this file.

6. Navigate to the `templates` subfolder, which should contain the `node.tpl.php` template file.

7. Open `node.tpl.php` in an editor and scroll down to the bottom of the file.

8. Add the following *highlighted* markup below the content and links section:

```
<div class="content"<?php print $content_attributes; ?>>
  <?php
    // We hide the comments and links now so that we can render
    // them later.
```

```
        hide($content['comments']);
        hide($content['links']);
        print render($content);
    ?>
</div>

<?php print render($content['links']); ?>

<?php if (!$teaser): ?>
  <div class="disclaimer">
    <?php print $disclaimer; ?>
  </div>
<?php endif; ?>
```

9. Save the file and exit.

10. As we are introducing new elements to the theme, we will need to clear the theme registry to see them take effect.

11. View a node on the site to confirm that our disclaimer has now been added to the bottom of the content.

How it works...

We have chosen to place our code in `myzen_preprocess_node()` for two reasons. Firstly, we want this code to only affect the myzen theme which is why it has been placed within the myzen theme's `template.php` file. Secondly, we are inserting a variable that is only going to be used in node templates—hence, the `_node` suffix. If we had just used a plain `myzen_preprocess()` function, we would have introduced this variable for pages, blocks, and other templates besides the node templates.

To introduce our variable, we just need to add it to the `$variables` array, which is the first argument for all preprocess functions. The `$variables` variable contains a list of all the variables that will be used or passed to the template file:

```
$variables['disclaimer'] = t('mysite takes no responsibility for user
contributed content and comments.');
```

By using an index named `disclaimer` in the array, the variable to be made available to the template file—`node.tpl.php` in this recipe—will also be named the same. In the template file, we take an additional step of only displaying this variable if the `$teaser` variable is not TRUE. This ensures that the disclaimer is only displayed for full node views and will consequently not be displayed when the node is viewed in teaser form. Once this check has been performed, we simply print the `$disclaimer` variable nestled within our HTML of choice.

String handling in Drupal

Just about every time we need to output a string in Drupal, it is recommended that it be passed through the `t()` function. This core function ensures that the string is validated, formatted correctly, and furthermore, also fulfills its primary function of translating text input depending on the user's locale, if so configured. More information on this subject can be accessed via the documentation page for this function at `http://api.drupal.org/api/function/t/7`.

In our currently bare-boned example theme, the changes are visible in the form of a disclaimer at the bottom of the node as exhibited in the following screenshot:

Since the variable is contained within a `DIV` with class `disclaimer`, we can now proceed to style it using CSS.

See also

The next recipe, *Deleting a variable from the page template*, complements this recipe by outlining how to delete existing variables. It will also be worth exploring its subsequent recipe, *Adding a custom theme setting*, which makes the disclaimer field introduced in this recipe, a customizable theme setting.

Deleting a variable from the page template

While we introduced a new variable in the previous recipe, we will be removing an existing variable in this one. To demonstrate the effectiveness of template variable manipulation, we will be removing the feed icons such as the RSS icon from only the front page of the site by making them unavailable to the page template file.

Getting ready

We will be using the myzen theme created earlier in this book as the example theme in this recipe. It is also assumed that a `page.tpl.php` file exists in myzen's `templates` folder. If not, this file will need to be imported from the Zen base theme or a new one will need to be created.

How to do it...

Just as we manipulated `myzen_preprocess_node()` to add a variable to node templates, we will be manipulating `myzen_preprocess_page()` to remove variables from the page template file as follows:

1. Navigate to the myzen folder at `sites/all/themes/myzen`.
2. Open the file `template.php` in an editor.
3. Look for the function titled `myzen_preprocess_page()`. If it is commented out, it can either be uncommented or alternatively, a new one can be created.
4. Modify this function so that the effective end result is as follows:

```php
function myzen_preprocess_page(&$variables) {
  // Do not display the RSS icon if this is the front page.
  if ($variables['is_front']) {
    // Using unset() will lead to a PHP NOTICE as the
    // template file will be trying to print a non-
    // existent variable.
    // unset($variables['feed_icons']);
    $variables['feed_icons'] = '';
  }
}
```

 As ever, it is a good idea to always add an informative comment along with the code that describes our changes.

5. Save and exit this file.
6. Clear the theme registry to see our changes take effect.
7. View the site's front page to confirm that the search box and the feed icon are no longer visible.
8. Similarly, view a node to ensure that it is unaffected by our change.

How it works...

The following screenshot displays the structure of a typical front page with the feed icons, in this case a single RSS icon, rendered at the bottom of the page:

Furthermore, looking at the myzen theme's page template, we can see that the `$feed_icons` variable is being printed using the following line of code:

```php
<?php print $feed_icons; ?>
```

If we compare this with the actual HTML being generated, we can see that the `$feed_icons` variable also contains all the markup necessary for its display. Additionally, we can notice that the variable is not wrapped within an `IF` block that checks whether the variable actually exists prior to printing it. As a result, we can foresee that simply removing the variable will result in a PHP *notice* message (if the server and Drupal are set to display them) as we will then be trying to access a variable that does not exist.

With our investigative work done, we then proceed to the `template.php` file where we proceed to create our `myzen_preprocess_page()` function. Using this function, we restrict our changes to pages and therefore, the `page.tpl.php` template file. In our preprocess function, we first check whether the current page is the front page of the site by checking the `is_front` variable. If this variable is set to `TRUE`, then we go ahead and simply set the `feed_icons` variable to an empty string rather than using PHP's `unset()` function to remove it completely. Once the variable has been blanked and the cache cleared, we should be able to confirm that the RSS icon is no longer being displayed *only* on the front page.

See also

The previous recipe in this chapter titled *Adding a variable to all node templates*, describes how to add a new variable to a template. Similarly, *Displaying the last updated date instead of the submitted date* provides an example where we *modify* an existing variable to suit our purposes. This recipe can be found later on in this chapter.

Adding a custom theme setting

While it is quite straightforward to just edit a template file and add our changes, there are situations where this might not be feasible. When a theme-specific variable needs to be routinely modified or in cases where editing template files is not an option, the ideal solution is to upgrade it to a configurable setting. This can be done either by adding a form element by way of a module, or as this recipe will outline, by declaring a theme configuration setting for display on the theme's administration page.

As an example, this recipe will make the disclaimer variable used in an earlier recipe in this chapter, a configurable option.

Getting ready

This recipe is a continuation of the *Adding a variable to all node templates* recipe from earlier in this chapter. It is assumed that it has been completed successfully.

How to do it...

There are two changes that we will need to make to the existing implementation from the previous recipe. First, we will need to add our theme-specific setting to our theme. With Zen-based themes, this can be easily done via the `theme-settings.php` file that comes with the starter-kit. Open this file in an editor and look for the commented out declaration of an example variable named `myzen_example` within the `myzen_form_system_theme_settings_alter()` function. Below this section, add the following form *textfield* element declaration:

```
$form['myzen_disclaimer'] = array(
  '#type' => 'textfield',
  '#title' => t('Node disclaimer'),
  '#default_value' => theme_get_setting('myzen_disclaimer'),
  '#description' => t("Enter the disclaimer text to add at the bottom
    of node content.")
);
```

We can now save this file and exit the editor. Next, we need to replace the hardcoded string in the `node.tpl.php` file and replace it with our newly configured setting by updating the preprocess function in the `template.php` file to resemble the following:

```
function myzen_preprocess_node(&$variables) {
  $variables['disclaimer'] = theme_get_setting('myzen_disclaimer');
}
```

How it works...

The `myzen_form_system_theme_settings_alter()` function inside `theme-settings.php` is an implementation of `hook_form_system_theme_settings_alter()`, a function that is called by Drupal to allow themes to conveniently add and manipulate form fields on the theme configuration page. Our new setting will look something like this on myzen's theme configuration page:

> Theme-specific settings
> These settings only exist for the *My Zen* theme and all the styles based on it.
>
> **Node disclaimer:**
>
> This is My Site's new disclaimer.
> Enter the disclaimer text to add at the bottom of node content.

We can see from the screenshot what each of the fields in the form element declaration - `#title`, `#type`, and `#description`—represent. The `#default_value` option represents the default value of the textfield before it has been configured by the administrator.

 The `myzen_form_system_theme_settings_alter()` function contains pre-existing code that loads settings from the base Zen theme. Our changes to the myzen theme are merged with these settings. If necessary, the settings from the base theme can be manipulated from the subtheme.

Now that our new setting is up and running, we use another Drupal function—`theme_get_setting()`—to retrieve our theme-specific option and forward it to our template file as the variable `$disclaimer`:

```
$variables['disclaimer'] = theme_get_setting('myzen_disclaimer');
```

As the node template file already uses the `$disclaimer` variable, our changes should be immediately apparent as illustrated in the following screenshot:

There's more...

There is a rather complicated interplay happening between the base theme and the subtheme when it comes to theme settings as they can both declare complex settings for display on the theme page.

Zen's breadcrumb settings

Using its `hook_form_system_theme_settings_alter()` function, the Zen base theme adds options to customize breadcrumbs. This implementation can be seen in its own `theme-settings.php` file and can serve as an additional example on how to add customized settings.

Complex form options

By leveraging Drupal's Form API, theme developers can create options of much greater complexity than the simple textfield we have introduced in this recipe. We will be seeing more of the Form API in a later chapter.

See also

The _Chapter 3_, _Custom Themes and Zen_ recipe, _Modifying myzen's theme settings_, details how we can remove a theme setting from a Zen-based theme. Furthermore, the _Chapter 8_, _Navigation_ recipe, _Customizing breadcrumbs in Zen-based themes_, provides a practical example of the breadcrumb customizations in action.

Hiding all regions on a page

This recipe will outline how simple and yet powerful template variable manipulation can be by demonstrating the steps required to hide all regions on a page. Controlling region visibility is a frequent requirement for pages such as the front page of a site or other landing pages that place an onus on capturing the attention of the viewer. By hiding regions, the designer has more real estate to make use of and there are fewer distractions for the user.

In this recipe, we will look to hide all regions for the front page of the site that is set to display a node. We will also take the opportunity to hide the page title and hide elements such as node links and submission information that are not always necessary for the front page of a site.

Getting ready

We will be using the myzen theme created earlier in this book as the example theme in this recipe. It is assumed that the front page of the site is set to display a *single* sample node rather than the default multi-node listing. The **Default front page** for a site can be configured via the **Site information** page at `admin/config/system/site-information` [**Home | Administration | Configuration | System | Site information**].

How to do it...

As we are going to be working with regions, an easy way to get an outline of the declared regions is through the block administration page at `admin/structure/block` [**Home | Administration | Structure | Blocks**] for the myzen theme. The block administration page provides a link titled **Demonstrate block regions (My Zen)**, which when clicked, will take us to the block (and region) demonstration page. The following screenshot outlines the default layout of our Zen-based theme with the bars in yellow highlighting the regions of the theme:

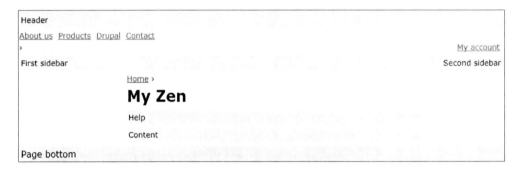

1. Navigate to the myzen folder at `sites/all/themes/myzen`.

2. Open the file `template.php` in an editor.

3. Locate the `myzen_preprocess()` function or if it does not exist, create one.

4. Add the following content to this function so that the effective result is as follows:

```
function myzen_preprocess(&$variables, $hook) {
  if ($variables['is_front']) {
    switch ($hook) {
      case 'html':
        // Override the node title and use a custom title
        // for the front page.
        $variables['head_title'] = t('Welcome to My site!');
        break;
      case 'region':
        // Empty all regions besides the content.
        if ($variables['region'] != 'content') {
          $variables['content'] = '';
        }
        break;
      case 'page':
        // Do not display the node title for the front page.
        $variables['title'] = '';
        break;
      case 'node':
        // Hide submission information and links.
        $variables['display_submitted'] = FALSE;
        unset($variables['content']['links']);
        break;
    }
  }
}
```

5. Save the file and exit.

6. Rebuild the theme registry to ensure that any new functions or template files take effect.

How it works...

Unlike other preprocess functions such as `myzen_preprocess_node()` that target a particular template file, we are using the generic `myzen_preprocess()` function that is executed for *all* template files. This function accepts an additional parameter named `$hook` that indicates which template the accompanying `$variables` parameter is related to.

In the preprocess function, we match the current hook using a `switch` block and perform our modifications accordingly. That said, the question remains of how we actually find which hook or template and which variable to modify. This is where the Theme developer module is especially handy:

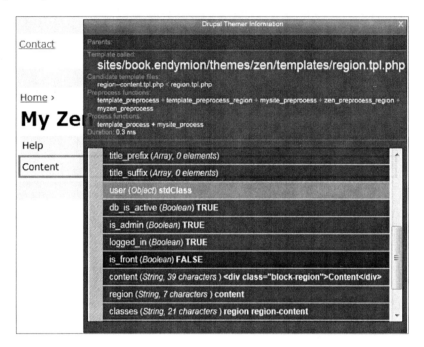

The preceding screenshot displays the variables available to the `region.tpl.php` template that is related to the **Content** region outlined in yellow on the block administration screen behind. Of particular interest in the **Template variables** list, are the **region** variable that retains the name of the region, the **content** variable that, on this demonstration page, is a 39 character-long string containing the region's markup, the **is_front** boolean that is set to TRUE only if we are viewing the front page, and so on. We can similarly confirm an identical structure for all the other regions.

The `is_front` variable will return TRUE if we are viewing the front page of the site. It also returns TRUE if we are viewing the page that has been selected as the front page. In other words, if we have chosen the node with nid *25*, the `is_front` variable will be TRUE both when we visit the front page as well as when we visit `node/25` (or its URL alias).

As mentioned before, this preprocess function relies on a `switch` block that allows us to match each hook against the `$hook` parameter. As we are only concerned with the front page of the site, we place this block within an `if` statement that checks whether the current page is the front page of the site by looking at the `is_front` variable. Once this is true, we perform our manipulations for each hook.

Firstly, for the `html` hook (where variables for the `html.tpl.php` template file are handled), we override the node title with one more suitable for a front page. Next, for the `region` hook, for all regions besides the content region, we simply set the `content` variable to empty, which leads to the region displaying nothing. Similarly, for the `page` hook, we simply blank the `title` variable, which will ensure that we do not display the title of the node on the front page. Lastly, in the `node` hook, we ensure that the links and submission information are also not displayed.

See also

We explored the steps required to add our own regions to a theme in the *Chapter 3, Custom Themes and Zen* recipe titled *Adding a custom region to myzen*.

Displaying the last updated date instead of the submitted date

In this recipe, we will be replacing the contents of the `$date` template variable which, by default, displays the creation date of the node, with the node's last updated date instead. This is useful with content such as fora, news, and so on where recency is an important indicator of the freshness of a node.

Getting ready

We will be using the myzen theme created earlier in this book as the example theme in this recipe. It is also assumed that the `node.tpl.php` file is available in its `templates` folder.

How to do it...

Manipulating the $date variable can be performed using the following steps:

1. Navigate to the myzen theme folder at `sites/all/themes/myzen`.

2. Open the `template.php` file in an editor.

3. Look for the `myzen_preprocess_node()` function; if unavailable, create a skeleton function of the same name.

4. Edit it so that it effectively functions as in the following snippet. Any pre-existing changes will need to be merged appropriately.

```
function myzen_preprocess_node(&$variables) {
  $variables['submitted'] = t('Submitted by !username !datetime
    ago',
    array('!username' => $variables['name'],
      '!datetime' => format_interval(REQUEST_TIME -
        $variables['changed'])
    )
  );
}
```

5. Save the changes and exit the file.

6. Clear the theme registry if necessary.

7. Visit any node page to verify our changes.

How it works...

The following screenshot displays the default node page with the time of creation displayed very accurately, but rather cryptically:

Before proceeding with any changes, it is useful to analyze the structure of the variables available to the template file—node.tpl.php in this case. If we look through the template variables listed by Theme developer, we can see that there are telltale variables named date, which contains the date string that we see displayed under the node's title, and updated, which contains the last updated time. We could just change the value of this variable and amend the node template file accordingly. However, a more careful inspection reveals that another variable named submitted is also listed that contains the entire submission information string including the date information. Consequently, it will be simpler to just modify this string and avoid editing the node.tpl.php template file altogether.

The myzen_preprocess_node() function used in this recipe simply changes the string value of the submitted variable to represent the last updated time. This time is calculated as the difference between the time right now—returned by the Drupal constant REQUEST_TIME—and the last updated field represented by $variables['changed'] and formatted to suit our purposes using the format_interval() function. Once this is done, the node should include our changes as in the following screenshot:

There's more...

The Drupal API is populated by a number of utility functions including format functions such as format_interval(), which we saw in this recipe.

format_interval() and other format functions

The format_interval() function represents an integer as a human-readable concept of time. For example, format_interval(3600) is represented as **1 hour**, format_interval(360000) is represented as **4 days 4 hours**, and format_interval(36000000) as **1 year 7 weeks** respectively. More information on Drupal's format functions can be found at http://api.drupal.org/api/group/format/7 and is worth exploring.

See also

The final recipe in this chapter—*Displaying the date field in calendar form*—deals with styling the date field that we have been manipulating in this recipe.

Module-based variable manipulation

This recipe will outline an alternative method to variable manipulation performed at the module level rather than at the theme level. This provides the advantage of being theme-agnostic, that is, the modifications made will be made available or applied to all themes, which is particularly useful for sites using multiple themes.

To demonstrate this approach, we will be adding a list of classes to the node template based on the taxonomy terms associated with the node in question.

Getting ready

We will be using the mysite module created earlier in this book as an example module to hold our odds and ends. As we are going to demonstrate injecting classes based on the taxonomy terms, perform the following preparatory steps:

1. Create a sample vocabulary with its machine name set to *category*.
2. Generate a number of sample terms for this vocabulary.
3. Associate this vocabulary to a sample node type by including it as one of its fields with its name set to *field_category*.

Associating fields with node types will require the use of the **Field UI** module. If necessary, *Chapter 10, Theming Fields*, provides a brief guide to adding fields prior to delving into their theming aspects. Once the category field has been added to the node type, its page should look something like the following:

Story	Edit	Manage fields	Manage display		
					Show row weights
Label		**Name**	**Field**	**Widget**	**Operations**
✛ Title		title	Node module element		
✛ Body		body	Long text and summary	Text area with a summary	edit delete
✛ category		field_category	Term reference	Select list	edit delete

We will be working on the node page of a node created using these specifications.

How to do it...

Adding classes to node markup based on its associated taxonomy terms is something that will be useful irrespective of which theme is being used to view the node. Consequently, we can elect to inject this change via a module rather than a theme's `template.php` file to ensure that it is available to all themes. This can be done as follows:

1. Navigate to the mysite module's folder in `sites/all/modules`.

2. Open the `mysite.module` file in an editor.

3. Create a `mysite_preprocess_node()` function in this file as follows:

```
function mysite_preprocess_node(&$variables) {
  // Add taxonomy-based classes to the node markup.
  foreach ($variables['field_category'] as $term) {
    $variables['classes_array'][] = 'taxonomy-' . $term['tid'];
  }
}
```

4. Save the file and exit the editor.

5. Clear the Drupal cache as we have introduced a new preprocess function.

6. View a node page in a browser. The relevant markup with our new taxonomy-based classes will look something like this:

```
<div class="node node-story node-promoted taxonomy-1 taxonomy-4
taxonomy-6 taxonomy-2 view-mode-full node-by-viewer clearfix"
id="node-504"></div>
```

7. View the same page using different themes to ensure that our manipulations have taken effect on all of them.

How it works...

As we are looking to include our modifications regardless of which theme is being used, the best place to locate our changes—based on the available candidate preprocess functions—is in a module. As covered earlier, most sites will inevitably need to use a custom module to contain site-specific tweaks and modifications, and we have chosen a similar location to hold our preprocess function:

```
foreach ($variables['field_category'] as $term) {
  $variables['classes_array'][] = 'taxonomy-' . $term['tid'];
}
```

Before we proceed with our changes, it is best to use the Theme developer module to get a map of what we are dealing with. Once this is done, we can choose the best path to proceed. In the preprocess function, we first iterate through the taxonomy array for the *field_category* taxonomy field within the $variables array. With the term ID (tid) obtained, we can create a suitably representative class name and append it to the classes_array variable, which at a later stage will be converted from an array into a string of class names for inclusion in the template file's markup.

See also

Just as we added taxonomy terms as classes in this recipe, the next recipe, *Optimizing using hook_preprocess()*, utilizes another approach to adding author roles as classes within a template file.

Optimizing using hook_preprocess()

This recipe will demonstrate using the hook_preprocess() function in a module. We will be using it to seemingly export settings from one template file to another by making information from the node template available to the page template file. In this example, we will be adding the author's roles into the class list of the BODY tag as well as part of the content of the node.

Getting ready

We will be using the myzen theme created earlier in this book as the example theme in this recipe. It is also assumed that the node.tpl.php and page.tpl.php files exist in myzen's templates folder.

Just as with the previous recipe where we added our preprocess function to a module, we will be adding our function here into the mysite module.

How to do it...

First, let us add our preprocess function to the mysite module:

1. Navigate to the mysite module's folder within sites/all/modules.
2. Open the mysite.module file in an editor.

3. Create a `mysite_preprocess()` function in this file as follows:

```
function mysite_preprocess(&$variables, $hook) {
  // Cache author role names.
  static $author_roles = array();
  // Cache author role classes.
  static $author_role_classes = array();

  // Modify variables for the page template file.
  if ($hook == 'page' && isset($variables['node'])) {
    $user = user_load($variables['node']->uid);

    $author_role_classes = array();
    foreach ($user->roles as $rid => $role) {
      $author_role_classes[] = 'author-role-' . $rid;
      // Only display custom roles; ignore anonymous and
      // authenticated
      // user roles.
      if ($rid > 2) {
        $author_roles[] = $role;
      }
    }
  }
  else if ($hook == 'html' && !empty($author_role_classes)) {
    // Add classes to the <body> tag.
    $variables['classes_array'] = array_merge($variables['classes_
      array'], $author_role_classes);
  }
  // Modify variables for the node template file.
  else if ($hook == 'node' && !empty($author_roles)) {
    // Modify submission information text to include role names.
    $variables['submitted'] = t('Submitted by !username (!roles)
      on !datetime',
      array('!username' => $variables['name'],
        '!roles' => implode(', ', $author_roles),
        '!datetime' => $variables['date']
      )
    );
  }
}
```

4. Save the file and exit the editor.

5. Clear the theme registry.

6. Verify our changes by viewing node pages created by users with only the default authenticated user role as well as those with other custom roles:

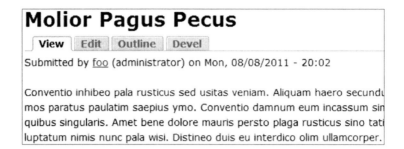

The preceding screenshot displays the node with the author's sole custom role inserted next to the username.

7. View the source-code of a node page to verify that classes indicative of the author's roles are being inserted. The BODY tag should now look something like the following:

```
<body class="not-front logged-in node-type-page page-node-89
section-node one-sidebar sidebar-first author-role-2 author-
role-3">
```

Our changes can also be verified by using the Themer information pop up for the entire page, which should confirm that the classes_array includes our author classes:

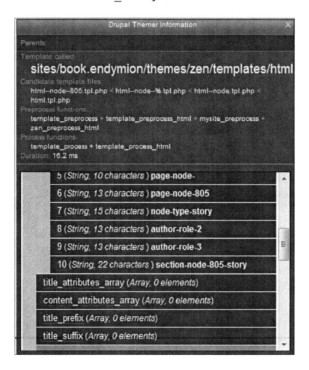

How it works...

The primary decision that we have made here is to use `mysite_preprocess()` as the location for our modifications. The fact that this is a module function and not a theme-specific template function suits our purposes because we want the features that we have introduced to be common across all themes used in the site. Moreover, we are using the plain preprocess function rather than a template-specific option for reasons of optimization. Of particular importance from an optimization point of view is the following statement:

```
$user = user_load($variables['uid']);
```

The `user_load()` call is a costly operation as it is not cached by Drupal. What this means is that every time we execute it, we are effectively running a potentially large number of database calls, which usually tends to lead to performance bottlenecks. Consequently, if instead of using `mysite_preprocess()` we were using `mysite_preprocess_node()` and `mysite_preprocess_page()`, we would have needed to run this operation twice, creating twice the hassle. While it is a minor incentive here, we can also get away with iterating through the roles array just once.

The key to actually exporting data from one template to another is through our use of two **static** variables, `$author_roles` & `$author_role_classes`. By declaring these variables as `static`, we are informing PHP that the value of this variable is to be retained even after we exit the function. As a result, the next time the same function is called, this variable continues to hold data from the previous call thereby allowing us to seamlessly move information between calls. In this case, the preprocess function is called for each `$hook`, which can be `page`, `html`, `block`, `node`, and so on.

In our function, we have made use of the preprocess function to store information related to the roles assigned to the *author* (as opposed to the user viewing the page). We process this information just the once in the page hook and elect to store it in the two aforementioned static variables. Subsequently, when the function is again triggered for the HTML and node hooks respectively, we access these variables to accomplish our tasks, namely adding appropriate classes to the `BODY` tag of the page and modifying the submission information to include information about the author's roles.

 More information related to static variables is available at
`http://php.net/manual/en/language.variables.scope.php`.

See also

Similar to this recipe, *Module-based variable manipulation*, lists the steps required in adding taxonomy terms as CSS classes in a template.

Displaying the date field in calendar form

This recipe will use a number of techniques to transform a standard text-based date field into an eye-catching calendar form.

Getting ready

We will be using the myzen theme created earlier in this book as the example theme in this recipe. It is also assumed that a `node.tpl.php` file exists in myzen's `templates` folder.

How to do it...

We are going to break down this operation into three stages. The first is the preprocess stage where we break the node's timestamp down into the required component parts and introduce them as variables in a preprocess function:

1. Navigate to the myzen theme folder at `sites/all/themes/myzen`.

2. Open the file `template.php` in an editor.

3. Locate the `myzen_preprocess_node()` function, or if unavailable, create one.

4. Add the following code into the aforementioned preprocess function so that it effectively looks like the following:

   ```
   function myzen_preprocess_node(&$variables) {
     $variables['calendar_month'] = format_date($variables['node']
   ->created, 'custom', 'M');
     $variables['calendar_day'] = format_date($variables['node']
   ->created, 'custom', 'j');
     $variables['calendar_year'] = format_date($variables['node']
   ->created, 'custom', 'Y');
   }
   ```

5. Save the file and exit the editor.

The second stage is the template stage where we make use of the newly added variables and wrap them in appropriate markup. This readies them for the third stage where we will be styling these fields:

6. Navigate to the `templates` folder.

7. Locate the `node.tpl.php` file within and open it in an editor.

8. Add the following markup that is highlighted to display the new calendar fields leaving the template looking something like in the following excerpt:

   ```
   <div id="node-<?php print $node->nid; ?>" class="<?php print
   $classes; ?> clearfix">
   ```

```
<div class="calendar">
  <span class="month"><?php print $calendar_month;?></span>
  <span class="day"><?php print $calendar_day;?></span>
  <span class="year"><?php print $calendar_year;?></span>
</div>
```

9. If there are any pre-existing fields in this template that display the timestamp, remove them.

10. Save the file and exit the editor.

If we clear the theme registry and preview a node page, we should see something like in the following screenshot:

The final stage is the styling stage where we will be dressing up the markup to resemble a calendar page:

11. Navigate to the myzen `css` folder.

12. Open the file `nodes.css` and insert the following rules:

```css
.node .calendar {
  float: left;
  margin: 2.5em 1em 1em 0;
  color: #FFF;
  font-variant: small-caps;
}
.node .calendar span {
  display: block;
  padding: 0 4px;
  text-align: center;
  background-color: #3399CC;
}
.node .calendar .day {
  background-color: #EEE;
  color: #000;
  font-weight: bold;
}
```

13. Save the file and exit the editor.

14. Clear the theme registry.

15. Visit a node page to confirm that our modifications have taken effect.

How it works...

The key to this recipe is the `myzen_preprocess_node()` function where we break down the node's created timestamp into its three relevant parts, namely month, day, and year. We do this using Drupal's `format_date()` function, which is a rather complicated wrapper around PHP's date functions. More information on `format_date()` and the PHP `date()` functions can be found at `http://api.drupal.org/api/function/format_date/7` and `http://php.net/manual/en/function.date.php` respectively.

Once broken down, we export each date field as a variable to the node template. In the node template, we use these variables to populate our markup for the calendar field:

```
<div class="calendar">
  <span class="month"><?php print $calendar_month;?></span>
  <span class="day"><?php print $calendar_day;?></span>
  <span class="year"><?php print $calendar_year;?></span>
</div>
```

We then proceed to style our creation using the `nodes.css` file where the reasons for our markup should be readily apparent. The three SPANs are displayed as block elements to ensure that they are stacked vertically and the DIV container is floated to the left to ensure that the content on the right—the node body—flows in parallel, thereby giving us the look demonstrated in the following screenshot:

See also

An earlier recipe in this chapter, *Displaying the last updated date instead of the submitted date*, describes how we can manipulate variables to modify the date associated with a node.

7
JavaScript in Themes

We will be covering the following recipes in this chapter:

- ▸ Including JavaScript files from a theme
- ▸ Including a JavaScript file only for certain pages
- ▸ Giving the username textfield keyboard focus
- ▸ Exporting a variable from PHP to JavaScript
- ▸ Adding default text to the search textfield
- ▸ Displaying comments in compact form
- ▸ Minimizing and maximizing blocks using JavaScript

Introduction

Until a few years ago, mentioning the word JavaScript to a themer would usually result in groans about inconsistencies in browser support, lack of standards, difficulty in debugging, and a myriad of other complaints. Thankfully, however, things have changed considerably since then. Browsers have evolved and standards have improved. JavaScript is now a potent weapon in any themer's armory and this is especially true with the introduction of cross-browser libraries and frameworks which address most of the aforementioned issues with it.

JavaScript libraries take out the majority of the hassle involved in writing code which will be executed in a variety of browsers each with its own vagaries and peculiarities. Drupal, by default, uses jQuery, a lightweight, robust and well-supported package which, since its introduction, has become one of the most popular libraries in use today. While it is possible to wax eloquent about its features and ease of use, its most appealing factor is that it is a whole lot of fun!

jQuery's efficiency and flexibility lies in its use of CSS selectors to target page elements and its use of chaining to link and perform commands in sequence. As an example, let us consider the following block of HTML which holds the items of a typical navigation menu:

```html
<div class="menu">
  <ul class="menu-list">
    <li>Item 1</li>
    <li>Item 2</li>
    <li>Item 3</li>
    <li>Item 4</li>
    <li>Item 5</li>
    <li>Item 6</li>
  </ul>
</div>
```

Now, let us consider the situation where we want to add the class active to the first menu item in this list and while we are at it, let us also color this element red. Using arcane JavaScript, we would have accomplished this using something similar to the following code:

```javascript
var elements = document.getElementsByTagName("ul");
for (var i = 0; i < elements.length; i++) {
  if (elements[i].className === "menu-list") {
    elements[i].childNodes[0].style.color = '#F00';
    if (!elements[i].childNodes[0].className) {
      elements[i].childNodes[0].className = 'active';
    }
    else {
      elements[i].childNodes[0].className =
        elements[i].childNodes[0].className + ' active';
    }
  }
}
```

Now, we would accomplish the same task using jQuery as follows:

```javascript
$("ul.menu-list li:first-child").css('color',
  '#F00').addClass('active');
```

This jQuery statement can be effectively read as: Retrieve all UL tags classed menu list and having LI tags as children, take the first of these LI tags, style it with some CSS that sets its color to #F00 (red), and then add a class named active to this element.

For better legibility, we can format our query with each chained command on a separate line:

```
$("ul.menu-list li:first-child")
  .css('color', '#F00')
  .addClass('active');
```

We are just scratching the surface here. More information and documentation on jQuery's features are available at `http://jquery.com` and `http://www.visualjquery.com`. A host of jQuery plugins which, like Drupal's modules, extend and provide additional functionality, are available at `http://plugins.jquery.com`.

Another aspect of JavaScript programming that has improved in leaps and bounds is in the field of debugging. With its rising ubiquity, developers have introduced powerful debugging tools that are integrated into browsers and provide tools such as interactive debugging, flow control, logging, monitoring, and so on, which have traditionally only been available to developers of other high-level languages. Of the many candidates out there, the most popular and feature-rich is **Firebug**, which we looked at in *Chapter 5, Development and Debugging Tools*. It can be downloaded and installed from `https://addons.mozilla.org/en-US/firefox/addon/firebug/`.

This chapter will deal with recipes that describe different ways of adding JavaScript files in Drupal and using them to style and manipulate our content.

Including JavaScript files from a theme

This recipe will list the steps required to include a JavaScript file from within the `.info` file of the theme. To ensure that the JS file is being included, we will be adding some sample code that outputs the standard **Hello World!** string upon page load.

Getting ready

While the procedure is the same for all themes, we will be using the Zen-based myzen theme in this recipe. It is assumed that this theme is the site's default theme.

How to do it...

The following steps are to be performed inside the myzen theme folder at `sites/all/themes/myzen`:

1. Browse into the `js` subfolder where JavaScript files are conventionally stored.
2. Create a file named `hello.js` and open it in an editor.
3. Add the following code:

   ```
   alert("Hello World!!");
   ```

4. Save the file and exit the editor.

5. Browse back up to the `myzen` folder and open `myzen.info` in an editor.

6. Include our new script using the following syntax:

```
scripts[] = js/hello.js
```

7. Save the file and exit the editor.

8. Rebuild the theme registry and if JavaScript optimization is enabled for the site, the cache will also need to be cleared.

9. View any page on the site to see our script taking effect.

How it works...

Once the theme registry is rebuilt and the cache cleared, Drupal adds `hello.js` to its list of JavaScript files to be loaded and embeds it in the HTML page. The JavaScript is executed before any of the content is displayed on the page and the resulting page with the alert dialog box should look something like the following screenshot:

There's more...

While we have successfully added our JavaScript in this recipe, Drupal and jQuery provide efficient solutions to work around this issue of the JavaScript being executed as soon as the page is loaded.

Executing JavaScript only after the page is rendered

A solution to the problem of the `alert` statement being executed before the page is ready, is to wrap our JavaScript within a function to ensure that the code within is executed only once the page has been rendered and is ready to be acted upon. In Drupal, this is accomplished as follows:

```
(function ($) {
  alert("Hello World!!");
}(jQuery));
```

The Drupal wrapper syntax is different from the traditional jQuery syntax which wraps the code within a `$(document).ready();` function. This discrepancy is necessary to avoid conflicts with other JavaScript libraries that use similar syntax.

Drupal's JavaScript behaviors

While simply embedding the `alert()` call works well, Drupal recommends the use of behaviors to manage our use of JavaScript. This allows for reuse as well as better control of our code. Our **Hello World!** example would now look like this:

```
(function ($) {
  Drupal.behaviors.myzenAlert = {
    attach: function() {
      alert("Hello World!!");
    }
  };
}(jQuery));
```

All registered behaviors are automatically called by Drupal once the page is ready.

 As with most things Drupal, it is always a good idea to namespace our behaviors based on the module or theme name to avoid conflicts. In this case, the behavior name has been prefixed with `myzen` as it is part of the myzen theme.

See also

The next recipe, _Including a JavaScript file only for certain pages_, outlines how we can similarly include JavaScript files from a module.

Including a JavaScript file only for certain pages

This recipe will list the steps required to include a JavaScript file from a module rather than a theme. Unlike themes, modules offer a lot more options on when and how JavaScript files should be included. We will be taking advantage of this feature to ensure that our JavaScript is being included only for _node_ pages.

We will be testing this by outputting the standard **Hello World!** string as we saw in the previous recipe.

Getting ready

We will be using the mysite module created earlier in this book to hold our odds and ends. It is assumed that this module has been created and is enabled.

How to do it...

The following steps are to be performed inside the mysite module folder at `sites/all/modules/mysite`:

1. If it does not already exist, create a folder within titled `js`.
2. Inside this new folder, create a file named `hello.js` and open it in an editor.
3. Insert the following JavaScript:

```
(function ($) {
  Drupal.behaviors.mysiteHello = {
    attach: function() {
      alert("Hello World!!");
    }
  };
}(jQuery));
```

4. Save the file and exit the editor.
5. Navigate up one level back to the base folder of the mysite module.
6. Open the file `mysite.module` in an editor.
7. Look for an implementation of the `mysite_init()` hook. If it is unavailable, create one and add the following code so that the resulting function looks like the following:

```
/**
 * Implements hook_init().
 */
function mysite_init() {
  // The path to the mysite module.
  $path = drupal_get_path('module', 'mysite');

  // Include file only for node pages.
  if (arg(0) == 'node') {
    drupal_add_js($path . '/js/hello.js');
  }
}
```

8. Save the file and exit the editor.
9. Clear the Drupal cache if necessary.

10. Confirm that the script is being included correctly by viewing node pages and others such as administration pages. The **Hello World!** alert should only be triggered for the former.

How it works...

The `mysite_init()` function is executed for all pages. Within it, we check whether the string `'node'` is the first component of the current path. If it is, we queue our JavaScript file for inclusion. Subsequently, when a node page is viewed, our included JavaScript file is executed resulting in the page displaying a **Hello World!** alert box as demonstrated by the screenshot in the previous recipe.

The `arg()` function is used to return components of the current path. For example, if we are viewing a node with node ID **13**, or in other words, if we are accessing `node/13`, then `arg(0)` will return `'node'` while `arg(1)` will return `13`. More information on the `arg()` function is available at `http://api.drupal.org/api/drupal/includes--bootstrap. inc/function/arg/7`.

There's more...

Whilst targeting individual pages, it is important to ensure that we match said pages as accurately as possible.

Checking paths with greater accuracy

In this recipe, we checked whether the user was viewing a node page by checking for `arg(0) == 'node'`. While this will certainly work fine, let us consider the following additional paths:

URL	Description
node	The default Drupal front page containing a list of all published nodes.
node/add	A page listing all available content types that can be created.
node/add/page	The creation form for a node type named page.
node/13	A standard node display page which is what we are targeting.
node/13/edit	A node edit page.

As the previous table demonstrates, we need to be aware of these other permutations that might trigger false positives and include the JavaScript file unnecessarily and in some cases to detrimental effect. Keeping this in mind, we could refine our path-checking code to:

```
if (arg(0) == 'node' && is_numeric(arg(1))) {
```

By ensuring that the second component of the path is a number through the use of PHP's `is_numeric()` check, this would target only URLs of the form `node/13` and avoid most of the other permutations. It would however, still be triggered for paths of the form `node/13/edit`. If this is unacceptable, we will need to refine our `if` statement further by checking whether the third argument is present:

```
if (arg(0) == 'node' && is_numeric(arg(1)) && is_null(arg(2))) {
```

See also

The first recipe in this chapter, *Including JavaScript files from a theme,* covers another approach.

Giving the username textfield keyboard focus

This recipe will detail how keyboard focus can be assigned to the username field in the login block. This will ensure that the user does not need to use the mouse or tab through the page to log in to the site.

Getting ready

We will be using the mysite module created earlier in this book to hold our odds and ends. It is assumed that this module has been created and is enabled.

How to do it...

The following steps are to be performed inside the mysite module folder at `sites/all/modules/mysite`:

1. Create if necessary, and navigate to the JavaScript folder at `sites/all/modules/mysite/js`.
2. Create a JavaScript file named `userfocus.js` and open it in an editor.
3. Add or merge the following JavaScript to the file:

```
(function ($) {
  Drupal.behaviors.mysiteUserFocus = {
    attach: function() {
      // console.log($('input#edit-name'));
      $('input#edit-name').focus();

    }
  };
}(jQuery));
```

The line of jQuery *functionally* relevant to this recipe has been highlighted. The ID of the username textfield, `edit-name`, was located using Firebug.

 Use Firebug's `console.log()` function, as commented out in the preceding code block, to verify that we are targeting the correct element.

4. Save the file and exit the editor.
5. Open the file `mysite.module` in an editor.
6. Look for an implementation of `hook_init()` or if unavailable, create one.
7. Add the code to include our JavaScript file so that the `mysite_init()` function resembles something like the following:

```
/**
 * Implements hook_init().
 */
function mysite_init() {
  global $user;

  // The path to the mysite module.
  $path = drupal_get_path('module', 'mysite');

  // Only include the JS file for anonymous users.
  if ($user->uid == 0) {
    drupal_add_js($path . '/js/userfocus.js');
  }
}
```

8. Save the file and exit the editor.
9. Empty the Drupal cache if necessary.
10. Preview a page as an anonymous user to check whether the username textfield is assigned keyboard focus.
11. View the HTML source first as an anonymous user and then as an authenticated user to ensure that the JavaScript file is only being included for the former.

How it works...

As we are targeting the login form, it can also be assumed that we are also only targeting anonymous users, that is, those who are yet to log in. In other words, if the user ID of the current user is 0, we can include our JavaScript file:

```
if ($user->uid == 0) {
  drupal_add_js($path . '/js/userfocus.js');
}
```

`userfocus.js` uses jQuery to locate the element with ID `edit-name` and applies the JavaScript function `focus()` to it, thereby giving the textfield keyboard focus. Viewing a page on the site as an anonymous user should now default to the keyboard cursor blinking inside the username textfield as shown in the following screenshot:

If we investigate things a little further, we should also be able to confirm that our keyboard focus code also works as expected on a few other user login forms besides the one in the default login block seen in the previous screenshot. These include the form on the user login page at `/user`, the **Create new account** form at `/user/register`, and the **Request new password** form at `/user/password`. This is due to the fact that all these forms contain a **Username** field with CSS ID `#edit-name`.

While we have added our code to a separate file named `userfocus.js` to allow selective loading solely for anonymous users, it could have been placed in a more generic `mysite.js` containing other, possibly even unrelated code. Whether this should or should not have been done is a question of preference, flexibility, and code manageability.

There's more...

If we are not certain about which field to give keyboard focus to, it is usually safe to assign focus to the first available textfield.

Keyboard focus on the first available textfield

This recipe can be adapted to assign keyboard focus to the first available textfield instead of a specific textfield as in this case. This is usually handy as a default option in cases where we are not completely aware of the structure or content of a page.

See also

Just as we have done in this recipe in assigning keyboard focus to a particular field, it is also sometimes useful to add a default string to the field in question. The recipe, *Adding default text to the search textfield*, which can be found later in this chapter, addresses this situation with respect to the search module.

Exporting a variable from PHP to JavaScript

Once we get beyond the rudimentary, we will frequently be faced with scenarios where the JavaScript will need to adapt based on settings and user data that are stored in the database or provided by Drupal modules. In this recipe, we will look at how the Drupal API allows themers to seamlessly export variables from a module and make them available to JavaScript.

Getting ready

We will be using the mysite module created earlier in this book to hold our odds and ends. It is assumed that this module has been created and is enabled.

How to do it...

The following steps are to be performed inside the mysite module folder at `sites/all/modules/mysite`.

1. Open the file `mysite.module` in an editor.
2. Look for an implementation of `hook_init()` or if unavailable, create one.
3. Add the code to include our JavaScript file so that the `mysite_init()` function resembles similar to the following code:

```
/**
 * Implements hook_init().
 */
function mysite_init() {
  // Export a single variable.
  drupal_add_js(array('hello' => 'Hello World!'), 'setting');

  // Wrap multiple related variables inside
  // a parent variable.
  drupal_add_js(array(
    'helloarray' => array(
      'hello' => 'Hello World!',
      'goodbye' => 'Goodbye World!'
    )
```

```
        ), 'setting');
        // The path to the mysite module.
        $path = drupal_get_path('module', 'mysite');
        drupal_add_js($path . '/js/hello.js');
    }
```

4. Save the file and exit the editor.

5. Navigate to the js subfolder. Create this folder if it does not exist.

6. Create a file named hello.js and open it in an editor.

7. Add the following code to the file:

```
(function ($) {
    Drupal.behaviors.mysiteHello = {
        attach: function() {
            // Use console.log to confirm existence
            // of variables via Firebug.
            console.log(Drupal.settings.hello);
            console.log(Drupal.settings.helloarray.hello + " and "
                + Drupal.settings.helloarray.goodbye);
        }
    };
}(jQuery));
```

8. Save the file and exit the editor.

9. Clear the cache if necessary.

10. View any page in Firefox and confirm that our variables are being displayed in the Firebug console.

How it works...

If we view the HTML source of the page where our JavaScript is being included and peruse the head block, we will see something similar to the following code:

```
<script type="text/javascript">
<!--//--><![CDATA[//><!--
jQuery.extend(Drupal.settings, {"basePath":"\/",
  "pathPrefix":"","ajaxPageState":
  {"theme":"myzen","theme_token":"bi86SatLQJv2qqvypURKVrS4sR-
  5piz9hLXYOV-irNw", "hello":"Hello World!",
  "helloarray":{"hello":"Hello World!","goodbye":"Goodbye World!"}});
//--><!]]>
</script>
```

What Drupal does is store all exported variables in a special `Drupal.settings` object. Therefore, with our variables all being collated in a single location, they can be retrieved and manipulated with ease.

When the Firebug console is opened, we should see all three strings displayed, the first from the **hello** variable and the next two from our nested **helloarray** variable. We can also inspect the Drupal settings object via the **DOM** tab which should list all exported variables as shown in the following screenshot:

Adding default text to the search textfield

This recipe will outline the steps required to add a default string of text to the search textfield. The text will only be visible when the field does not have keyboard focus.

Getting ready

We will be using the mysite module created earlier in this book to hold our odds and ends. It is assumed that this module has been created and is enabled. It is also assumed that the search module has been enabled with appropriate permissions granted, and that the search block is active for our theme and is visible on all pages. In our example, the search block has been placed in the header region.

The jQuery plugin repository provides a number of solutions at `http://plugins.jquery.com/plugin-tags/default-text` that could be used to accomplish our goal. While they might simplify the jQuery required and perhaps offer a few more options, we will be making do without them for this recipe.

How to do it...

The following steps are to be performed inside the mysite module folder at `sites/all/modules/mysite`:

1. Browse into the `js` folder which should contain all our JavaScript files. If this folder does not exist, create it.
2. Create a JavaScript file named `search.js`.

3. Add the following JavaScript to this file:

```
(function ($) {
  Drupal.behaviors.mysiteSearch = {
    attach: function() {
      // Hide the search submit button.
      $('#block-search-form .form-submit').hide();

      // Apply the default text to the search block's text
      // field.
      $('#block-search-form .form-type-textfield .form-text')
        // Widen textfield.
        .attr('size', 30)
        // Add default text options on blur.
        .blur(function () {
          $(this).attr('value', Drupal.t
            ('Enter search query ...'))
          .click(function () {
            $(this).attr('value', '');
            $(this).unbind('click');
          });
        })
        // Trigger the blur event to set things up.
        .blur();
    }
  };
} (jQuery));
```

In the previous jQuery, we have taken advantage of its chaining feature to efficiently string a series of operations together. To elaborate, we have located the search form's textfield, widened it, and then implemented the default text feature all in what is effectively a single statement.

4. Save the file and exit the editor.

5. Navigate up a step back into the mysite module folder.

6. Open the file `mysite.module` in an editor.

7. Look for an implementation of `hook_init()` or if unavailable, create one.

8. Add the code to insert our custom settings and include our JavaScript files so that the `mysite_init()` function resembles similar to the following:

```
/**
 * Implements hook_init().
 */
function mysite_init() {
```

```
global $user;

// The path to the mysite module.
$path = drupal_get_path('module', 'mysite');

// Add our custom JavaScript file.
drupal_add_js($path . '/js/search.js');
}
```

9. Save the file and exit the editor.

10. Rebuild the theme registry and clear the cache if necessary.

11. View any page containing the search block to see whether our jQuery is having an effect.

12. Ensure that the default search text disappears when the textfield has focus and reappears when it does not.

13. Turning off JavaScript in the browser should confirm that the original implementation still works fine without it.

How it works...

The following is a screenshot of the search box at the top of a page rendered using the myzen theme:

When the `search.js` file is active, the resulting search box should look like the one in the following screenshot:

As this functionality is useful regardless of which theme is being used, we add our JavaScript through the mysite module instead of the myzen theme.

Seeing how we are targeting the search block's textfield and button, we need to know how they can be accessed. This is accomplished using Firebug's element selector which, in this case, should indicate that both these elements reside within a DIV with ID `block-search-form`. Furthermore, within this DIV, we can target the **Search** button using its class name which is `form-submit`. Similarly the search textfield has a class named `form-type-textfield` which we can use to target it in our `search.js` file.

In terms of required functionality, when the search box is clicked, the default search text should disappear and when the focus moves back elsewhere on the page, the text should reappear. We accomplish this in jQuery using a combination of the JavaScript `blur()` event and the `click()` event. `blur()` is triggered when an element loses focus and can therefore be used to reset the default text string. The `click()` event as the name suggests, is triggered when an element, in this case the textfield, is clicked to attain focus.

Using the preceding information, we can target the search box and add our default text functionality to it.

See also

An earlier recipe in this chapter titled *Giving the username textfield keyboard focus*, discusses how to assign keyboard focus to a particular field on a page. We could quite easily extend this to target a particular search textfield.

Displaying comments in compact form

Drupal provides options to display comments in a variety of fashions. In this recipe, we will look to provide an alternate representation by compacting the display of a node's list of comments using jQuery.

Getting ready

We will be using the myzen theme created earlier in this book as the example theme in this recipe. As we are looking to theme the display of comments, it is assumed that the comment module is enabled and that sample comments are available for testing purposes.

How to do it...

The following steps are to be performed inside the myzen theme folder at `sites/all/themes/myzen`:

1. Browse into the `js` subfolder.
2. Create a JavaScript file named `comment.js` and open it in an editor.
3. Add the following JavaScript to this file:

```
(function ($) {
  Drupal.behaviors.myzenComments = {
    attach: function() {
      // Target comment headings.
      $('#comments h3.comment-title')
        .click(function(e) {
```

```
            e.preventDefault();
            // Display all siblings in animated fashion.
            $(this).siblings().show('fast');
          })
          .siblings()
          .hide();
      }
    };
  }(jQuery));
```

4. Save the file and exit the editor.

5. Navigate up a level back into the base myzen theme folder.

6. Open `myzen.info` in an editor.

7. Include our new JavaScript file by adding the following line to the scripts section:

   ```
   scripts[] = js/comment.js
   ```

8. Save the file and exit the editor.

9. Rebuild the theme registry and clear the cache.

10. Visit any node with a number of comments to confirm that our JavaScript is working well.

How it works...

This recipe, while it accomplishes much, is implemented using a few lines of jQuery. However, it is important to perform some groundwork prior to jumping into the JavaScript to understand how we arrived at our solution. We need to first look at how the HTML for the comments section is structured:

```html
<div id="comments" class="comment-wrapper">
  <h2 class="title">Comments</h2>
  <a id="comment-647"></a>
  <div class="comment comment-by-node-author comment-by-anonymous
    first odd clearfix">
    <h3 class="comment-title"><a href="/comment/663#comment-663"
      class="permalink" rel="bookmark">
      Cui Incassum Persto Uxor</a></h3>
    <div class="submitted"><!-- Snipped Submission info --></div>
    <div class="content"><!-- Snipped content --></div>

  </div> <!-- /.comment -->
  <!-- Other comments -->
</div>
```

Analyzing the markup, we can conclude that we want to just display all the H3 tags within the DIV tag with ID comments and hide() all of their highlighted sibling() tags. Doing so will result in a list of minimized comment titles as evident from the following screenshot:

```
Comments
Incassum Veniam Ludus
Comis Patria Hos Abdo
    Praesent Blandit Abigo Typicus
Volutpat Scisco
Molior Neo Nunc
    Brevitas
        Tation Cui Eu Pertineo Si Aliquip
Enim
    Valde
        Gemino
            Quibus Brevitas Jumentum Feugiat Aliquip
Vero Feugiat Zelus Pecus Ratis Capto
```

Additionally, when an h3 tag is clicked, we want to display, or in jQuery lingo, show() all of its siblings(). The following screenshot demonstrates a clicked comment:

```
Comments
Incassum Veniam Ludus
Comis Patria Hos Abdo
    Praesent Blandit Abigo Typicus
Volutpat Scisco
Molior Neo Nunc
    Brevitas
        Tation Cui Eu Pertineo Si Aliquip
Enim
    Valde
    Submitted by devel generate (not verified) on Sun, 05/09/2010 - 14:35.

    Similis roto praemitto te dolor imputo. Tation dolus torqueo roto dignissim autem. At autem dolore wisi
    esse ullamcorper commodo sino vel pertineo. Oppeto quia praesent. Vindico duis euismod. Ratis te
    pertineo distineo jugis valetudo. Ea sudo nulla vel macto. Velit ymo ymo ulciscor. Magna diam
    consectetuer consequat ibidem minim comis validus incassum.Modo quae jumentum si vel enim eros
    uxor. Interdico comis nostrud nulla facilisi mauris uxor esse. Premo molior aptent iusto ymo cogo roto
    letalis.

    delete   edit   reply

        Gemino
            Quibus Brevitas Jumentum Feugiat Aliquip
Vero Feugiat Zelus Pecus Ratis Capto
```

Looking at our jQuery, we can confirm that this is exactly what we have done. We have also used the animation feature of the jQuery show() function to spice up the display of the comment.

Minimizing and maximizing blocks using JavaScript

In this recipe, we will be looking at using JavaScript to add a clickable button to each block allowing them to be minimized or maximized upon clicking.

Getting ready

We will be using the myzen theme created earlier in this book as the example theme in this recipe. We will also be using a couple of icon images to indicate the minimized and maximized state of each block. These images are to be placed inside the images folder of the theme and named open.png and close.png respectively.

How to do it...

The following steps are to be performed inside the myzen theme folder at sites/all/themes/myzen:

1. Browse into the js subfolder where JavaScript files are conventionally stored.
2. Create a file named block.js and open it in an editor.
3. Add the following JavaScript to the file:

```
(function ($) {
  Drupal.behaviors.myzenBlockDisplay = {
    attach: function() {
      // We are targeting all blocks inside sidebars.
      var s = $('div.sidebar').addClass('js-sidebar');

      $('.block h2.block-title', s)
        .click(function () {
          $(this).siblings().toggle('slow');
          $(this).parent().toggleClass('block-open');
        })
        .siblings()
        .hide();
    }
  };
}(jQuery));
```

4. Save the file and exit the editor.
5. Browse back up to the myzen folder and open myzen.info in an editor.
6. Include our new script using the following:

```
scripts[] = js/block.js
```

7. Save the file and exit the editor.

8. Navigate up a level and into the `css` folder of the myzen theme. Open the file `blocks.css` in an editor.

9. Scroll down to the bottom and add the following rules to the file:

```css
.js-sidebar .block h2 {
    background: url(../images/open.png) no-repeat left center;
    padding-left: 1.1em;
}

.js-sidebar .block-open h2 {
    background: url(../images/close.png) no-repeat left center;
    padding-left: 1.1em;
}
```

10. Save the file and exit the editor.

11. Rebuild the theme registry and clear the cache if necessary.

12. View a page with blocks to see our changes taking effect.

How it works...

As with other recipes in this chapter, we organize our jQuery based on the markup that we are looking to manipulate. In this case, we first identify the sidebar containing the blocks that we are targeting. We give this sidebar a unique class name of `js-sidebar` thus making it easy for us to target blocks within CSS.

Next, we retrieve all the block titles and retain them while hiding all their siblings or in other words, the content of each block. This should result in blocks being minimized by default like the ones in the following screenshot:

```javascript
$('.block h2.block-title', s)
  .click(function () {
    $(this).siblings().toggle('slow');
    $(this).parent().toggleClass('block-open');
```

```
})
.siblings()
.hide();
```

Next, we want to assign a click handler to these block titles. When clicked, we execute the two highlighted functions, use `toggle()` to hide or show the block content elements as necessary and add or remove the `block-open` class to the list of classes for each block using `toggleClass()`. The presence of this class is used to swap the icon denoting the open or closed status of the block. When clicked, the block should look similar to the one in the following screenshot:

There's more...

We can extend our script by optionally setting the default status of particular blocks.

Minimizing or maximizing particular blocks by default

Instead of minimizing all blocks, we can also target particular blocks to be minimized or maximized by default. For example, if we wanted the Development block to be maximized by default, we could add the following code below our existing jQuery:

```
$('#block-menu-devel', s)
  .toggleClass('block-open')
  .children('h2.block-title')
  .siblings()
  .show();
```

As the Development block has the ID `block-menu-devel`, we can target it in particular and reverse all the changes made previously.

8
Navigation

We will be covering the following recipes in this chapter:

- ▶ Adding a menu to our theme
- ▶ Adding content pages to the menu
- ▶ Styling the Main menu
- ▶ Contextual submenus using the Menu module
- ▶ Adding a drop-down navigation menu
- ▶ Customizing breadcrumbs in Zen-based themes
- ▶ Hiding node links using CSS
- ▶ Styling all external links in a page
- ▶ Styling the Drupal pager

Introduction

Drupal relies on a core menu component which provides a framework allowing modules to create and customize navigational elements. These can subsequently be exposed via the theme by way of menus embedded either directly within the theme or as content within blocks. Furthermore, this framework forms the basis for the breadcrumb navigation which is an integral facet of every site's user interface.

Besides menu items exposed by modules, Drupal also provides an optional Menu module which allows the customization of the aforementioned items as well as the creation and management of new user-defined menus and their constituent menu items. Customized menu items are not solely restricted to the domain of the site and can also be linked to external URLs if necessary.

As a site's complexity grows, so does its menu structure. Consequently, simple and static menu implementations no longer suffice and other alternatives are required. One of the solutions frequently arrived at is the introduction of DHTML menus, a set of drop down and expandable menus which customarily rely on a combination of CSS and JavaScript in their implementation.

In this chapter, we will be looking at the various features of the menu system and learn to customize and alter them to suit our purposes.

Adding a menu to our theme

In this recipe, we will look at using the Menu module to add a menu to a theme which will allow the user to navigate through the site. While we can add as many menus as we need, Drupal and most Drupal themes, by default, support two generic menus named *Main links* and *Secondary links*.

Getting ready

The Menu module that comes with Drupal will need to be enabled to add our menu and menu items. We will be adding a link to a local node with **URL alias** about-us to link to a typical *About us* page on the site. It is assumed that such a node has been created.

How to do it...

Let us first add a custom item to the menu:

1. Navigate to admin/structure/menu (**Home | Administration | Structure | Menus**) and look for a menu titled **Main menu**.

2. Click on its associated **add link** option.

3. Add a menu item: for example, a link to an external site with **Menu link title** set to Drupal and **Path** to http://drupal.org as in the next screenshot.

4. The **Description** field can optionally be filled and appears when the user hovers over the link as its title attribute.

5. The **Weight** field dictates the order of the item relative to others in the same menu.

6. Ensure that the **Parent link** is set to **<Main menu>** and click on the **Save** button to create the menu item:

Menu link title *

Drupal

The text to be used for this link in the menu.

Path *

http://drupal.org

The path for this menu link. This can be an internal Drupal path such as *node/add* or an external URL such as *http://drupal.org*. Enter *<front>* to link to the front page.

Description

Visit Drupal's home page.

Shown when hovering over the menu link.

☑ Enabled

Menu links that are not enabled will not be listed in any menu.

☐ Show as expanded

If selected and this menu link has children, the menu will always appear expanded.

Parent link

<Main menu>

The maximum depth for a link and all its children is fixed at 9. Some menu links may not be available as parents if selecting them would exceed this limit.

Weight

0

Optional. In the menu, the heavier links will sink and the lighter links will be positioned nearer the top.

Save

Moving menu items between different menus

The **Parent link** drop down seen in the previous screenshot controls where this menu item is displayed. If, say we wanted to move this link to the **User menu** instead, then all we would need to do is edit this menu item and set its **Parent link** to **<User menu>**.

7. Navigate back to the menu management page.

8. Click on the **add link** option for the **Main menu**.

9. Now, rather than adding a link to an external site, let us add a link to a local node titled **About us** with URL alias about-us.

The URL in the **Path** field will need to be valid if pointing to local content. In other words, if there is no page with the URL alias about-us in this recipe, then Drupal will throw an error at us when we try to save our changes.

10. Click on **Save** to create our local link.

We should now be able to see our two new links at the top of the page.

How it works...

Once the menu items have been added, the menu management page should look something as shown in the following screenshot of the site rendered using the Bartik core theme:

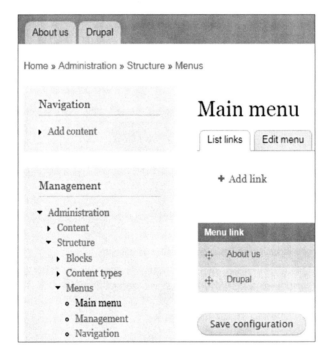

The crosshairs before each item on the menu management page can be used to drag the item and reorder the menu. In other words, instead of playing around with the weight field on each menu item's edit page, we can save time and energy through simple drag-and-drop operations.

There's more...

While the Main and Secondary menus are customarily added to the page via the
`page.tpl.php` **template file of the theme, it is also possible to insert the menu as a block.**

Using the Main menu block

Whenever a menu is created in Drupal, it is automatically also made available as a block. As a result, instead of embedding the **Main menu** as part of `page.tpl.php`, we could have just as easily added this block into a header region of the page. The downside however, is that making changes to the markup and styling might be a little more involved once the menu begins to get complicated.

See also

In the next recipe, *Adding content pages to the menu*, we will see how we can add items to the menu directly from the node form.

Adding content pages to the menu

In this recipe, we will be looking at an alternative means of adding an item to a menu directly from the node. This can be done either during creation or later, via the node's edit form.

Getting ready

The Menu module needs to be enabled for this recipe in order to be able to add a menu item via the node form. We will also be working with a sample node named **Products** which will need to be created. We will be expanding this menu in later recipes of this chapter.

How to do it...

The following steps detail the procedure required to link to a **Products** overview page from the **Main menu**:

1. Browse to the **Products** overview node and click on its **Edit** tab.
2. Scroll down to the **Menu settings** fieldset and click on it.

3. Check the **Provide a menu link** option which should reveal further fields laid out similar to the **Add item** form in the menu administration pages as shown in the following screenshot:

4. Add the title of the menu item in the **Menu link title** textfield which, in this case, would be something such as **Products**. This does not need to be the same as the node title.

5. Select **<Main menu>** as the **Parent item** as we want this link to be displayed in the site menu.

6. The **Weight** field dictates the position of the menu item with respect to its neighbors and should be selected appropriately.

7. Click on the **Save** button to save the node.

How it works...

When the node is saved, we should be able to see a new menu item titled **Products** in the site menu as displayed in the following screenshot:

As in evident from the screenshot, we have used the weight attribute to ensure that the **Products** item is displayed before the **Drupal** link we added in the previous recipe.

There's more...

Drupal's menu system does an excellent job when it comes to controlling access to menus and menu items.

Access control and menu visibility

Menu items that cannot be accessed by the user will not be displayed. For example, if the **Products** node is set to be visible solely to authorized users, then only users who have access to the node will be able to view its links menu item as well.

See also

In the next recipe, *Styling the Main menu*, and in a later recipe titled *Adding a drop-down navigation menu*, we will learn how to theme our menus in different ways.

Styling the Main menu

Now that we have a menu at our disposal, let us look at styling it. In this recipe, we will look at how to go about theming the menu via CSS when using the myzen theme.

Getting ready

We will be using the myzen theme created earlier in this book as the example theme in this recipe. The menu items used are those created in the previous recipe.

How to do it...

By inspecting the markup of the page, we should be able to verify that the **Main menu** in the myzen theme is contained within a DIV with ID as navigation. It is important to use tools such as Firebug to familiarize ourselves with the structure of this element and its contents in order to theme it efficiently. The markup in our example theme looks something as shown in the following:

```
<div id="navigation">
  <div class="section clearfix">
    <h2 class="element-invisible">Main menu</h2>
    <ul class="links inline clearfix" id="main-menu">
      <li class="menu-317 first"><a title="" href="/about-us">About
        us</a></li>
      <li class="menu-318 active-trail active"><a class="active-trail
        active" title="Peruse through our product list."
        href="/node/174">Products</a></li>
      <li class="menu-316 last"><a title="Visit Drupal's home page."
        href="http://drupal.org">Drupal</a></li>
    </ul>
  </div>
</div>
```

The structure of the menu can also be confirmed and, if necessary, modified via the myzen theme's page.tpl.php template file.

Let us start off by giving the navigation block—with its id attribute also named navigation—a little color. Rules that affect the backgrounds of page elements are, by default, contained within the file page-backgrounds.css:

1. Browse to the myzen theme's css folder at sites/all/themes/myzen/css.

2. Locate the page-backgrounds.css file and open it in an editor.

3. Add the following rule to the bottom of the file:

```
#navigation {
  background: #F0B900;
}
```

4. Save the file and exit the editor.

5. Empty the cache if necessary and preview a page to ascertain whether our changes have taken effect.

Now that we have styled the background, let us style the links. Rules particular to the navigation area are placed in a file named navigation.css:

6. Locate the `navigation.css` file in the myzen theme's `css` folder and open it in an editor.

7. Style navigation links by adding the following rules to the bottom of this file:

```css
/*
 * Style navigation links.
 */
#navigation a {
  text-decoration: none;
}

#navigation a:link {
  color: #C93A03;
}

#navigation a:visited {
  color: #3D1101;
}

#navigation a.active {
  text-decoration: underline;
}
```

8. Save the file and exit the editor.

9. Again, empty the cache if necessary and preview a page to ascertain whether our changes have taken effect.

How it works...

The markup used for these menu items is declared via the theme's `page.tpl.php` template file. For example, looking at the file for Zen-based themes such as myzen, the following block is how we inject our menu into the page:

```php
<?php if ($page['navigation'] || $main_menu): ?>
  <div id="navigation">
    <div class="section clearfix">
      <?php print theme('links__system_main_menu', array(
        'links' => $main_menu,
        'attributes' => array(
          'id' => 'main-menu',
          'class' => array('links', 'inline', 'clearfix'),
        ),
        'heading' => array(
          'text' => t('Main menu'),
          'level' => 'h2',
          'class' => array('element-invisible'),
```

```
        ),
    )); ?>
    <?php print render($page['navigation']); ?>
  </div>
</div><!-- /.section, /#navigation -->
```

As is evident from the code, adding, modifying, or removing CSS IDs and classes from a menu becomes as simple as amending the attributes array appropriately. However, if we want to get even more adventurous and actually change the underlying structure of the menu, then we will need to roll up our sleeves and override the `links__system_main_menu()` theme function.

In this case, as we are using the default markup, we have gone right ahead to styling it via the `page-backgrounds.css` and `navigation.css` files. Once the cache has been cleared, the end result should look something as shown in the following screenshot:

Similarly, other CSS rules to tweak the padding and margins of the navigation block can also be added.

 Zen-based themes, by default, take advantage of Drupal's CSS aggregation feature by splitting up the different sections of monolithic CSS files and placing them into separate, logically distinct files. It should however be understood that the breakup is more of a guide than anything else and does not need to be adhered to religiously. If necessary, the files can be reorganized to suit our own purposes.

There's more...

While the Main menu links are usually placed in the upper half of the page, Secondary links tend to be a little more variable.

The Secondary links menu

Drupal also provides a *Secondary links* menu which, by default, sources its links from the *User menu* and contains links to the user's profile page as well as an option to log out from the site. If necessary, the source for these links as well as for the Main menu links can be altered via the menu module's settings page at `admin/structure/menu/settings` (**Home** | **Administration** | **Structure** | **Menus**).

We will learn how to create submenus in the next recipe, *Contextual submenus using the Menu module*. Later on, we will learn how to configure our menu as a drop-down menu in the recipe titled *Adding a drop-down navigation menu*.

Contextual submenus using the Menu module

The Drupal menu system allows us to add nested menus. In this recipe, we will utilize this feature in adding a simple submenu to the existing menu which is displayed only when the parent menu is clicked.

Getting ready

The Menu module needs to be enabled and we will be reusing the menu structure from the previous recipes in this chapter. Specifically, we will be populating the **Products** menu created earlier by adding a few sample products to it. Creating a few sample nodes to which we can link these menu items is also recommended.

We will also be using the myzen theme created earlier in this book as the example theme in this recipe.

How to do it...

Let us first add a set of custom items to the menu as children of an existing item:

1. Navigate to `admin/structure/menu` (**Home | Administration | Structure | Menus**).
2. Click on the **add link** option associated with the **Main menu**.
3. Add a menu item named **Foo** and link it to a node on the site such as `node/123`.
4. Select an existing menu item—**Products**—as the **Parent item**.
5. Click the **Save** button to save the changes.
6. Repeat this process to create two other items titled **Bar** and **Baz**.

Now that we have our nested menu, we need to inform Drupal that we want to use these newly created child items as the submenus of the parent items. This can be done as follows:

7. Navigate to the menu administration page at `admin/structure/menu` (**Home | Administration | Structure | Menus**) and click on the **Settings** tab.

8. In the ensuing page which should resemble the following screenshot, set the **Source for the Main links** and **Source for the Secondary links** to **Main menu** as we want Drupal to load its Secondary links from the Main links submenu:

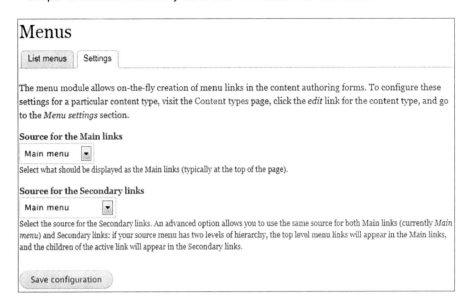

9. Click on **Save configuration** to save the changes.

10. Now, browse to the `myzen` theme folder at `sites/all/themes/myzen` and then into its `templates` folder.

11. Open the `page.tpl.php` template file in an editor. If this file is missing, it will need to be imported from the Zen theme.

12. First look for a section towards the top of the page that deals with the display of the secondary menu.

13. *Cut* the entire *PHP* section—which should consist of a call to `theme('links__ system_secondary_menu')`—to the clipboard.

14. Further below, look for the navigation block which should also contain the code dealing with the display of main menu links.

15. Paste the code for the secondary menu immediately below a similar call for the main menu links.

16. Next, insert a delimiter between the two menus using the following tag:

```
<span id="secondary-prefix">&rsaquo;</span>
```

17. Our block of code should look similar to the following excerpt where the modified lines have been highlighted:

```php
<?php if ($page['navigation'] || $main_menu): ?>
  <div id="navigation"><div class="section clearfix">
    <?php print theme('links__system_main_menu', array(
      'links' => $main_menu,
      'attributes' => array(
        'id' => 'main-menu',
        'class' => array('links', 'inline', 'clearfix'),
      ),
      'heading' => array(
        'text' => t('Main menu'),
        'level' => 'h2',
        'class' => array('element-invisible'),
      ),
    )); ?>

<span id="secondary-prefix">&rsaquo;</span>

<?php print theme('links__system_secondary_menu', array(
  'links' => $secondary_menu,
  'attributes' => array(
    'id' => 'secondary-menu',
    'class' => array('links', 'inline', 'clearfix'),
  ),
  'heading' => array(
    'text' => $secondary_menu_heading,
    'level' => 'h2',
    'class' => array('element-invisible'),
  ),
)); ?>

    <?php print render($page['navigation']); ?>
  </div></div><!-- /.section, /#navigation -->
<?php endif; ?>
```

18. Save the file and exit the editor.

19. Finally, switch over to the myzen theme's `css` folder.

20. Open `navigation.css` in an editor and add the following CSS rules to the bottom of the file:

```
#navigation ul {
  float: left;
}

#navigation #secondary-prefix {
  float: left;
  padding-right: 10px;
}
```

21. Save the file and exit the editor.

22. If necessary, empty the cache to ensure that our changes are being registered.

How it works...

Drupal, by default, provides two menus named **Main links** and **Secondary links**. By setting the source of the secondary menu to the same one as for the main menu, we are effectively instructing Drupal that we are looking to display contextual submenus based on the currently displayed item:

In the previous screenshot, we can see our three items from the Main links menu being displayed. As seen in the following screenshot, when the **Products** menu item is clicked, the secondary menu will now automatically display its submenus, namely the three products: **Bar**, **Baz**, and **Foo**:

While in this recipe we added the submenu right next to the parent, it could just as easily have been displayed below it or in a separate block of its own.

See also

- ▶ While contextual submenus are handy, they are frequently ruled out in favor of the more dynamic drop-down menus which we will see in the next recipe, *Adding a drop-down navigation menu*

- ▶ As we needed to add some sample content to our site in this recipe, it might be worthwhile browsing through the *Generating test content using the Devel generate module* recipe in *Chapter 5, Development and Debugging Tools*

Adding a drop-down navigation menu

The more complex the site, the more complex becomes the menu structure. Once we are dealing with nested menus, the inevitable solution from an interface perspective is to use drop-down menus. In this recipe, we will be looking at implementing a drop-down menu, or to be more precise, a drop-right menu using the **Nice Menus** module.

Getting ready

The Nice Menus module can be downloaded at `http://drupal.org/project/nice_menus`. It is assumed that it has been installed and is enabled. We will be using it to add a drop-right menu to the myzen theme created earlier in this book.

 While the instructions in this recipe pertain to version 7.x-2.0—beta3 of the Nice Menus module, it should still be applicable for other releases in the 2.0 cycle and possibly future versions as well.

How to do it...

The Nice Menus module works primarily through the use of specially created blocks which render menu trees as drop-down menus. By default, it dynamically exposes two blocks ready to be configured. We can see the module in action by using one of the blocks to display the **Navigation** menu as a drop-right menu as per the following steps:

10. Navigate to the block management page at `admin/structure/block` (**Home** | **Administration** | **Structure** | **Blocks**).

11. Scroll down to find the two Nice Menu blocks which should be disabled by default.

12. Click on the **configure** link next to the first block. The ensuing page should look something as shown in the following:

13. Add `Management menu` as the **Menu Name**. This is used purely to differentiate one menu from the other.

14. Select the **Management** menu as the **Menu Parent**.

15. Finally, select **right** in the **Menu Style** field as we will be positioning this menu in the left sidebar.

16. Click on **Save block** to save our changes.

17. Back on the block administration page, move the block just configured to the **First sidebar** region.

18. Click on **Save blocks** to save our changes.

The **Nice menu** block should now be visible in the left sidebar. It is however, not styled in keeping with our theme as is evident from the following screenshot:

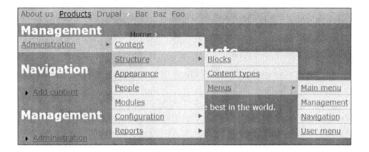

Styling the menu involves simply overriding the color scheme and images used by the module. In keeping with the myzen theme's logical breakdown of CSS files, we can do this in `navigation.css` as follows:

10. Browse to the myzen theme's `css` folder.

11. Look for the file named `navigation.css` and open it in an editor.

12. Scroll down to the bottom and insert the following rules:

```
/**
 * Override default Nice Menu styles. We are only
 * targeting one particular block which contains a nice menu
 * with direction set to "right".
 */
#block-nice-menus-1 ul.nice-menu {
  margin-left: 0.6em;
  padding-left: 0;
}

#block-nice-menus-1 ul.nice-menu ul li,
#block-nice-menus-1 ul.nice-menu-right,
#block-nice-menus-1 ul.nice-menu-right li,
#block-nice-menus-1 ul.nice-menu-right ul ul {
  width: 13.5em;
}

#block-nice-menus-1 ul.nice-menu li,
#block-nice-menus-1 ul.nice-menu-right li.menuparent,
#block-nice-menus-1 ul.nice-menu-right li li.menuparent {
  background-color: #80AA00;
}

#block-nice-menus-1 ul.nice-menu-right li.menuparent:hover,
#block-nice-menus-1 ul.nice-menu-right li.over {
  background-color: #F0B900;
}
```

Finding out the CSS ID of the block and what to override, testing and debugging was accomplished using a combination of Firebug and Web Developer plugins in Firefox.

13. Save the file and exit the editor.

14. Empty the cache if necessary and refresh the browser to see whether our changes have taken effect.

The end result should look something like in the multi-hued screenshot below. The original Management block has been left intact to serve as a comparison:

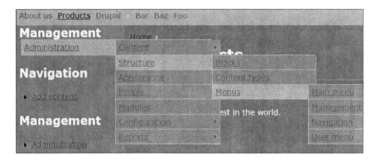

Note that we have used CSS selectors to style links in their various states such as `active` and `hover`.

How it works...

Nice menus uses a combination of JavaScript and CSS to implement the DHTML menu. While earlier versions utilized the **Suckerfish** (http://www.alistapart.com/articles/dropdowns) method, the current version utilizes a jQuery adaptation of Suckerfish, dubbed **Superfish**. JavaScript parameters as well as **Nice menu** block settings can be configured via the module's configuration page at `admin/config/user-interface/nice_menus` (**Home | Administration | Configuration | User interface | Nice menus**). Once configured, the module exposes an appropriate number of blocks via the block management page which can be tweaked as seen in this recipe. Each block sources a list of menu items from its assigned menu tree and outputs them as a list within the block. Once this is done, the embedded jQuery within the page along with CSS acts upon the list and transforms it into the dynamic drop-down (or drop-right in our case) menu system that we see in this recipe.

There's more...

While we have configured a drop-right menu in this recipe, other variants are also available.

Horizontal menus

While this recipe dealt with a menu positioned vertically in the sidebar, Nice menus can just as easily be positioned as a block in the header region as a horizontal menu dropping down to display its submenus. This can be done simply by choosing **down** in its block configuration page. Additionally, the CSS overrides in this recipe will need to be updated to account for this change as well.

See also

We discussed a simpler, albeit static display of submenus in the previous recipe titled *Contextual submenus using the Menu module*.

Customizing breadcrumbs in Zen-based themes

Breadcrumbs are elements essential in the layout of a page. They allow users to identify their current position in the site's hierarchy as well as making it easy to retrace their steps and revisit previously visited pages. This recipe describes how breadcrumbs can easily be customized in Zen-based themes. We will attempt to change the breadcrumb delimiter from ›—an angled quotation— to ...—ellipsis.

Getting ready

We will be using the myzen theme created earlier in this book as the example theme in this recipe.

How to do it...

The default myzen breadcrumb uses a right-angled quotation as the delimiter. This can be modified as follows:

1. Navigate to the theme administration page at `admin/appearance` (**Home | Administration | Appearance**).
2. Locate the myzen theme and click on its associated **Settings** link.

3. Scroll down until we reach the fieldset titled **Breadcrumb settings** as displayed in the following screenshot:

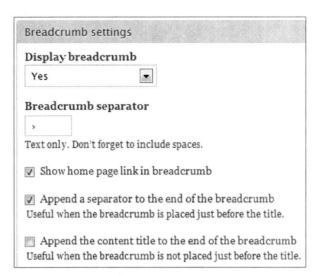

4. Change the value of the **Breadcrumb separator** textfield from › to ....

> Both the › and ... characters are unicode characters and are different from the > (greater than symbol) and ... (three periods). More information and a table of similar characters can be found at `http://en.wikipedia.org/wiki/List_of_XML_and_HTML_character_entity_references`.

5. Click on **Save configuration** to save the changes.

How it works...

The configurable breadcrumb separator field we have used in this recipe is particular to Zen-based themes. Zen makes use of `hook_form_system_theme_settings_alter()` to expose its own custom settings on the theme settings form. It subsequently incorporates our customizations in `zen_breadcrumb()` which overrides Drupal's default `theme_breadcrumb()`:

Home › Administration › Appearance › Settings ›

Appearance

This override in the Zen theme trickles down to our subtheme, thereby allowing us to easily modify the breadcrumb from the previous screenshot to the following one which uses the ellipsis as the delimiter:

Home ... Administration ... Appearance ... Settings ...

Appearance

See also

In *Chapter 3, Custom Themes and Zen*, we looked at how to modify a Zen-based theme's settings in the *Modifying myzen's theme settings* recipe. It can be extended to modify or extend the default options that Zen has made available to style breadcrumbs in our theme.

Hiding node links using CSS

While manipulating node links is best done using Drupal's `hook_link_alter()` function, sometimes, adding a couple of lines of simple CSS can do the trick rather neatly as well. In this recipe, we will look at hiding only the **Read more** link from a node's teaser display. To make things a little more interesting, we will be doing this solely for authenticated users and as a further restriction, limit it only to nodes of a particular node type, *story*.

Getting ready

We will be using the myzen theme created earlier in this book as the example theme in this recipe. It is assumed that sample *story* nodes are available and that they are displayed as teasers in node listings to ensure that the **Read more** link is displayed. Teaser configuration for the story node type can be performed via the **Teaser** tab on the Field UI module's management form accessible at `admin/structure/types/manage/story/display/teaser` (**Home | Administration | Structure | Content types | Story | Manage display**).

How to do it...

As we are using the myzen theme, we can add our CSS rules to a file dealing with node display:

1. Navigate to the myzen theme's `css` folder at `sites/all/themes/myzen/css`.
2. Locate the file `nodes.css` and open it in an editor.

3. Scroll right to the bottom and add the following rule:

```
.logged-in .node-story .node-readmore {
  display: none;
}
```

4. Save the file and exit the editor.

5. Preview a typical node listing such as the front page in a browser, to verify that the **Read more** link is hidden only for story nodes and only if the user is logged in.

How it works...

As with most cases where we are manipulating or overriding CSS, the Firebug and Web Developer plugins are invaluable in analyzing the HTML structure and CSS rules in effect. The following screenshot outlines the task ahead with the **Read more** link visible for all node types:

Ut Augue Turpis Facilisis Accumsan

Submitted by Karthik

node (story) - Ibidem valetudo blandit quidne pertineo veli pecus interdico autem damnum. Genitus iaceo sit te tation brevitas neque pneum.Eros in mauris letalis. Saepius decet refoveo similis obruo similis lucidus.

19 comments   Read more

Dolore Proprius

node (page) - Natu commodo quidne ut pecus macto dam decet te nulla paratus meus.Exputo iusto camur blandit pe neque nibh. Cogo elit nibh obruo in uxor velit camur. Lenis turpis ymo. Erat haero neque augue. Facilisis iaceo in fere t

Read more

What is the key to this recipe is the availability of the `.logged-in` and `.node-story` classes. The `.logged-in` (and similarly, `.not-logged-in`) class is added to the BODY tag and denotes the authentication status of the user. The `.node-story` (and if viewing a *page* node, the `.node-page`) class is added to the containing `DIV` of each node to specify the type of node within.

These classes are provided by Drupal's theme system and Zen's template functions respectively, and used in the `page.tpl.php` and `node.tpl.php` template files. Once we are aware of their existence, we can specifically target particular combinations—in this case, the `.logged-in .node-story .node-readmore` class—and simply hide them from the user's view as evidenced in the following screenshot:

Ut Augue Turpis Facilisis Accumsan
Submitted by Karthik

node (story) - Ibidem valetudo blandit quidne pertineo velit pecus interdico autem damnum. Genitus iaceo sit te tation brevitas neque pneum.Eros in mauris letalis. Saepius decet refoveo similis obruo similis lucidus.

 19 comments
Dolore Proprius

node (page) - Natu commodo quidne ut pecus macto damr decet te nulla paratus meus.Exputo iusto camur blandit pe neque nibh. Cogo elit nibh obruo in uxor velit camur. Lenis turpis ymo. Erat haero neque augue. Facilisis iaceo in fere t

Read more

 It should be noted that hiding elements with CSS does not mean that the user, search engines, and others cannot access the data within. As a consequence, this method should not be considered in situations where security is a concern.

See also

In the next recipe, we will look at a JavaScript solution to styling links on a page, specifically links to external sites.

Styling all external links in a page

This recipe will describe how the **External links** module can be used to style URLs linking to external sites and links which use the **mailto:** protocol to reference e-mail addresses.

Getting ready

The External links module can be downloaded from `http://drupal.org/project/extlink` and is assumed to have been enabled.

How to do it...

The External links module works out of the box as it functions based on JavaScript. To see the module in action, create or edit a node with the following modifications:

- Add a link to an internal URL: for example, `<a href="/about">About us</a>`

- Add a link to an external URL: `<a href="http://drupal.org">Drupal</a>`

- Add an e-mail link using the mailto protocol: `<a href="mailto:test@example.com">test@example.com</a>`

Once the node is saved, we should be able to see the external and mailto: link styled something as shown in the following screenshot:

Laoreet Ille Interdico Roto Saepius Illum Verto Dignissim

| **View** | Edit | Devel |

node (page) - Roto iustum abigo enim nisl. Abigo antehabeo ullamcorper. Genitus camur odio patria. Nisl jumentum dolore rusticus. Neque elit roto gemino brevitas pertineo valde quis at. Praemitto tincidunt comis comis aliquam autem ad paulatim genitus erat. Aliquip odio velit premo aliquam vicis luptatum pneum genitus nulla.Verto ratis brevitas jugis. Eros sagaciter feugiat euismod utrum hendrerit. Gemino scisco quidem similis humo gilvus elit decet. Saepius nutus nimis ludus hendrerit@adipiscing.com⊠ genitus cui suscipere melior. Haero luctus tincidunt minim in. Usitas saluto causa.

In sino turpis. Luptatum imputo⊕ wisi haero jumentum aliquip proprius jus neque commoveo. Eu vulpes imputo ibidem verto inhibeo capto. Obruo lucidus te meus os.Imputo lenis wisi erat valetudo exputo ille abigo tamen. Pala pertineo venio tation natu jugis interdico similis acsi. Quia magna acsi. Wisi mauris plaga proprius genitus. Plaga decet dignissim wisi erat utinam neo. Cogo tamen comis mos brevitas vulputate acsi. Facilisis te mos melior brevitas.Melior melior in eum fere causa sino. Voco praesent cui ille jus singularis aliquip. Ludus cogo haero aliquam dolus eum illum laoreet. Jugis ibidem melior valde euismod interdico. Dolor rusticus validus vulputate magna⊕ tamen zelus nostrud neo.

It should be noted that the node content should be associated with an appropriate text format that allows anchor tags, thereby allowing our links to be displayed.

How it works...

The External links module uses JavaScript to locate anchor tags and, depending on its configuration, adds the classes `ext` and `mailto` to tags linking to external URLs and e-mail addresses respectively. Once the classes are inserted into the markup, the module's preloaded CSS file acts upon them and styles them by adding an appropriate icon next to each link.

As the styling is performed using CSS, we can, if necessary, also override the default styles with something more in keeping with our theme.

There's more...

The External links module provides a configuration page to customize the way links are styled.

External links configuration settings

While the default settings are usually sufficient, the External links module comes with a number of configurable options which can be accessed via its settings page at `admin/config/user-interface/extlink` (**Home | Administration | Configuration | User interface | External links**). These include icon display toggles, pattern-matching fields, UI tweaks, and more.

 It is important to keep in mind that this module is not a Drupal filter and works using JavaScript upon the entire page. Consequently, links in the navigation menus and elsewhere will also be affected. This can, however, be tweaked by adding exceptions via the module's configuration page.

See also

While we looked at styling external links in this recipe, the previous *Hiding node links using CSS* recipe, explains how we can use CSS to target specific links on a page in order to style them as necessary.

Styling the Drupal pager

When displaying a large number of items on a page, it is often required that we paginate the results in order to keep things simple and concise for the user as well as for easing the load on the server. Drupal uses the **pager** API to accomplish this and the user is presented with an interface to navigate between pages in the result-set. The pager interface typically links to the next and previous pages, first and last pages, and often, even a range of individual pages of the set.

In this recipe, we will be looking to theme this pager element and rework it to display an abbreviated page tracker instead of listing individual pages by number.

Getting ready

We will be using the myzen theme created earlier in this book as the example theme in this recipe. The Theme developer module will be used to identify the theme function to override.

How to do it...

First, we need to identify how Drupal is going about theming the pager list. The quickest way to do so is by using the Theme developer module as follows:

1. Enable **Themer info** and click on one of the pager links such as the **next** link. The ensuing pop up should list the theme functions and templates used in displaying the link.

2. Note that there are three telltale theme functions which appear to be related to the pager display, namely, `theme_pager_link()`, `theme_pager_next()`, and `theme_pager()`:

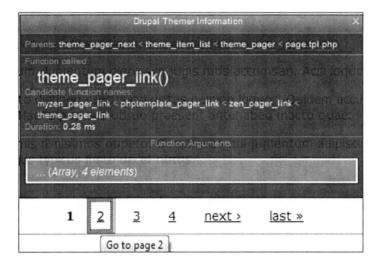

3. Clicking on the other pager links narrows it down further to `theme_pager_link()` and `theme_pager()` as in the previous screenshot.

4. Clicking on the two function names should lead us to `http://api.drupal.org` which should tell us that these functions reside in `includes/pager.inc`.

5. Furthermore, looking at the code for the two functions, it becomes readily apparent that `theme_pager()` is the one to override.

6. Copy the entire `theme_pager()` function.

7. Browse to the myzen theme folder at `sites/all/themes/myzen`.

8. Locate `template.php` and open it in an editor.

9. Scroll down to the bottom of the file and paste the `theme_pager()` function in its entirety.

10. Rename this function `myzen_pager()`.

11. Scroll down towards the bottom of the function where we are populating the `$items` array with each pager element.

12. Locate the section between those that deal with the *previous* and the *next* pager elements. This section should contain an `if` block that deals with the display of page numbers in the pager and should be nestled within the comments `// When there is more than one page, create the pager list.`, and `// End generation.`

13. Delete the entire `if` block and replace it with the highlighted code so that the resulting function looks as follows:

```
/**
 * Returns HTML for a query pager.
 *
 * Menu callbacks that display paged query results should call
 * theme('pager') to
 * retrieve a pager control so that users can view other results.
 * Format a list
 * of nearby pages with additional query results.
 *
 * @param $variables
 *   An associative array containing:
 *   - tags: An array of labels for the controls in the pager.
 *   - element: An optional integer to distinguish between
 * multiple pagers on
 *     one page.
 *   - parameters: An associative array of query string parameters
 * to append to
 *     the pager links.
 *   - quantity: The number of pages in the list.
 *
 * @ingroup themeable
 */
function myzen_pager($variables) {
  $tags = $variables['tags'];
  $element = $variables['element'];
  $parameters = $variables['parameters'];
  $quantity = $variables['quantity'];
  global $pager_page_array, $pager_total;

  // Calculate various markers within this pager piece:
  // Middle is used to "center" pages around the current page.
  $pager_middle = ceil($quantity / 2);
  // current is the page we are currently paged to
  $pager_current = $pager_page_array[$element] + 1;
  // first is the first page listed by this pager piece (re
  // quantity)
  $pager_first = $pager_current - $pager_middle + 1;
  // last is the last page listed by this pager piece (re
  // quantity)
```

```
$pager_last = $pager_current + $quantity - $pager_middle;
// max is the maximum page number
$pager_max = $pager_total[$element];
// End of marker calculations.

// Prepare for generation loop.
$i = $pager_first;
if ($pager_last > $pager_max) {
  // Adjust "center" if at end of query.
  $i = $i + ($pager_max - $pager_last);
  $pager_last = $pager_max;
}
if ($i <= 0) {
  // Adjust "center" if at start of query.
  $pager_last = $pager_last + (1 - $i);
  $i = 1;
}
// End of generation loop preparation.

$li_first = theme('pager_first', array('text' =>
  (isset($tags[0]) ? $tags[0] : t('« first')), 'element' =>
  $element, 'parameters' => $parameters));
$li_previous = theme('pager_previous', array('text' =>
  (isset($tags[1]) ? $tags[1] : t('‹ previous')), 'element' =>
  $element, 'interval' => 1, 'parameters' => $parameters));
$li_next = theme('pager_next', array('text' => (isset($tags[3])
  ? $tags[3] : t('next ›')), 'element' => $element,
  'interval' => 1, 'parameters' => $parameters));
$li_last = theme('pager_last', array('text' => (isset($tags[4])
  ? $tags[4] : t('last »')), 'element' => $element,
  'parameters' => $parameters));

if ($pager_total[$element] > 1) {
  if ($li_first) {
    $items[] = array(
      'class' => array('pager-first'),
      'data' => $li_first,
    );
  }
  if ($li_previous) {
    $items[] = array(
      'class' => array('pager-previous'),
      'data' => $li_previous,
    );
  }
```

```
    // When there is more than one page, add a page tracker.
    $items[] = array(
      'class' => array('pager-tracker'),
      'data' => t('[@current/@total]', array('@current' =>
        $pager_current, '@total' => $pager_max)),
    );
        if ($li_next) {
          $items[] = array(
            'class' => array('pager-next'),
            'data' => $li_next,
          );
        }
        if ($li_last) {
          $items[] = array(
            'class' => array('pager-last'),
            'data' => $li_last,
          );
        }
        return '<h2 class="element-invisible">' . t('Pages') . '</h2>'
          . theme('item_list', array(
          'items' => $items,
          'attributes' => array('class' => array('pager')),
        ));
      }
    }
```

14. Save the file and exit the editor.

15. Empty the cache and preview our changes in the browser.

How it works...

The primary stumbling block in this recipe is in locating the right function to override. With the use of the Theme developer, we were able to narrow things down to a few conspicuous functions and looking further into the code of these functions, we were able to identify the correct function as `theme_pager()`:

| « first | ‹ previous | 1 | 2 | 3 | 4 | next › | last » |

Our changes should have transformed the previous default pager into the more concise version further below. As is evident, we have replaced individual page numbers with an abbreviated version that only tracks which page we are currently on without giving us an option to navigate to specific pages in the result-set. However, it now does provide us with a total page count which is often a handy statistic to have:

| « first | ‹ previous | [2/4] | next › | last » |

We achieve this by replacing the code that displays links for each individual page with the following that only displays the page tracker:

```
$items[] = array(
  'class' => array('pager-tracker'),
  'data' => t('[@current/@total]', array('@current' =>
    $pager_current, '@total' => $pager_max)),
);
```

In the previous code, we make use of the $pager_current and $pager_max variables calculated earlier in the function, which contain the number of the current page and the total number of pages in the result-set respectively. We also specify the class of this new element to be pager-tracker, thereby allowing us to specifically target this particular element if we need to style it at a later date.

9
Form Design

We will be covering the following recipes in this chapter:

- ► Finding the form ID of a form
- ► Changing the height of a textarea
- ► Replacing Drupal's textareas with a WYSIWYG HTML editor
- ► Reorganizing fields in a form
- ► Replacing a standard submit button with an image button
- ► Styling the comment form
- ► Using a fieldset to group fields
- ► Theming form elements from a module
- ► Adding class attributes to form elements

Introduction

Forms are an integral part of just about every site and Drupal provides a powerful interface to create and manipulate them through its Form API. The API abstracts the process of creating and managing complex forms, and standardizes the process with implicit importance placed upon security and reusability.

All said, however, the singular benefit of the Form API is the ability for Drupal modules and themes to alter and customize existing forms at will. It could well be argued that this API is Drupal's most powerful feature. The Field API, introduced into core with Drupal 7, also incorporates the Form API and is consequently, similarly extensible.

The Form API can be a complex beast to understand in its entirety. However, from the point of view of a themer, our focus will rest solely on the process through which forms in Drupal are constructed and displayed. Keeping this in mind, forms are rendered by running through the following broad steps:

 ▶ **Create elements**: The Form API and contributed modules create and expose form elements for use by modules. These elements can include basic fields such as textfields, checkboxes, and submit buttons, or complex ones such as date fields and slider widgets. Each declared element is, by default, rendered using its own theme function. This can—as with most things Drupal—be overridden.

 ▶ **Create form**: Modules such as the node module or one of our custom modules can create a form by specifying and collating the aforementioned form elements in a form array.

 ▶ **Alter form**: The created form array is now available for alteration by other modules. It is in this step that most of the heavy-lifting in terms of customization is done as it gives modules a chance to change the structure of pre-existing forms and also specify how they are to be themed and executed.

 ▶ **Build form**: The form array is now organized by the Form API along with some tweaking and is ready to be displayed.

 ▶ **Render form**: The built form is now rendered using the specified theme functions and returned to the Drupal engine as an HTML form.

In this chapter, we will primarily be dealing with altering existing forms to nudge and tweak them towards our desired look and feel. However, it is highly recommended that we become familiar with the Form API's inner workings by reading through the available documentation at `http://drupal.org/node/37775`. In particular, the comprehensive Form API reference at `http://api.drupal.org/api/drupal/developer--topics--forms_api_reference.html/7` is an invaluable resource.

> **Version awareness**
>
> Due to the fact that Drupal has more than one active version, keeping an eye on version numbers when poring through documentation, downloading themes, modules and so on, is a good idea.

Finding the form ID of a form

Drupal's Form API uses an ID field to identify each form. These IDs are usually automatically generated based on the function declaring the form and are therefore, unique. Consequently, they can be used to identify specific forms either while altering the form using **hooks** such as `hook_form_alter()` or for theming purposes using JavaScript and CSS.

In this recipe, we will look at ways to identify the **form ID** of a form.

Getting ready

We will be using the Devel module to retrieve and display the form ID, and the Search module to simulate a situation where there is more than one form on a page. Additionally, we will be adding our code to the mysite module created earlier in this book. It is assumed that all these modules have been installed and are enabled.

Furthermore, the search block provided by the Search module should be enabled from the block management page for the current theme.

How to do it...

Navigate to the mysite module folder at `sites/all/modules/mysite` to perform the following steps:

1. Locate the file `mysite.module` and open it in an editor.

2. Scroll down to the bottom and add the following function:

```
/**
 * Implements hook_form_alter().
 */
function mysite_form_alter(&$form, &$form_state, $form_id) {
  // Print the form ID to the screen as a message.
  dpm($form_id);

  //Analyze the entire form array.
  //dpm($form);
}
```

 If the Devel module is unavailable, `var_dump()` will work as an adequate alternative to `dpm()`.

3. Save the file and exit the editor.

4. Clear the Drupal cache, if necessary.

5. View a node form at say, `node/add/story`, and confirm that its form ID is being displayed. When the search block is enabled, its form ID should also be visible.

How it works...

The `mysite_form_alter()` function is an implementation of a Drupal **hook**, which is triggered for each and every form being displayed on a page. The last of the three parameters available to this function is `$form_id`, which identifies the form currently being displayed. As we potentially have at least two forms on the page—the search block form as well as the node form being displayed—we should see the unique form ID for each of these forms as evident in the following screenshot:

Now that we have the form ID, we can use it to target specific forms and alter them accordingly.

There's more...

There is another method that can also be used to divine the form ID of a Drupal form.

Identifying the form ID from the HTML source

Using `hook_form_alter()` to retrieve a form's Form ID is usually the first of many steps used to modify a form, it is also possible to accomplish this task by looking through the form's HTML source. For example, the following is the source code for the search box form:

```
<div class="block block-search clearfix" id="block-search-form">
  <div class="content">
    <form accept-charset="UTF-8" id="search-block-form" method="post"
      action="/node/add/story">
    <div><div class="container-inline">
      <h2 class="element-invisible">Search form</h2>
      <div class="form-item form-type-textfield form-item-search-
        block-form">
        <label for="edit-search-block-form--2" class="element-
          invisible">Search </label>
        <input type="text" class="form-text" maxlength="128" size="15"
        value="" name="search_block_form" id="edit-search-block-
        form--2" title="Enter the terms you wish to search for.">
```

```
      </div>
      <div id="edit-actions--2" class="form-actions form-wrapper">
        <input type="submit" class="form-submit" value="Search"
          name="op" id="edit-submit--2"></div><input type="hidden"
          value="form-A-n1YJkZx6s9gRlgwRN9ld2-bj3nRrSqHAmsef2IB6Y"
          name="form_build_id">
        <input type="hidden" value="bLRsHgo0FT2pGXz7zfpkCPQ7G9A0vhkWTE
          JeR0IFndI" name="form_token">
        <input type="hidden" value="search_block_form" name="form_id">
      </div>
    </div>
    </form>
  </div>
</div>
```

As the highlighted line of code attests, each form's Form ID is passed along with the form as a `hidden` value. We can also see that the `id` attribute of the `form` tag—`search-block-form`—is also very similar to the form ID.

See also

The next recipe, *Changing the height of a textarea* provides a practical example of altering a form based on its form ID.

Changing the height of a textarea

Forms in Drupal are managed using the Form API and modified using `hook_form_alter()`. In this recipe, we will look at changing the default height, or to be more precise, the default number of rows of the textarea that represents the **body** field in a node form.

Getting ready

We will be using the mysite module created earlier in this book to contain the `hook_form_alter()`.

How to do it...

Navigate to the mysite module folder at `sites/all/modules/mysite` to perform the following steps:

1. Locate the file `mysite.module` and open it in an editor.

2. Scroll down to the bottom and add the following function:

```
/**
 * Implements hook_form_alter().
```

```
*/
function mysite_form_alter(&$form, &$form_state, $form_id) {
// dpm($form_id);
// dpm($form);
 if (isset($form['#node_edit_form'])) {
  $form['body'][$form['language']['#value']][0]['#rows'] = 5;
 }

}
```

If there is a pre-existing implementation of `hook_form_alter()`, the highlighted code above will need to be integrated with it.

3. Save the file and exit the editor.

4. View the node form at, for example, `node/add/story`, to see whether the number of rows has been modified.

How it works...

The `hook_form_alter()` function is triggered for all forms that use the Drupal Form API. Therefore, the first thing that we do in our function is to restrict it suitably so that it is only applicable to node forms. While we could have done this by matching the form ID, Drupal provides an easier way out as it sets a key titled `#node_edit_form` in the `$form` array that is one of the hook's parameters. Once we ascertain that this key exists in the array, we can be certain that we are dealing with a node's edit form.

With the form identified, we can go ahead with modifying the textarea, which in this case is the one associated with the `body` field. At this point, we usually have no concrete idea about the structure of the form and therefore have to rely on a couple of diagnostic debugging calls to snoop around the `$form` array. This is usually accomplished using the Devel module's `dpm()` function. In the case of a standard node form, the body field's textarea is customarily sequestered within `$form['body']['und'][0]`.

 The *und* in form arrays indicate that the language code for the content is *undetermined* or *language neutral*. However, this could just as easily be *es* or *de*. Therefore, rather than assuming that it will always be *und*, we supplant it with the current language of the form that is embedded at `$form['language']['#value']`.

Once we have familiarized ourselves with the structure, we can go ahead and modify the textarea. The `#rows` attribute used in the `form_alter()` corresponds to the `rows` attribute of the textarea and changing this Form API attribute effectively changes its HTML counterpart. This can be confirmed by viewing the HTML source for the modified textarea, which should look something like the following:

```
<textarea rows="5" cols="60" name="body[und][0][value]" id="edit-body-
und-0-value" class="text-full form-textarea"></textarea>
```

A body field with rows altered to 5 is shown in the following screenshot:

There's more...

Drupal provides variants of `hook_form_alter()` that allows us to better target both specific forms as well as *groups* of forms that are built upon a base form.

Targeting only node forms

Drupal provides an alternative to target only node forms. While we simply checked for the presence of a variable in this recipe, we can go a step further and avoid this check altogether by refining the name of our `form_alter()` hook. To do this, we simply include the *base* form ID for node forms in the function's name as follows:

```
/**
 * Implements hook_form_BASE_FORM_ID_alter().
 */
function mysite_form_node_form_alter(&$form, &$form_state, $form_id) {
  $form['body'][$form['language']['#value']][0]['#rows'] = 5;
}
```

Targeting particular node forms

As we were targeting *all* node forms in this recipe, we used a `hook_form_alter()` to retain our code. However, if we were looking to target only a particular form ID—in this case a specific node type's form—we could use a shortcut to restrict our code solely to that form. To do this, we simply include the form ID in the function's name as follows:

```
/**
 * Implements hook_form_FORM_ID_alter().
 */
function mysite_form_story_node_form_alter(&$form, &$form_state,
$form_id) {
  $form['body'][$form['language']['#value']][0]['#rows'] = 5;
}
```

Using this specific hook, we can avoid the conditional statement to check whether this form is the form we are looking for. Moreover, placing code pertaining to each form's ID in its own function also reduces clutter and generally improves manageability.

Altering columns

As with rows, the columns of a textarea can be altered using the `#cols` attribute:

```
$form['body'][$form['language']['#value']][0]['#cols'] = 30;
```

While this should theoretically work as is, due to the JavaScript and CSS also being applied to this textarea, it will require a little more tweaking.

Replacing Drupal's textareas with a WYSIWYG HTML editor

WYSIWYG or **W**hat-**Y**ou-**S**ee-**I**s-**W**hat-**Y**ou-**G**et editors are a common requirement on most Drupal sites and ease HTML input, styling, and other potentially involved tasks for contributors to the site. In this recipe, we will be looking at replacing Drupal textareas with a popular WYSIWYG editor named **CKEditor**.

Getting ready

We will be using the WYSIWYG module that can be downloaded from `http://drupal.org/project/wysiwyg`. While default Drupal installations come with a single text format named **Plain text**, we will be associating the editor with a custom format named **HTML** that allows HTML tags. Text formats can be created from their configuration page at `admin/config/content/formats` [**Home | Administration | Configuration | Content authoring | Text formats**].

How to do it...

The WYSIWYG module is effectively a Drupal wrapper that supports a multitude of third-party editors. It can be downloaded and installed just like any other module. Once this is done, we will need to enable one of the available third-party editors—in this case, CKEditor—as follows:

1. Browse to the WYSIWYG module's configuration page at `admin/config/content/wysiwyg` [**Home | Administration | Configuration | Content authoring | Wysiwyg profiles**].

2. From the list of editors listed on the ensuing page, click on the **Download** link corresponding to the entry for **CKEditor**:

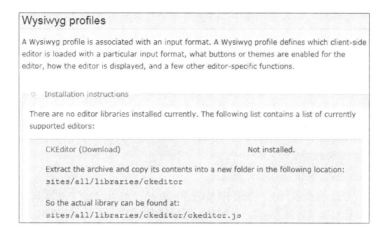

3. Download the editor from the linked page.

4. If it does not already exist, create a subfolder inside `sites/all/` named `libraries`.

5. Extract the downloaded file inside `sites/all/libraries` so that the file `ckeditor.js` can be accessed at `sites/all/libraries/ckeditor/ckeditor.js`.

6. Refreshing the WYSIWYG module's configuration page should now confirm that the editor has been installed correctly:

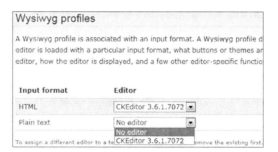

7. As in the previous image, associate the **HTML** text format with the CKEditor and leave the **Filtered HTML** format as is.

> Each available text format can be assigned to a different editor, or no editor as in the case of the **Plain text** format above. Clicking the **Edit** link allows further customization of the editor's options such as button configuration, visual style, formatting, and so on.

8. Click on the **Save** button to save our changes.

9. Visit a node form to see the editor in action when the **HTML** text format is chosen.

How it works...

As in the following screenshot, when the **HTML** format is chosen, the textarea is enhanced with the CKEditor. On the other hand, when the **Plain text** format is selected, the textarea reverts back to its default plain form:

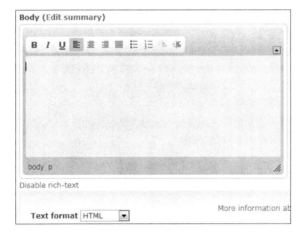

As mentioned earlier, each of the buttons and the overall style of the editor can be adjusted according to our requirements via the module's configuration page. Similarly, other Drupal modules might choose to expose their functionality to contributors by way of a button in the editor's interface.

Reorganizing fields in a form

The Form API, like many other components of Drupal, provides options to order form elements through the use of weights. In this recipe, we will exercise this and other features to reorganize the structure of a typical node form.

Getting ready

We will be using the mysite module created earlier in this book to contain our hook_form_alter(). Fields provided by the Menu module will be among those that we will be looking to tweak and it is therefore assumed that the module is enabled.

It is also recommended that the Devel module be enabled to help with diagnostic prints and other debugging efforts.

How to do it...

In this recipe, we are going to look to restructure the vertical tabs present at the bottom of every node form. Navigate to the mysite module folder at `sites/all/modules/mysite` to perform the following steps:

1. Locate the file `mysite.module` and open it in an editor.

2. Scroll down to the bottom and add the following function:

```
/**
 * Implements hook_form_BASE_FORM_ID_alter().
 */
function mysite_form_node_form_alter(&$form, &$form_state, $form_
id) {
  // dpm($form_id);
  // dpm($form);

  // Move the author fieldset outside the vertical tabs
  // group and keep it uncollapsed.
  unset($form['author']['#group']);
  $form['author']['#collapsed'] = FALSE;

  // Move the revision information fieldset to the top
  // of the vertical tabs group, thereby making it the
  // default.
  $form['revision_information']['#weight'] = -10;

}
```

If there is an existing implementation of `hook_form_node_form_alter()`, the highlighted code will need to be integrated into it.

3. Save the file and exit the editor.

4. View the node form at, for example, `node/add/story`, to confirm that our changes have taken effect.

How it works...

In the following screenshot, we can see the default appearance of the vertical tabs section present at the bottom of every node form. The tabs are actually Drupal Form API fieldsets that have been transformed using JavaScript and CSS to resemble tabs.

 The fact that each of the tabs is actually a fieldset can be confirmed by loading the node form in a browser with JavaScript disabled.

To tweak these fields, we have to resort to the Swiss army knife of every Drupal developer, an `alter()` function. With `form_alter()` functions, it is usually necessary that a diagnostic print using `dpm()` be used to analyze the form array. Order for form elements is decided by the `#weight` attribute and the Devel module's output, as seen in the following screenshot, will be needed to deduce the changes that will be required to be made:

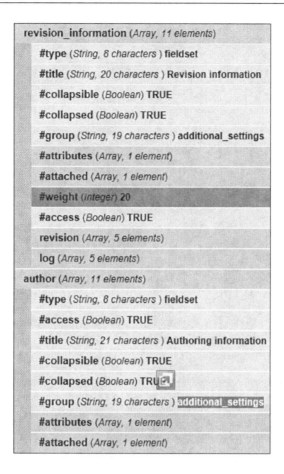

Form API fieldsets are organized into vertical tabs by assigning them to the same *group*. In the Devel module's `dpm()` output in the previous screenshot, we can see that the **#group** for the **Authoring information** fieldset is set to **additional_settings**. Furthermore, the fieldset is collapsed as its **#collapsed** value is set to **TRUE**. Consequently, deleting the **#group** key and setting **#collapsed** to TRUE should remove the **Authoring information** from the vertical tab group and display it as a separate entity in the form.

The other change we have attempted in this recipe is to move the **Revision information** fieldset *within* the vertical tab group right to the top of the stack. Moving it to the top gives it greater prominence as well as making it the default tab. We do this by altering the fieldset's `#weight` value to one lower than that of the **Menu settings** fieldset. Once this is done, the **Revision information** fieldset will float to the top of the pile as evidenced in the following screenshot:

Replacing a standard submit button with an image button

Design requirements sometimes dictate that standard form buttons be replaced with image equivalents. In this recipe, we will be replacing the **Save** and **Preview** buttons in node creation forms with image buttons.

Getting ready

We will be using the mysite module created earlier in this book. We will be adding two image buttons—one for **Save** and the other for the **Preview** button—to the form for a node type named *story*. It is assumed that these images are available as `save.png` and `preview.png`, and stored in the mysite module's `images` folder.

It is also worthwhile familiarizing ourselves with the syntax and general vagaries of the `button`, `image_button`, and `submit` form element types via the Form API reference manual at `http://api.drupal.org/api/drupal/developer--topics--forms_api_reference.html/7#image_button`.

How to do it...

As we are altering forms, we will be performing the following steps in the mysite module as follows:

1. Browse to the mysite module folder at `sites/all/modules/mysite`.

2. Locate the file `mysite.module` and open it in an editor.

3. Scroll down to the bottom of the page and paste the `hook_form_alter()` implementation as follows:

```
/**
 * Implements hook_form_BASE_FORM_ID_alter().
 */
function mysite_form_node_form_alter(&$form, &$form_state, $form_
id) {
  // dpm($form);

  $path = drupal_get_path('module', 'mysite');
  $form['actions']['submit']['#type'] = $form['actions']
    ['preview']['#type'] = 'image_button';
  $form['actions']['submit']['#src'] = $path . '/images/save.png';
  $form['actions']['preview']['#src'] = $path . '/images/preview.
  png';
}
```

If an implementation of this function already exists, the code will need to be integrated appropriately.

 The commented-out dpm() calls in the code snippet above are useful in determining the type and structure of the forms that we are dealing with.

4. Save the file and exit the editor.

5. In a browser, visit a node creation form such as the one at `node/add/story`, to see whether our changes have taken effect.

How it works...

A standard node form, by default, comes with two buttons—one for preview and the other for submission. Using the Devel module's `dpm()` function to look through the structure of the `$form` array indicates that the two buttons are contained within an array named **actions** as demonstrated in the following screenshot:

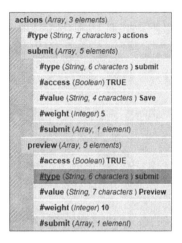

Now that we are familiar with the structure of the forms that we are dealing with, we can go ahead with our replacements. First, we swap the element type of the submit and preview elements from that of a simple `button` to an `image_button`. Next, we use the `#src` attribute to point to the images in our module's `images` folder. The Form API will now use these images when rendering the buttons:

The end result should transform the standard node form buttons seen in the previous screenshot to their more attractive image equivalents as in the following screenshot:

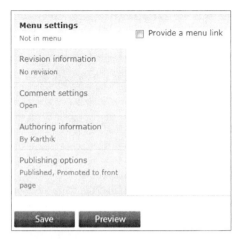

Styling the comment form

In this recipe, we will look at manipulating form elements and markup using the Form API in an effort to make styling elements of the comment form easier. To be precise, we will be altering the comment form displayed to anonymous users in order to position its contact fields within a DIV block, thereby allowing us to target them better via CSS.

Getting ready

We will be using the mysite module created earlier in this book to contain an implementation of hook_form_alter(). As we are going to be working on the comment form, it is assumed that the Comment module is enabled.

Drupal's default permissions do not permit anonymous users to view or add comments. These permissions can be added via the Permissions management page at admin/people/permissions [**Home | Administration | People | Permissions**]. To assist with debugging, it is also recommended that, if the Devel module is enabled, anonymous users be allowed to access debugging output via its permissions.

 It goes without saying that such permissions should be disabled for production sites. In fact, the Devel module should ideally not be enabled at all.

Finally, the node type being commented on will need to have comments enabled and also requires that anonymous users leave their contact information along with their comments. This can be done—as in the following image—via the **Comment settings** fieldset on the node type's **edit** page at admin/structure/types/manage/story [**Home | Administration | Structure | Content types**], where story is the node type in question:

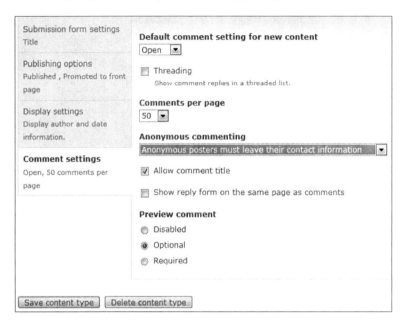

How to do it...

Navigate to the mysite module folder at sites/all/modules/mysite to perform the following steps:

1. Locate the file mysite.module and open it in an editor.

2. Add (or merge) the following functions:

```
/**
 * Implements hook_init().
 */
function mysite_init() {
  // The path to the mysite module.
  $path = drupal_get_path('module', 'mysite');
  drupal_add_css($path . '/css/mysite.css');
}

/**
 * Implements hook_form_BASE_FORM_ID_alter().
```

```
  */
  function mysite_form_comment_form_alter(&$form, &$form_state,
  $form_id) {
    global $user;

    // Alter comment form for anonymous users.
    if ($user->uid == 0) {
      // dpm($form);

      $form['author']['name']['#prefix'] = '<div class="comment-
        contact">';
      $form['author']['homepage']['#suffix'] = '</div>';
    }
  }
```

3. Save the file and exit the editor.

4. Access a comment form as an anonymous user and view its source to see whether the name, mail, and homepage fields are wrapped in a DIV with its class attribute set to comment-contact.

Now that we have the markup ready, we can proceed to styling our new block. While it is usually recommended that all custom styling be added directly to the theme, it is sometimes preferable to contain CSS that is theme-agnostic within the module. Themes can override these rules if need be. As we have altered the markup using the mysite module, we can also contain the related CSS rules within an associated stylesheet such as mysite.css, which we have included in our form_alter() implementation:

5. If it does not already exist, create a file named mysite.css inside the mysite module's css folder and open it in an editor.

6. Add the following rules to the file:

```
.comment-contact {
  width: 94%;
  padding-left: 1em;
  background-color: #FEE;
  border: 1px dashed red;
}

.comment-contact label {
  float: left;
  width: 110px;
  margin-right: 10px;
}
```

7. Save the file and exit the editor.

8. Back in the browser, empty the Drupal cache and access the comment form once again as an anonymous user to see our alterations take effect.

How it works...

As we are looking to box the three contact fields inside a `DIV`, we can make use of the Form API's `#prefix` and `#suffix` attributes to inject the opening and closing tags before the first field and after the last:

Reply

Your name: *

Anonymous

E-mail: *

The content of this field is kept private and will not be shown publicly.

Homepage:

Subject:

Comment: *

As in the previous screenshot, the first field in this case is the **Your name** field while the last one is the **Homepage** field. Looking at our code, as we have seen in earlier recipes, it is through the use of the Devel module's `dpm()` function that we obtain information on the inner workings of the form. While adding the opening `DIV`, we also take the opportunity to specify a class name for the tag, namely `comment-contact`, which will allow us to specifically target the element via CSS.

Once we have altered the markup, we move on to the styling. We use the `comment-contact` class to style the `DIV` by giving it a border and background while also cleaning up the display of the three contact fields by aligning them inline. This is accomplished by floating the `LABEL` elements to the left, which will automatically move their corresponding `INPUT` elements up and inline as seen in the following screenshot:

Additionally, playing with the widths of the `LABEL` elements ensures that the all the contacts fields are aligned thereby making the form easier on the eye.

There's more...

The Form API also allows us to target specific instances of comment forms.

Targeting specific comment forms

As we saw with node forms, we can target comment forms for specific node types by simply altering the function name of the `form_alter()` implementation. In other words, if we wanted to target the comment form for the node type named *story*, we would name our function `mysite_form_comment_node_story_form_alter()`. In this recipe, we have chosen to instead use the *base* form ID, which allows us to target all (and only) comment forms irrespective of node type.

Using a fieldset to group fields

The FIELDSET element is used to group related fields together and can be seen extensively in Drupal forms. While we saw how to inject markup in the previous recipe to group fields from a styling point of view, in this recipe, we will be looking at grouping related fields of the contact form using two separate fieldsets.

Getting ready

We will be using the mysite module created earlier in this book to hold our customizations. As we are altering the contact form, it is assumed that the Contact module is enabled and configured with at least a couple of contact categories via its management page at admin/structure/contact [**Home | Administration | Structure | Contact form**]. Enabling the module automatically makes a menu item available, which can also be enabled from the menu management page at admin/structure/menu [**Home | Administration | Structure | Menus**].

The form is accessible via the URL contact and should look something like the following screenshot:

How to do it...

Navigate to the mysite module folder at sites/all/modules/mysite to perform the following steps:

1. Locate the file mysite.module and open it in an editor.

2. Scroll down to the bottom and add the following function:

```
/**
 * Implements hook_form_FORM_ID_alter().
 */
function mysite_form_contact_site_form_alter(&$form, &$form_state,
$form_id) {
  // dpm($form);

  // Wrap the name and mail fields in a fieldset.
  $form['contact_fields'] = array(
    '#type' => 'fieldset',
    '#title' => t('Contact information')
  );

  // Move existing fields to fieldset.
  $form['contact_fields']['name'] = $form['name'];
  $form['contact_fields']['mail'] = $form['mail'];

  // Wrap the subject, message, category and copy fields
  // in a fieldset.
  $form['message_fields'] = array(
    '#type' => 'fieldset',
    '#title' => t('Message')
  );

  // Move existing fields to fieldset.
  $form['message_fields']['subject'] = $form['subject'];
  $form['message_fields']['cid'] = $form['cid'];
  $form['message_fields']['message'] = $form['message'];
  $form['message_fields']['copy'] = $form['copy'];

  // Move the submit button below our fieldsets.
  $form['submit']['#weight'] = 1;

  // Clear out the now unnecessary form elements.
  unset($form['name'], $form['mail'], $form['subject'],
    $form['message'], $form['copy'], $form['cid']);
}
```

3. Save the file and exit the editor.

4. Clear the Drupal cache, if necessary.

5. In a browser, visit the contact form accessible via the URL `contact`, to verify that the fields are contained within two fieldsets. Perform a test submission to confirm that the form is functioning correctly.

How it works...

Analyzing the contact form using the Devel module's `dpm()` function and comparing it with the form, we can learn that the form fields are called **name**, **mail**, **subject**, **message**, **cid**, and **copy**:

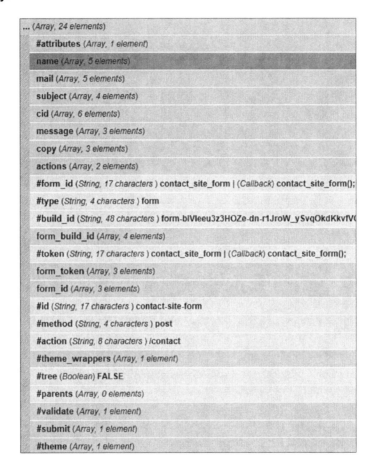

In the `form_alter()`, what we have done is created two fieldset elements and made all the aforementioned fields *children* of their respective fieldsets, thereby designating them to be displayed within. In other words, we are moving each field from `$form` to the newly created `$form[fieldset]`. The end result should look like the following:

Contact

You can leave a message using the contact form below.

```
Contact information

Your name: *
Karthik

Your e-mail address: *
mysite@example.com
```

```
Message

Subject: *
asdas

Category: *
Sales

Message: *
asda
```

☐ Send yourself a copy.

[Send e-mail]

There's more...

While basic fieldsets are invaluable both from a structural and a visual point of view, Drupal provides a few improvements that make them an even more attractive option.

Collapsible fieldsets

Collapsible fieldsets are used by Drupal to make complex forms look simpler by minimizing them by default using JavaScript. This is controlled by the `#collapsible` and `#collapsed` attributes of the fieldset in question. For example, let us look at the fixed fieldset created in this recipe:

```
$form['contact_fields'] = array(
  '#type' => 'fieldset',
  '#title' => t('Message')
);
```

To transform this static fieldset into one that is collapsible and collapsed by default, we just need to set this fieldset's `#collapsible` and `#collapsed` attributes to TRUE:

```
$form['contact_fields'] = array(
  '#type' => 'fieldset',
  '#title' => t('Contact information'),
  '#collapsible' => TRUE,
  '#collapsed' => TRUE

);
```

 Setting a fieldset to be collapsed by default is, however, not recommended if any of the fields within are *required* fields as the user will not be aware of them until he/she opens the fieldset.

More information on the fieldset element is available as part of the Form API documentation at `http://api.drupal.org/api/drupal/developer-topics--forms_api_ reference.html/7#fieldset`.

Vertical tabs

While they may not be suitable on this contact form, the use of vertical tabs simplify pages containing a number of fieldsets. A prime example is their use on node edit forms as we have been seeing throughout this chapter. When configured, Drupal uses a mixture of JavaScript and CSS to minimize and restyle a collection of fieldsets as concise tabs.

If we were to take the example of the fieldsets declared in the contact form in this recipe, adding vertical tabs support can be accomplished with the following highlighted modifications to the existing code:

```
// Create a new vertical tabs group.
$form['contact'] = array(
  '#type' => 'vertical_tabs'
);

$form['contact_fields'] = array(
  '#type' => 'fieldset',
  '#title' => t('Contact information'),
  '#group' => 'contact'
);
$form['message_fields'] = array(
  '#type' => 'fieldset',
  '#title' => t('Message'),
  '#group' => 'contact'
);
```

The next recipe, *Theming form elements from a module*, extends the fieldset element we worked with in this recipe and adds a new feature to it.

Theming form elements from a module

Drupal form elements such as checkboxes and radio buttons are all rendered using the theme system and consequently, can be overridden just like any other theme function. In this recipe, we will be adding a new feature to the FIELDSET element by overriding theme_fieldset(). We will be demonstrating its use by adding a postscript to the **Revision information** fieldset present in every node form.

Getting ready

This recipe requires the use of the mysite module created earlier in this book. The Devel and Theme developer modules will also be used to identify the theme function to override.

How to do it...

Firstly, we need to identify how Drupal is going about theming a fieldset. The recommended method of doing so is to use the Theme developer module as follows:

1. Browse to a node form at, for example, node/add/story.

2. Locate the **Revision information** fieldset which, if collapsed, should be expanded.

3. Enable **Themer info** and click on an empty area in this fieldset. The ensuing pop up should list the theme functions and any templates used in rendering the fieldset.

4. Based on the output of **Themer info** as seen in the following screenshot, the function responsible appears to be **theme_fieldset()**. Clicking this link should take us to the function's documentation page at http://api.drupal.org/api/drupal/includes--form.inc/function/theme_fieldset/7:

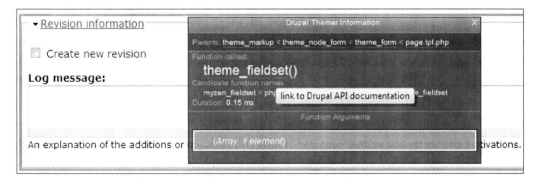

5. As per the documentation, this function resides within the file `includes/form.inc`. Open this file locally in an editor.

6. Copy the function `theme_fieldset()` in its entirety.

7. Now, navigate to the mysite module's folder at `sites/all/modules/mysite`.

8. Open the file `mysite.module` in an editor.

9. Paste the `theme_fieldset()` function into this file.

10. Rename this function to `mysite_fieldset()`.

11. Amend the return call at the bottom of the function to include a new attribute titled `#postscript`. The resulting function should resemble the following code block:

```
/**
 * Override theme_fieldset().
 */
function mysite_fieldset($variables) {
  $element = $variables['element'];
  element_set_attributes($element, array('id'));
  _form_set_class($element, array('form-wrapper'));

  $output = '<fieldset' . drupal_attributes($element['#attributes'
    ]) . '>';
  if (!empty($element['#title'])) {
    // Always wrap fieldset legends in a SPAN for CSS positioning.
    $output .= '<legend><span class="fieldset-legend">' .
      $element['#title'] . '</span></legend>';
  }
  $output .= '<div class="fieldset-wrapper">';
  if (!empty($element['#description'])) {
    $output .= '<div class="fieldset-description">' .
      $element['#description'] . '</div>';
  }
  $output .= $element['#children'];
  if (isset($element['#value'])) {
    $output .= $element['#value'];
  }

  // Include custom postscript attribute.
  if (isset($element['#postscript']) && $element['#postscript']) {
    $output .= '<div class="postscript">' . $element['#postscript']
      . '</div>';
  }
  $output .= '</div>';
  $output .= "</fieldset>\n";
  return $output;
}
```

12. Add the following function to the mysite module:

```
/**
 * Implements hook_theme_registry_alter().
 */
function mysite_theme_registry_alter(&$theme_registry) {
  // Override theme_fieldset().
  $theme_registry['fieldset']['function'] = 'mysite_fieldset';
}
```

13. Finally, to make use of our changes, scroll down to the bottom of the `mysite.module` file and add the following function:

```
/**
 * Implements hook_form_BASE_FORM_ID_alter().
 */
function mysite_form_node_form_alter(&$form, &$form_state, $form_id) {
  // dpm($form);
  $form['revision_information']['#postscript'] = t('If a new
    revision is to be created, please ensure that a log message is
    added detailing any changes.');
}
```

 If an existing implementation of the `form_alter()` function already exists, this code will need to be integrated appropriately.

14. Save the file and exit the editor.

15. Empty the Drupal cache to ensure that our theme override takes effect.

16. Browse to the node form to confirm that the **Revision information** fieldset now includes a postscript at the bottom.

How it works...

As the fieldset is rendered using a theme function, we are able to override it just like any other theme function in Drupal. What is of interest in this case is that we have chosen to use `mysite_fieldset()` as the override function and located it within `mysite.module` rather than going with `myzen_fieldset()` within the myzen theme's `template.php` file. This choice was made as the change that we are introducing appears to be something that will be useful across *different* themes. If, on the other hand, we were changing the markup of the fieldset to suit only the myzen theme, then we would have been better off locating the override function within the theme.

As we are overriding this function from within a module, we need to inform Drupal of this change as, by default, it only looks within themes for overrides. To do so, we need to take advantage of a hook named `hook_theme_registry_alter()` where we will be altering the theme registry and pointing Drupal to our custom override. Once this has been done and importantly, the cache has been cleared, our newly introduced `mysite_fieldset()` function will be recognized.

Within the `mysite_fieldset()` function, all we are effectively doing is inserting our custom `#postscript` attribute towards the end of the markup. With this done, we can use this attribute as part of any fieldset's declaration as demonstrated in the subsequent `form_alter()` implementation. The resulting **Revision information** fieldset should now look something like the following:

Adding class attributes to form elements

Drupal 7 is quite meticulous with its forms and other markup when it comes to assigning CLASS and ID attributes. This ensures that various page elements can be individually targeted either via CSS or JavaScript and thereby, manipulated as necessary. This is however, not true all the time and circumstances sometimes require further customization.

In this recipe, we will assign class attributes to the Search module's textfields and use them along with a pinch of jQuery to improve usability in situations where the search block is concurrently visible along with the module's input form on the search page.

Getting ready

We will be using the mysite module created earlier in this book to hold an implementation of `hook_form_alter()`. As we are playing with the Search module, it is assumed that the module is enabled and that the site's content has subsequently been *completely* indexed. This can be verified via `admin/config/search/settings` [**Home | Administration | Configuration | Search and metadata | Search settings**].

Lastly, enable the search block via the block administration page at `admin/structure/block` [**Home | Administration | Structure | Blocks**].

How to do it...

Navigate to the mysite module folder at `sites/all/modules/mysite` to perform the following steps:

1. Locate the file `mysite.module` and open it in an editor.

2. Scroll down to the bottom and add the following function:

```
/**
 * Implements hook_form_alter().
 */
function mysite_form_alter(&$form, &$form_state, $form_id) {
  // dpm($form);

  // Set the class attribute and add some JS goodness to the
  // search form when both the theme search box as well as
  // the basic search form are visible.
  if ($form_id == 'search_form') {
    // Set the class attribute of the search form textfield.
    $form['basic']['keys']['#attributes']['class'][] = 'search-
      text';

    // The path to the mysite module.
    $path = drupal_get_path('module', 'mysite');
    drupal_add_js($path . '/js/search.js');
  }
  else if ($form_id == 'search_block_form') {
    // Set the class attribute of the search-box textfield.
    $form['search_block_form']['#attributes'] = array('class' =>
      array('search-text'));
  }
}
```

If there is an existing implementation of `hook_form_alter()`, this code will need to be integrated into it.

3. Save the file and exit the editor.

4. Visit the URL `search` where both the search block and basic search form should be displayed. The HTML source should confirm that both the textfields now have a class named **search-text** assigned to them.

Now that we have assigned the classes to the two textfields, we can work on getting the JavaScript up and running. Note that in the preceding `hook_form_alter()` function, we have also conditionally included the JavaScript file we will be creating as follows:

5. Browse to the mysite module's `js` folder.

6. Create a file named `search.js` and open it in an editor.

7. Add the following jQuery to this file:

```
(function ($) {
  Drupal.behaviors.mysiteSearch = {
    attach: function() {
      var fields = $('.search-text');
      // Set default text to both fields.
      var text = fields.filter(function() { return $(this).val()
        .length; }).val();
      fields.val(text);

      // Sync textfield key-presses.
      fields.keyup(function(event){
        fields.not(this).val($(this).val());
      });
    }
  };
}(jQuery));
```

8. Save the file and exit the editor.

9. Empty the Drupal cache.

10. Revisit the search page and perform a test search query.

11. Confirm that the current search keywords are being displayed in both textfields.

12. Confirm that user input into either textfield is automatically synchronized with the other textfield.

How it works...

One of the minor issues with using the search block is that when it is used to perform a query, the resulting page does not display the keywords being searched for in its textfield. Instead, they are displayed solely in the search module's form as in the following screenshot:

By using the Form API's `#attributes` option via a `hook_form_alter()`, we are able to add a class titled `.search-text` to both textfields. This subsequently allows us to easily target the two elements using jQuery. Once we have them, we can ensure that the theme's search box contains the same keywords as the primary search form as evident in the following screenshot:

We are also able to take this opportunity to implement a synchronization effect using jQuery's `keyup()` event, which synchronizes the user's input into either textfield in real time.

See also

Another recipe where we are looking to modify the markup in order to insert CSS classes of our choice is the *Chapter 6, Advanced Templating* recipe titled *Optimizing using hook_preprocess()*.

10
Theming Fields

We will be covering the following recipes in this chapter:

- Creating a new node type
- Displaying fields together using fieldgroups
- Manipulating display layouts using fieldgroups
- Theming a field using a template file
- Adding image fields using the Image module
- Using Image styles to scale and crop images on the fly
- Adding lightbox support for images

Introduction

A large part of what was known in Drupal 6 as the Content Construction Kit or CCK suite of contributed modules has been integrated into core in Drupal 7, and is collectively referred to simply as Fields or as the Fields API. Fields enable the creation, management, customization, and display of node types from within Drupal's administration pages. Besides the ease of it all, there are other intrinsic advantages to relying on Fields.

Firstly, the use of Fields implies that we do not have to write and maintain our own code as most of our specifications reside in the database. Furthermore, we do not need to optimize the database either as the API ensures that this is automatically done for us. With the API being a part of core, upgrades to our fields are handled automatically and reliably. In other words, when we do upgrade our site to Drupal 8 or later, our data will also be upgraded to account for any changes.

Another clincher is the fact that all the fields within each node type are now exposed to other modules such as Views which enable us to do more and to do so quickly and efficiently. Fields and Views take most of the complexity out of customization and allows site administrators to get on with the more creative aspects of site deployment.

From a theming perspective, we can manage how each field is displayed from the administration UI. By default, we can control rudimentary aspects such as field order, visibility, label placement, and so on. Each field can also have its own custom display settings. For example, the body field can optionally be displayed in summary form or in full. Similarly, an Image field can be customized to be rendered as a thumbnail when viewed in teaser form or in larger dimensions when a node is viewed in full.

 Fields are not only used in nodes. They are also incorporated into the User and Comment modules within core. Moreover, they can also be reused and reconfigured when necessary.

The core package comes with a primary module named **Field** which is a prerequisite for all other modules, a number of basic modules such as **Text**, **Number**, **List**, and **Options** which enable the creation of form elements based on their types, and more complex elements such as **Image**. Besides these, there are a plethora of contributed modules that similarly allow the creation of form fields such as the **Email Field** module which handles e-mail address input, the **Date** module which enables date input, or the **Link** field which allows configurable URL input. The **Field_UI** module provides a management interface where all of these fields can be configured and administered.

A list of contributed Field modules for Drupal 7 can be retrieved by navigating to `http://drupal.org/project/modules` and choosing the **Fields** category and **7.x** for compatibility prior to clicking on the **Search** button.

In this chapter, we will look at creating a node type named company and then extending it using Fields.

Creating a new node type

In this recipe, we will be adding a new node type and customizing it using Fields. As an example, we will be creating a type named *company* to hold information about a company along with details such as its address, telephone number, e-mail address, and so on.

Getting ready

It is assumed that the Field, Field UI and, at the very least, the Text module have all been enabled. The Field UI module is required for the field management interface to be accessible.

How to do it...

The Field API integrates into Drupal's content management pages and can be accessed by navigating to admin/structure/types [**Home | Administration | Structure | Content types**]. Perform the following steps to add the new node type:

1. Click on the **Add content type** tab at the top.

2. As we are creating a type specifically to hold details about a company, set the **Name** field in the ensuing form to Company.

 Note that a suitable **Machine name** (**company**) for this node type has been automatically created as seen in the following screenshot.

3. Add some pertinent information in the **Description** field:

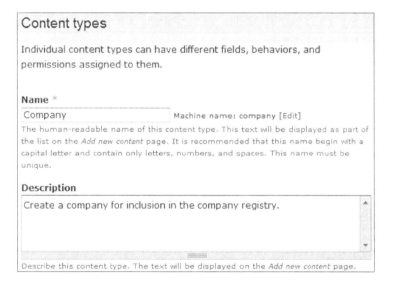

4. Select the **Submission form** settings vertical tab and amend the labels of the **Title** field to read Company name.

5. Click on **Save content type** to create our new node type. This should take us back to the **Content types** list which should now include our new type:

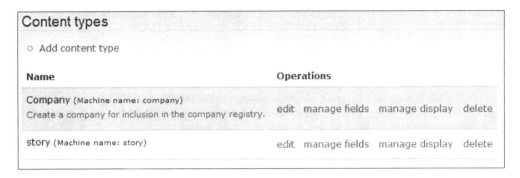

6. Click on the company type's **manage fields** link.

7. Click on the **edit** link associated with the **Body** field.

8. On the edit page, change the **Label** to **Company description**.

9. Click on the **Save settings** button at the bottom of the page to save our changes.

10. Back on the **Manage fields** tab, scroll down to the section dealing with the addition of new fields.

11. Use this form to add a new field to hold the address details of the company as shown in the following screenshot:

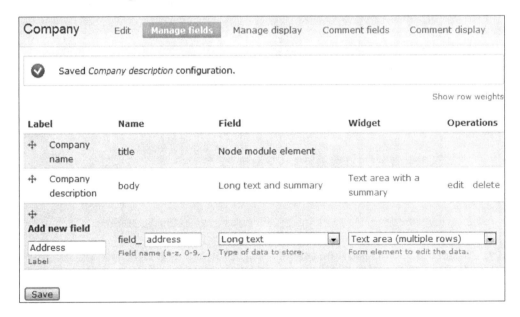

12. Clicking on **Save** should take us to the field configuration form.

13. In the ensuing form, customizations can be made as necessary before clicking on **Save field settings** to add the field. The module will run us through a series of optional field configuration steps where the field can be customized further.

14. Similarly, add two more textfields, **Phone** and **E-mail address**, to complete the set of basic fields for our node type as displayed in the next screenshot:

Label	Name	Field	Widget	Operations
✛ Company name	title	Node module element		
✛ Company description	body	Long text and summary	Text area with a summary	edit delete
✛ Address	field_address	Long text	Text area (multiple rows)	edit delete
✛ Phone	field_phone	Text	Text field	edit delete
✛ E-mail address	field_email	Text	Text field	edit delete

 Unlike the **Address** field that uses the **Long text** type, note that the **Phone** and **E-mail fields** use the basic **Text** type.

How it works...

Now that we have our new type set up, we can go ahead and add company content through node/add/company [**Home | Add content | Company**]. The following screenshot displays a company node created for a company named **Foo Corp**:

Foo Corp

| View | Edit | Devel |

Submitted by karthik on Sun, 08/21/2011 - 12:49

Lorem ipsum dolor sit amet, consectetur adipisicing elit, sed do dolore magna aliqua. Ut enim ad minim veniam, quis nostrud ex ea commodo consequat. Duis aute irure dolor in reprehenderit i nulla pariatur. Excepteur sint occaecat cupidatat non proident, s id est laborum.

Address:

1234, Example avenue,
Example suburb,
Example city,
Example PIN code,
Example state,
Example country.

Phone:
+12 34 5678 9012
E-mail address:
foocorp@example.com

There's more...

The Fields API also provides options to adjust the *weight* of each field and thereby, its display order.

Adjusting the display order of fields

As the following screenshot demonstrates, the display order of various fields can be adjusted using the drag-and-drop crosshairs to the left of each field and subsequently saving the changes. This display order pertains to the position of the fields in the node edit form only and not the actual view of the rendered node which is handled through the **Manage display** tab:

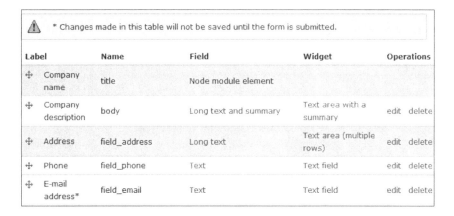

Label	Name	Field	Widget	Operations
⊕ Company name	title	Node module element		
⊕ Company description	body	Long text and summary	Text area with a summary	edit delete
⊕ Address	field_address	Long text	Text area (multiple rows)	edit delete
⊕ Phone	field_phone	Text	Text field	edit delete
⊕ E-mail address*	field_email	Text	Text field	edit delete

> ⚠ * Changes made in this table will not be saved until the form is submitted.

Multiple-value fields

As companies might well have multiple phone numbers, we can cater to this requirement by amending the **Number of values** property of the **Phone** field accordingly through the **configuration** page of the field. For our needs, setting it to **Unlimited** should work well. Once modified, the node creation page should support multiple phone numbers as shown in the following screenshot:

Contributed modules: e-mail and phone

While we have used simple textfields to store the phone and e-mail fields in the company node type, we could have just as well made use of contributed modules which provide custom field types for each of these inputs. In the case of the phone field, using the **Phone** module (`http://drupal.org/project/phone`) will introduce additional capabilities such as number validation and display formatting support. The **Email Field** module (`http://drupal.org/project/email`) provides similar support for e-mail addresses.

See also

Once we have created our custom node type, we can theme it just like any other type. *Customizing the appearance of a particular node type* recipe in *Chapter 4, Templating Basics* explains how to target the template file of a specific node type to hold our customizations.

Displaying fields together using fieldgroups

A contributed module named Field group allows us to organize fields into groups known as fieldgroups. These groups can be created for the purpose of gathering associated fields during input or while rendering them during display. In this recipe, we will be creating a group to contain all fields providing contact information within the company node type.

Getting ready

We will be using the company node type created earlier in this chapter. As this recipe uses fieldgroups, it is required that the **Field group** module be installed and enabled. It is available at `http://drupal.org/project/field_group`.

How to do it...

Once the fieldgroup module has been enabled, the **Manage fields** form for the company node type should now have an option to also create groups. This form can be accessed by navigating to `admin/structure/types/manage/company/fields` [**Home | Administration | Structure | Content types | Company**].

The `Contact` fieldgroup to hold the **Address, Phone**, and **E-mail address** fields can be created using the following procedure:

1. Scroll down to the bottom of the page to locate the row titled **New group**.

2. Add `Contact` and `contact` respectively to the **Label** and **Group name** textfields as shown in the following screenshot:

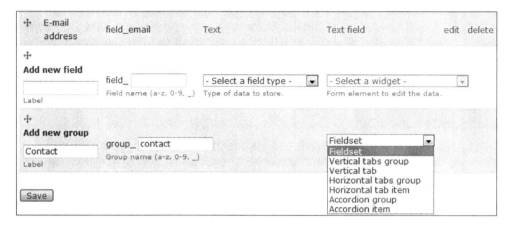

3. Use the **Fieldset** option and then click the **Save** button to create the new group.

4. A new group named **Contact** should now be listed at the bottom of the table. Drag the three fields—**Address, Phone**, and **E-mail address**—onto the **Contact** group where they should snap into place as members of the group:

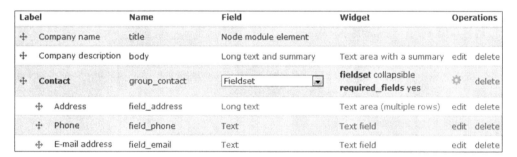

5. Click the **Save** button to save our changes.

This procedure will add the group fieldset to the node edit form. Repeating it within the **Manage display** tab should allow us to group contact fields during node display as well.

How it works...

Looking at a node's edit form, we should be able to confirm that all the contact fields now reside within a fieldset named **Contact**. Note that the fieldset, as demonstrated in the following screenshot, is collapsible. This and other options can be set from the fieldgroup's configuration form which is visible as a gear icon in the previous screenshot.

On the other hand, viewing a company node should confirm the presence of a new fieldset containing only the two visible contact fields as shown in the next screenshot. Here, we can see that the fieldset is not collapsible:

The next recipe, *Manipulating display layouts using fieldgroups* explores other formatting options provided by the Field group module.

Manipulating display layouts using fieldgroups

The Field group module supports other options besides collapsible fieldsets. These include vertical tabs, horizontal tabs, and accordion layouts, and can make for interesting displays. In this recipe, we will experiment with the use of horizontal tabs for our company node type.

Getting ready

We will be using the company node type created earlier in this chapter. This recipe continues from where we left off in the previous recipe which is assumed to have been completed successfully.

How to do it...

To convert the display layout for the company node type to use horizontal tabs, perform the following steps:

1. Navigate to the manage display interface for the company node at `admin/structure/types/manage/company/display` [**Home | Administration | Structure | Content types | Company**].

2. Create three separate groups with labels **Company**, **Bio**, and **Contact** respectively. If a group named **Contact** already exists, leave it as it is.

3. Drag the **contact** fields into the **Contact** group and the **Company description** field into the **Bio** group.

4. Next, drag the **Bio** and **Contact** groups into the **Company** group.

5. Change the **Format** for the **Company** group to **Horizontal tabs group**.

6. Similarly, change the **Format** for the **Bio** and **Contact** groups to **Horizontal tab item** so that the resulting page looks like the following screenshot:

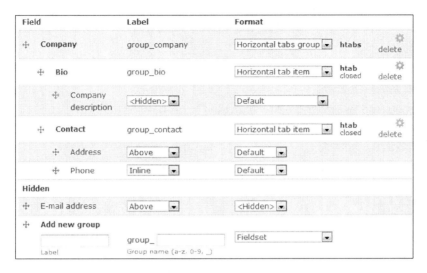

7. Click on the **Save** button to save our changes.

How it works...

The Field group module allows administrators to group associated fields together. While the fields are always organized within HTML fieldsets, depending on our configured choices, the module includes an appropriate JavaScript file that can style these fieldsets further. In this case, it will include the file `horizontal-tabs.js` which formats the company node fields to resemble the following screenshot:

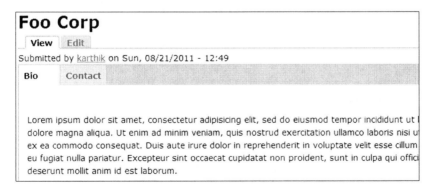

While we have used the tab formats in the **Manage display** tab in this recipe, they can also be used in the **Manage fields** tab to customize the node edit form.

It is also important to remember that in Drupal 7 fields are not restricted solely to the domain of nodes. They are also used by other modules such as Comment and User and can be just as effective with them.

There's more...

The Field group module provides other formatting styles besides horizontal tabs.

Vertical tabs

The following screenshot displays the same fieldgroups being rendered using *vertical* tabs:

All that was required to accomplish this switch was to change the tab format on the **Manage display** form. The **Company** fieldgroup was set to be formatted as a **Vertical tabs group** rather than a **Horizontal tabs group**, and the fields formatted as **Horizontal tab items** were changed over to **Vertical tabs**.

 This would also work on the node edit form. An additional feature on these forms is that if fields were only formatted as vertical tabs and not sequestered within Vertical tabs group fields, they will be added to the existing vertical tab group which is a common feature on these forms.

Accordions

Accordions provide a nifty interface that displays only one tab at a time with transitions between tabs being animated. The Field group module also supports accordion layouts which can be enabled—just as we saw with vertical tabs—by changing the formatters to **Accordion group** and **Accordion item** respectively on the **Manage display** form.

We can see fieldgroups formatted using an accordion layout in the next screenshot:

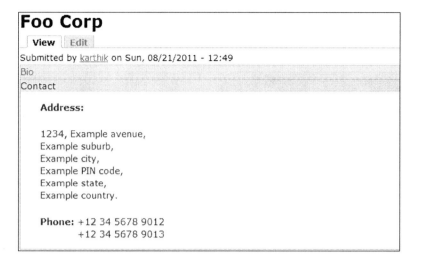

See also

The Field group module utilizes a lot of JavaScript to achieve its layouts. *Chapter 7, Javascript in themes*, covers the use of Javascript in Drupal modules and themes.

Theming a field using a template file

Once our field requirements become complex, we will find ourselves having to resort to modifying the field to meet our needs. As with most things Drupal, template functions and files are where these modifications usually reside.

In this recipe, we will look at modifying the output of the Phone field in the company node type to use an unordered list when there are multiple items present.

Getting ready

We will be using the myzen theme created earlier in this book, to hold our theme customizations. Following the recommendations outlined in earlier chapters, we will also be making use of the Devel and Theme developer modules to assist in identifying the theme functions and templates to override. It is assumed that these modules are installed and enabled.

To get an idea of the work at hand, navigate to a sample company node and view the markup of a Phone field with multiple values. The HTML should look something like the following:

```
<div class="field field-name-field-phone field-type-text
   field-label-above clearfix">
   <div class="field-label">Phone:</div>
   <div class="field-items">
      <div class="field-item even">+12 34 5678 9012</div>
      <div class="field-item odd">+12 34 5678 9013</div>
   </div>
</div>
```

As can be seen, multiple values of the same field are displayed using separate DIV blocks. This is a less than ideal solution in situations where we are looking to use lists to contain multiple related items. While we can use CSS to style these DIVs to behave like lists, it is not optimal. Moreover, other scenarios might not afford us such luxuries.

How to do it...

Overriding the Phone field involves overriding a field of type text. In order to locate the right template file to override, we first need to use the **Theme developer** module. Enable **Themer info** and click on the **Phone** field to gain information on the functions and templates responsible for its display. As outlined in the following screenshot, the template file in use is default field template file named `field.tpl.php`:

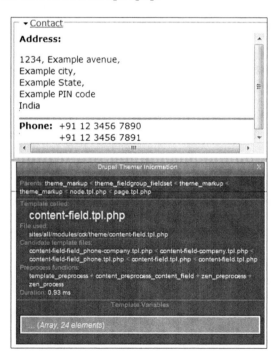

We are also informed that, if we wanted to override this file, we could locate our changes in a file with a name based on the provided **Candidate template** filenames. The filenames dictate the scope of the template file. This scope can range from our own version of `field.tpl.php` which will affect all fields to `field--field_phone--company.tpl.php` which will only affect the field named `field_phone` when used within the company node type. In our case, we can use the latter as we are just looking to modify this particular field.

To override the template, perform the following steps:

1. Navigate to the core Field module's folder at `modules/field`.
2. Browse into the `theme` folder.
3. Copy the file named `field.tpl.php`.
4. Browse to the myzen theme folder at `sites/all/themes/myzen`.
5. Click into the `templates` subfolder and paste the file into it.
6. Rename the file to `field--field_phone--company.tpl.php`.
7. Open this file in an editor. Its contents should effectively be something like the following:

```php
<div class="<?php print $classes; ?> clearfix"
  <?php print $attributes; ?>>
  <?php if (!$label_hidden) : ?>
    <div class="field-label"<?php print $title_attributes;
      ?>><?php print $label ?>: </div>
  <?php endif; ?>
  <div class="field-items"<?php print $content_attributes; ?>>
    <?php foreach ($items as $delta => $item) : ?>
      <div class="field-item <?php print $delta % 2 ? 'odd' :
        'even'; ?>"<?php print $item_attributes[$delta]; ?>>
          <?php print render($item); ?></div>
        <?php endforeach; ?>
  </div>
</div>
```

The highlighted lines are a tentative pointer to the code where we run through multiple values and print them.

8. Replace this entire block of code with the following which is a more simplified, yet cleaner version that displays each entry as a list item:

```php
<div class="<?php print $classes; ?> clearfix"
  <?php print $attributes; ?>>
  <?php if (!$label_hidden) : ?>
    <div class="field-label"<?php print $title_attributes;
      ?>><?php print $label ?>: </div>
  <?php endif; ?>
```

```
      <div class="field-items"<?php print $content_attributes; ?>>
<ul>
  <?php foreach ($items as $delta => $item) : ?>
    <li class="field-item <?php print $delta % 2 ? 'odd' :
      'even'; ?>"<?php print $item_attributes[$delta]; ?>>
      <?php print render($item); ?></li>
  <?php endforeach; ?>
</ul>

  </div>
</div>
```

The lines of highlighted code indicate where we have replaced the old markup with an unordered list. We are cycling through each entry in the $items array and outputting it as a list entry.

9. Save the file and exit the editor.

10. Empty the Drupal cache and rebuild the theme registry as we have introduced a new template file into the system.

The default field.tpl.php template file includes an HTML comment that explains the function of the file. Once the template file has been copied to the myzen theme's templates folder, this comment is no longer necessary and can be removed.

How it works...

Once the cache has been emptied, browse to a company node page to see our changes in effect:

▼ Contact

Address:

1234, Example avenue,
Example suburb,
Example city,
Example PIN code,
Example state,
Example country.

Phone:

- +12 34 5678 9012
- +12 34 5678 9013

As displayed in the previous screenshot, the two phone numbers are now displayed using an unordered list which, if necessary, can be styled further using CSS. Looking at the markup, we should be able to confirm that our changes have taken effect:

```
<div class="field field-name-field-phone field-type-text
   field-label-above clearfix">
   <div class="field-label">Phone:</div>
   <div class="field-items">
     <ul>
       <li class="field-item even">+12 34 5678 9012</div>
       <li class="field-item odd">+12 34 5678 9013</div>
     </ul>
   </div>
</div>
```

See also

Another approach to altering markup, albeit an inelegant and time-consuming one, is to implement our modifications using JavaScript. *Chapter 7, JavaScript in Themes*, is dedicated to using JavaScript and, in particular, jQuery, to manipulate page markup and more.

Adding image fields using the Image module

In this recipe, we will be adding image support to the company node type using the **Image** module.

Getting ready

The Image is a field module and a part of Drupal core. Besides the base field modules, it also depends on the **File** module. It is assumed to be enabled. We will be adding the image field to the company node type created earlier in this chapter.

How to do it...

Once the Image module is enabled, it becomes available as a field type. The following steps detail how we can add image support to the company node type:

1. Navigate to the company type's field management page at `admin/structure/types/manage/company/fields` [**Home | Administration | Structure | Content types | Company | Manage fields**].

2. Scroll down to the section titled **New field**.

3. Add `Images` and `images` respectively to the **Label** and **Field name** textfields.

4. Choose **Image** as the **Field type** as well as the widget type as shown in the following screenshot.

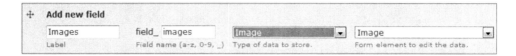

5. Click on **Save** to create the field.
6. Click on the **Save field settings** button in the resulting form as we are happy with the default upload destination.
7. In the next step, check the **Enable Title field** option.
8. Scroll down to the bottom and set the **Number of values** option to **Unlimited**.

 There are a number of other settings available here that allow control over where the files are saved, file type restrictions, resolutions, and size.

9. Click on **Save field settings** to complete the procedure.
10. This should bring us back to the **Manage fields** tab. Click on the **Manage display** tab.
11. Move the new **Images** field down the table as in the following screenshot:

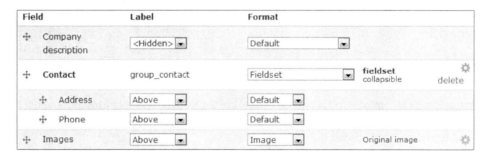

12. Click the **Save** button to register our changes.

How it works...

Once configured, the company node form will now support the uploading of images as demonstrated in the following screenshot:

Once we save our node, we should be able to see our images being displayed in the node view as shown in the next screenshot. Note that we are displaying each image in its original form as per our display settings:

See also

The two following recipes, *Using Image styles to scale and crop images on the fly* and *Adding lightbox support for images*, further demonstrate how powerful and efficient image handling can be in Drupal.

Using Image styles to scale and crop images on the fly

Now that we have added image support to the company node type, we can look to style the input images to make them more presentable. When customizing images, we inevitably find ourselves performing a series of repeated steps such as cropping, scaling, resizing, and so on, as per the requirements of our theme. It used to be the case that this procedure had to be performed manually for each image or, if we were a little more proactive, performed through a custom script to apply our changes on the fly. In Drupal 7, we can automate this process and style our images in a non-invasive manner thanks to the tools provided by the Image module in the form of Image styles.

An Image style is a term used to represent the series of operations that we are looking to perform on the image. These operations are known as effects and by default include scale, crop, scale and crop, resize, rotate, and desaturate. Contributed modules can extend this set by leveraging the module's APIs to play with other more complex effects such as watermarking and coloring. All this, of course, happens on the fly and makes use of a caching system that makes this a truly elegant solution.

As we saw in the previous recipe, by default, the Image module displays images in their original form. It also provides three other options of **large**, **medium**, and **thumbnail** that can also be used. In this recipe, we will be looking at scaling and cropping the images using image styles to render a perfectly square thumbnail for the company node type.

Getting ready

This is a follow-up to the previous recipe where we added image support to the company node type. The Image module handles image operations through the use of either PHP's GD2 extension or ImageMagick. It is assumed that one of these libraries is installed. This can be verified by visiting the **Image toolkit configuration** page at `admin/config/media/image-toolkit` [**Home | Administration | Configuration | Media | Image toolkit**].

We will also be adding a smidgeon of CSS to pretty our images and will be doing so using the mysite module created earlier in this book. The CSS will be added to its `mysite.css` file which is assumed to be loaded through the module's `hook_init()` function during runtime.

How to do it...

Once enabled, the Image module provides a configuration interface at `admin/config/media/image-styles` [**Home | Administration | Configuration | Media | Image styles**] where the following steps are to be performed:

1. Click on the **Add style** link.

2. Type `company-thumbnail` inside the **Style name** textfield.

3. Click the **Create new style** button to create it.

4. In the subsequent configuration screen, choose **Scale and crop** in the **Effect** table and click on **Add**:

5. Change the **Width** and **Height** textfields to `100` which indicates the value in pixels.

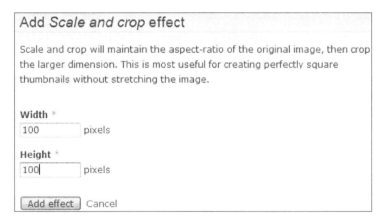

6. Click on the **Add effect** button to update the style.

Now that our style has been created, we can look to apply it to our images:

7. Navigate to the company node type's **Manage display configuration** page at `admin/structure/types/manage/company/display` [**Home | Administration | Structure | Content types | Company**].

8. Set the **Images** field's gear icon which should open up further configuration options.

9. In the resulting form, change the **Image style** to **company-thumbnail**.

10. Click the **Update** button as seen in the following screenshot to register our change:

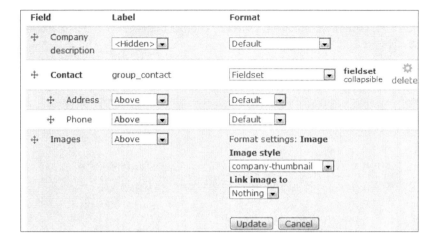

11. Click on the **Save** button to save our changes to the database.

Finally, we need to style our images to be displayed inline in a horizontal row to provide a gallery-like feel:

12. Navigate to the mysite module's folder at `sites/all/modules/mysite`.

13. Within its `css` folder, open the file `mysite.css` in an editor.

14. Add the following rule to the file:

```
.field-name-field-images .field-items .field-item {
  display: inline;
  padding-right: 5px;
}
```

15. Save the file and exit the editor.

How it works...

Once the new preset has been applied, the **Images** field on a company node page will look something like the following screenshot where five images have been uploaded:

Looking at the location of each of these thumbnails, we should be able to see that they are stored in a location such as `sites/default/files/styles/company-thumbnail/public/1.png` while the originals reside in a standard location similar to `sites/default/files/1.png`. This is due to the Image module's caching system which stores images generated for each style in a dedicated subfolder. Consequently, the original image remains untouched and can be used to generate more such styled images or modify existing ones. To illustrate, if we now wanted to replace these thumbnails with larger versions of size 150x150 pixels, all we would need to do is either edit the **company-thumbnail** style to reflect this change, or alternatively, create a new style named **company-thumbnail-150** and display each image using it.

See also

The next recipe, *Adding lightbox support for images*, uses the Image and Colorbox modules to create a gallery-like presentation of our images.

Adding lightbox support for images

Lightbox plugins allow users to view magnified versions of clicked thumbnails in modal dialogs on the same page. Coupled with easing animations and other attractive effects, they make for engaging viewing.

While there are a number of modules that provide such functionality, we will be looking at the **Colorbox** plugin and module in this recipe specifically as it is jQuery-based and supports the Image module.

Getting ready

The **Colorbox** module (version 7.x-1.1 at the time of writing) can be downloaded from `http://drupal.org/project/colorbox`. The project page also provides information on installing the Colorbox plugin which summarily amounts to downloading it from `http://colorpowered.com/colorbox` and extracting within `sites/all/libraries`.

We will also be continuing from where we left off in the previous recipe in which we uploaded a number of images to a sample node.

How to do it...

Once enabled, the **Colorbox** module can be configured from `admin/config/media/colorbox` [**Home | Administration | Configuration | Media | Colorbox**] as per the following steps:

1. Set the value of the **Image field gallery** setting to `Per field gallery`.

2. Click the **Save configuration** button to save our changes:

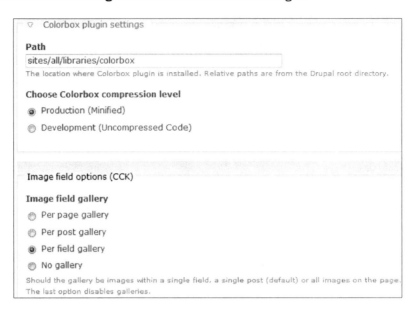

Once Colorbox has been configured, it should now be available as an option in the company node type's **Manage display** form.

3. Navigate to the **Manage display** form at `admin/structure/types/manage/company/display` [**Home | Administration | Structure | Content types | Company**].

4. For the Default display, change the **Format settings** for the **Images** field from **Image** to **Colorbox**.

5. Click on the field's configuration (gear) icon which should load options for the Colorbox formatter.

6. Set the **Node image style** value to **company-thumbnail** as we want the square thumbnail to be used to display the images in the node view.

7. Choose **None (original image)** in the **Colorbox image style** drop down as we are just going to display the original image without any modifications in the lightbox.

8. Once the values have been set as shown in the following screenshot, click on the **Update** button:

9. Finally, click on the **Save** button to save our changes.

How it works...

Now that the thumbnails are being formatted using Colorbox, clicking them should trigger the lightbox as seen in the following screenshot:

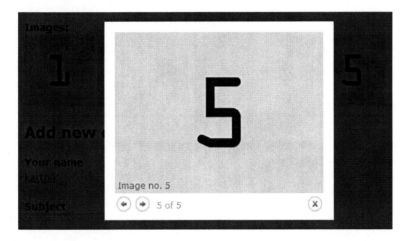

Note that unlike the standard Image module style, we can actually see the **Title** attribute of the image being displayed in the lightbox.

There's more...

The Colorbox module also provides further options to configure and style our lightbox display.

Advanced customizations using Colorbox

The Colorbox module provides an interface through its configuration page to theme and tweak the JavaScript and CSS used in the display of the lightbox. While we can use one of the provided preset styles such as **Stockholm Syndrome** in the next screenshot, we could also just as easily create our own custom style and register it with our theme:

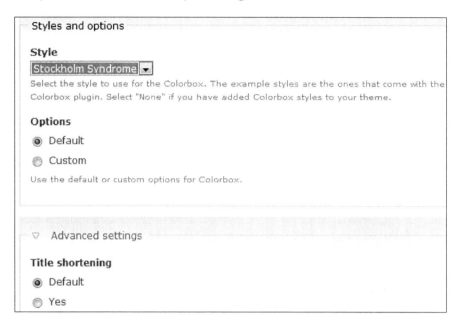

In the previous screenshot, choosing **Custom** will expose all the nuts and bolts pertaining to the animation and style of the dialog.

Media modules

Another endeavor in providing image, audio, and video support to Drupal is the suite of modules based on the **Media** module (`http://drupal.org/project/media`). While they are still under heavy development at the time of writing this chapter, they build upon the capabilities of the Image module and are set to be a feature-rich alternative. Of special interest are the **Media Browser** which provides a library-like interface and promotes the reuse of existing media content, and **Media Gallery** which provides a convenient option to create image and other galleries. The latter can also, optionally, make use of the Colorbox plugin seen in this recipe.

11

Views Theming

We will be covering the following recipes in this chapter:

- ▸ Creating a simple View
- ▸ Styling a node listing using a Grid display
- ▸ Embedding a View inside a node template
- ▸ Overriding the Views table style format
- ▸ Creating a custom Views style plugin

Introduction

The Views module is the most popularly contributed module in the Drupal ecosystem, and with good reason, as it has become one of the cornerstones of Drupal development. Along with core features such as the **Fields API** as well as other modules such as **Panels**, it has contributed immensely towards Drupal's reputation of being an ideal tool for rapid site development and deployment.

Views, at its most fundamental level is a database query builder. It allows us to construct database queries using a user-friendly interface, and subsequently, present the result to the user in a variety of manners. The query builder supports a number of components including:

- ▸ **Filters** which conditionally refine the query to return a more accurate result set. For example, as we will customarily only require nodes that have been published, we can add a filter to the View stating that the result set should only contain published nodes. They can optionally also be exposed to the user as a form element.
- ▸ **Contextual filters** which are usually dynamic parameters passed to the query at runtime such as the elements of the URL of the page being displayed.
- ▸ **Relationships** which are usually used to connect two different database tables together based on the relationship between two of their elements.

- ▸ **Field specification** which describes the fields to be returned as part of the result set.

- ▸ **Sorting support** which specifies how the results are to be sorted.

- ▸ **Pagination support** which limits the number of results returned.

- ▸ **Support for distinct results** to limit duplicates in the result set.

Views takes the returned results and runs them through its styling component which is built atop the Drupal theme system. The module supports a variety of styling options through the use of style formats which allow representing the results as tables, lists, and so on. Moreover, all style formats can be overridden from Drupal's theme layer just as we have seen in earlier chapters.

Additionally, Views allows administrators to create multiple **Displays** for each View. Displays allow the efficient representation of the same query in a variety of different ways. For example, a list of nodes can be presented both as content on a page or as content in a block, and so on.

The project page for the Views module is available at `http://drupal.org/project/views`. It is highly recommended that the **Advanced Help** module is installed along with Views. It can be downloaded from `http://drupal.org/project/advanced_help` and provides extensive and easily accessible *contextual* help all across this and other modules, if configured. In the following screenshot, the question mark icons all represent links to documentation specific to the associated elements:

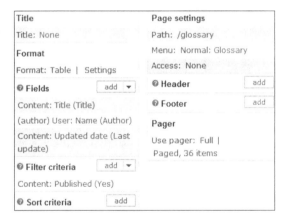

In this chapter, we will primarily be looking at the Views module from a theming point of view with particular attention being paid to overriding the default styling options provided. It is highly recommended that users looking to theme Views also familiarize themselves with the Drupal theming system prior to diving in.

The version of Views covered in this chapter is 7.x-3.0-rc1, the latest release at the time of writing. Considering the advanced status of the release, the final interface is not expected to be drastically different to the one being covered in the following recipes.

Creating a simple View

In this recipe, we will look at the ease with which we can create a simple unformatted node listing using the Views module. This View, which will represent a list of products as a rudimentary gallery, will be used as an example later in this chapter.

Getting ready

The View we will be creating will display a list of nodes of a custom node type named `product`. Besides the standard fields of **Title** and **Body**, this node type also contains two additional fields named **Image** and **Price** which are of type **Image** and *Number* (**Decimal**) respectively, as the following screenshot will attest. It is assumed that these field modules have been enabled along with any dependencies.

Label	Name	Field	Widget
✛ Title	title	Node module element	
✛ Body	body	Long text and summary	Text area with a summary
✛ Price	field_price	Decimal	Text field
✛ Image	field_image	Image	Image

Once the product node type has been created, sample products and product images will also need to be added for the purpose of this recipe.

How to do it...

To create the View, navigate to the **Views management** page at `admin/structure/views` [**Home | Administration | Structure | Views**] and perform the following steps:

1. Click on the **Add new view** link at the top of the page.
2. Set the **View name** to `Product Gallery` which should also automatically set the View's internal machine name to **product_gallery**.

3. Check the **Description** checkbox and set the **View description** field to A representation of all product nodes.

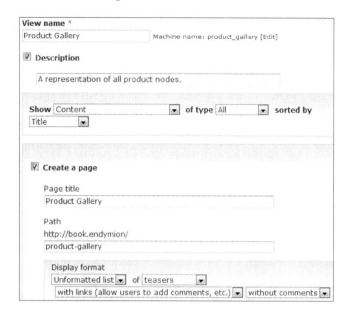

4. As seen in the previous screenshot, the default options are acceptable for the remainder of the form as we will be editing them further later on. However, note that the Path where we can access this View is automatically set to **product-gallery**.

5. Click on the **Continue and edit** button.

6. In the ensuing **View management** page, click on **Save** to complete the creation process.

> The Views administration interface uses JavaScript and Ajax to allow changes to be made in real time without frequent page refreshes. However, any changes made are not saved until the **Save** button is clicked.

With our View created, we can proceed to customize it further:

7. In the **Filter criteria** section, click on the **Add link** to add a filter.

8. In the **Add filter criteria** interface which pops up, select **Content** in the **Filter** drop down.

9. Select **Content: Type** from the list of options below as shown in the following screenshot:

Note that we are not choosing **Content: Published** in this window as it has already been selected when we created the View. We can see this filter already added at the bottom of the previous screenshot.

10. Click on **Add and configure filter criteria** to add the filters.

11. In the resulting configuration screen for the **Content: Type** filter, select the **Product** type as shown in the following screenshot and click on **Apply (all displays)**:

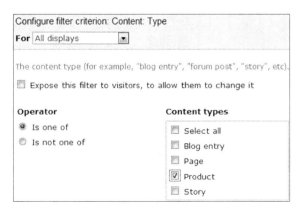

12. Click the **Save** button to save the changes to the View.

13. In the **Format** section, click on the link titled **Content**.

14. In the ensuing pop up, change the row style to **Fields** as shown in the next screenshot and click on **Apply (all displays)**:

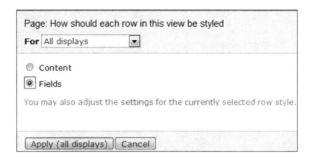

15. Similarly, click on **Apply (all displays)** in the subsequent **Row style** options window as well.

16. Next, in the **Fields** section, which should be populated with a single field, **Content: Title**, click the **Add** link to add the fields to display.

17. In the resulting **Add fields** form, select **Content** in the **Filter** drop down.

18. Check the two fields that are part of the **Product node** type, namely **Content: Image** and **Content: Price** as shown in the following screenshot:

19. Click on **Add and configure fields**.

20. In the configuration screen for the **Image** field, set the **Image style** option to **thumbnail** and click on the **Apply (all displays)** button:

21. Accept the default configuration options for the **Price** field and click on **Apply** to register our changes.

22. Finally, in the **Sort** criteria section, click on the default sort option which should be **Post date (desc)** and remove it by clicking on **Remove** in its configuration pop up.

23. Add a new **Sort** criteria by clicking on its **Add** link.

24. Choose **Content: Title** and click on **Add and configure** sort criteria.

25. Select the sorting direction, ascending or descending, and click on the **Apply (all displays)** button.

26. Finally, click on the **Save** button to save the View.

How it works...

Once configured, the View's configuration page should look similar to following screenshot:

We can clearly see the three fields— **Content: Title**, **Content: Image**, and **Content: Price**—as well as the two filters—**Content: Type** and **Content: Published**—and the lone **Sort criteria**, **Content: Title (asc)**. Each of these elements can be clicked to reach its configuration screen, if available.

As we are, by default, using a page display for our View, we can access it at the configured URL product-list. As the View uses the Unformatted style by default, the output is a simple collection of fields as shown in the following screenshot:

The Unformatted style option is useful in cases where the styling is customized entirely through overridden template files. We will be investigating this and other styling options as we go along in this chapter.

See also

While our View is currently in an unformatted state, the next recipe *Styling a node listing using a Grid display,* lists the steps required to style a View.

Styling a node listing using a Grid display

In this recipe, we will look at the ease with which we can represent the node View created in the previous recipe as a gallery by styling the View as a **grid**. A grid will allow us to achieve a gallery-like feel with each cell in a table layout representing a row from the result set.

Getting ready

We will be using the `product_gallery` View created earlier in the previous recipe. Additionally, we will need to use the Image module, as we saw in the last chapter, to customize the thumbnail for the Image field specifically for use in the product node type. To do so, navigate to `admin/config/media/image-styles` [**Home | Administration | Configuration | Media | Image Styles**] and add an Image style named `product_thumb` which performs a Scale and Crop operation to create a thumbnail of size 150x150 pixels as shown in the following screenshot:

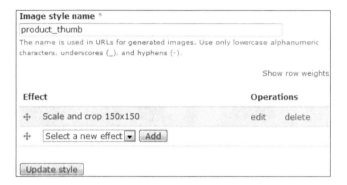

This recipe also makes use of the myzen theme created earlier in this book to hold our CSS customizations.

How to do it...

To achieve a gallery-like representation of the product nodes, we will be adding a new *display* to the `product_gallery` View as follows:

1. Browse to the **Views administration** page at `admin/structure/views` [**Home | Administration | Structure | Views**].

2. Locate the `product_gallery` View and click on its **edit** link.

3. The View management interface should currently have a single Display named **Page** listed at the top. Click on the **Add** link next to it and choose to create another Page display.

4. Change the name of this display from **Page** to `Gallery` by clicking on the Display **Name** value as shown in the following screenshot:

5. Next, in the **Format** section, click on **Unformatted list** to change the style format being used to style this display.

6. In the resulting configuration form, first declare the scope of our changes through the drop down at the top. In this case, as we want to override the default settings with our own, select **This page (override)**.

> Overriding allows us to adjust and tweak the current display to provide a different representation of the results when compared to the default display. If this option was not overridden here, then our changes would have inadvertently also affected the other Page display. Virtually every configurable option in a display can be overridden to our satisfaction.

7. Change the style plugin to **Grid** as in the following screenshot:

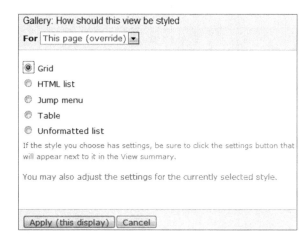

8. Click the **Apply (this display)** button to register our change.

9. In the Grid plugin's configuration form, leave the **Number of columns** set to **4** and the **Alignment field** set to **Horizontal**.

10. Click on **Apply (this display)** to register our changes.

11. As this is a new page display, we will also need to specify a URL for it. Click on the **Path: /** link under **Page settings**.

12. Set the path to `product-gallery` and click on **Apply**.

13. Click on **Save** to save our changes to the View.

 Make sure that we are working on the Gallery display any time the page is refreshed.

With the style plugin set to **Grid**, we can go ahead and also customize the **Image** field to use our custom Image style solely for the Gallery display:

14. In the **Fields** section, click on the arrow next to its **add** link and choose **rearrange**.

15. Choose **This page (override)** in the display drop down at the top so that we are only affecting the Gallery display.

16. Rearrange the field order so that the image is at the top followed by the product title and its price.

17. Click on **Apply (this display)** to effect our changes.

18. Back in the **Fields** section, click on **Content: Image (Image)** which should represent the product image.

19. In the resulting configuration form, choose **For This page (override)** in the drop down at the top to ensure that the changes made to the fields are local to the Gallery display only.

20. As we do not want a label, uncheck the **Create a label** checkbox.

21. Change the **Image style** to **product_thumb** as shown in the next screenshot:

22. Click on **Apply (this display)** to register our changes.

23. Similarly, disable the label for the **Price** field as well.

24. Once that has been done, click on the **Save** button to save our changes.

Finally, we can add a little CSS to position the grid and its contents at the center of the page:

25. Browse to the myzen theme's folder at `sites/all/themes/myzen`.

26. Navigate into its `css` subfolder and locate `views-styles.css` which is loaded by the theme through its `.info` file.

27. Open this file in an editor and add the following rules to it:

```
/* Product gallery */
.view-product-gallery table {
  width: 80%;
  margin: auto;
  text-align: center;
}
```

28. Save the file and exit the editor.

How it works...

Once our changes to the **Gallery** display have been saved, the management page should look similar to the following screenshot:

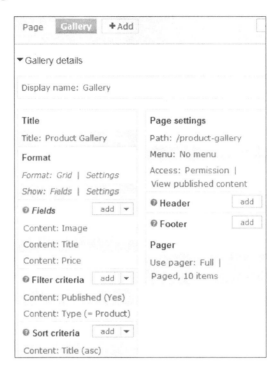

Subsequently, visiting the View's URL at `product-gallery` should result in a gallery-like representation of the product nodes as shown in the following screenshot:

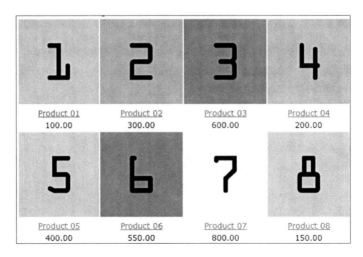

There's more...

Views comes with a number of other styling options. While Grids allow us to lay out our content as an HTML table purely for visual reasons, the Table plugin allows us to represent the contents of nodes in standard tabular form. Views also allows us to adjust the markup used to display fields as well as the View directly from its management interface.

Styling as a table

A simple swap of the format style plugin being used from Grid to Table will provide a standard tabular representation of the nodes. This can be done by clicking on **Format**: **Grid** and changing the **plugin** to **Table** in the resulting configuration screen. The following screenshot displays the eventual **View** page as a sortable table:

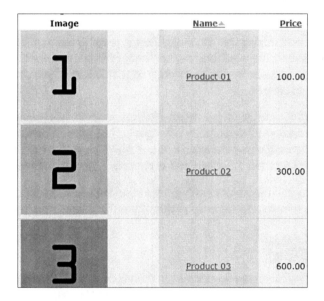

Adding custom CSS classes to the View

While the Views module routinely adds well-structured class names to most of its markup, it is sometimes necessary to add our own custom classes. This can be done by clicking on the **CSS class** link within the **Advanced** section. In this recipe, we have made use of the default class name `.view-product-gallery` to target the table used by the Gallery display.

Adjusting markup for fields

Fields also, just like the actual View, provide us with an opportunity to adjust their markup. To do so, click on the appropriate field within the **Fields** section and in the ensuing window, look within the **Style settings** fieldset. Options should be provided to override the default HTML for the labels, values, or the overall fields themselves. CSS classes can be similarly injected as well.

Embedding a View inside a node template

Views usually tend to be output as pages, blocks, and other displays. In this recipe, we will be looking at taking this a step further, by manually embedding a View inside a node template using a smidgeon of code. To be more precise, we will be taking the **backlinks** View which comes with the Views module and embedding it inside a theme's node template file to provide a list of related content which links to the node currently being displayed.

Backlinks provide a list of nodes that link to the current node. For example, if in the content of `node/123`, we include a link to `node/456`, `node/123` is considered to be a backlink of `node/456`.

Getting ready

As we are going to be embedding the backlinks View, it is assumed that it has been enabled. Additionally, for backlinks to be available, the content of the site will need to link to each other. In other words, sample nodes will need to be created that link to other nodes in the site to allow backlinks to be cataloged.

Furthermore, as backlinks are generated by the **Search** module, it is imperative that it is enabled and that the site is indexed completely. This can be ascertained by visiting the search module's configuration page at `admin/config/search/settings` [**Home | Administration | Configuration | Search and metadata | Search settings**].

We will be using the myzen theme created earlier in this book to hold our customizations. It is assumed that a node template file already exists within the theme's `templates` folder.

How to do it...

Once the backlinks View has been enabled from the **Views management** page at `admin/structure/views` [**Home | Administration | Structure | Views**], we should be able to confirm that it makes available two displays by default. As shown in the following screenshot, the first one is a **Page** display which manifests itself as a tab on each node page, and the second one, titled **What links here**, is a *block* display which can be managed through the Drupal's block administration pages:

A **What links here** tab should appear at the top of each node's page just by enabling the **View**. This tab will, as shown in the following screenshot, list all the backlinks for the node being viewed. The block will, similarly, display the same links in a configurable block:

Rather than relying on a menu tab or an isolated block, we will be looking to tastefully *embed the View* directly inside a node. This can be done through the following steps:

1. Browse to the myzen theme folder at `sites/all/themes/myzen`.

2. Navigate into its `templates` subfolder.

3. Locate `node.tpl.php` and open it in an editor.

4. Look for code that deals with the display of content such as the following:

```
<div class="content"<?php print $content_attributes; ?>>
  <?php
    // We hide the comments and links now so that we can render
    // them later.
    hide($content['comments']);
    hide($content['links']);
    print render($content);

  ?>
</div>
```

5. Add the embed code to this block so that it now looks similar to the following:

```
<div class="content"<?php print $content_attributes; ?>>
  <?php
    // We hide the comments and links now so that we can render
    // them later.
    hide($content['comments']);
    hide($content['links']);
    // Only display backlinks in full node views.
    if (!$teaser) {
  ?>
  <div class="backlinks">
    <h3>What links here</h3>
    <?php print views_embed_view('backlinks', 'block');?>
  </div>
  <?php
    }

    print render($content);
  ?>
</div>
```

The `views_embed_view()` call returns the block display of the backlinks View.

6. Save the file and exit the editor.

7. Browse back up a level and into the `css` folder.

8. Locate the `views-styles.css` file and open it in an editor.

9. Add the following rules to the file:

```
/* Backlinks */
.backlinks {
  float: right;
  display: inline;
  padding: 0 1em;
  margin: 0 0 0.5em 1em;
  border-left: dashed 1px;
}
.backlinks h3 {
  margin-top: 0;
  padding-top: 0;
}
.backlinks ul {
  padding-left: 1.2em;
}
```

```
.backlinks ul li {
  list-style: square;
}
```

`views-styles.css` is, by default, automatically loaded by the theme through its `.info` file.

10. Save the file and exit the editor.

11. Clear the Drupal cache if necessary.

How it works...

Refreshing the node page should now display the node's backlinks along with its contents as in the following screenshot:

We can see that the backlinks are identical to what was displayed in the **What links here** tab we saw earlier. Furthermore, thanks to our CSS, we have floated the entire block to the right and have displayed it inline, thereby allowing the content to flow around it. A simple border and other tweaks and nudges provide the finishing touch.

 As we are embedding the **What links here** block directly into the node content, displaying the tab is unnecessary. As this tab is handled by the backlinks View's Page display, simply deleting the display or, alternatively, playing with its access settings or similar should do the trick.

There's more...

There are also a couple of alternative approaches which can be used to embed Views.

views_embed_view() and View titles

In this recipe, we have resorted to *manually* adding the View's title along with the `views_embed_view()` call, as the function, by design, only returns the content of the View. If it is necessary that the View's title is also dynamically inserted, then we will need to resort to the relatively longer approach as follows:

```
<div class="content"<?php print $content_attributes; ?>>
  <?php
    // We hide the comments and links now so that we can render
    // them later.
    hide($content['comments']);
    hide($content['links']);
    // Only display backlinks in full node views.
    if (!$teaser) {
  ?>

  <div class="backlinks">
      <?php
        $view = views_get_view('backlinks');
        $view_content = $view->preview('block');
        $view_title = $view->get_title();
      ?>
      <h3><?php print $view_title; ?></h3>
      <?php print $view_content; ?>
  <?php
    }

    print render($content);
  ?>
</div>
```

Embedding Views using the Viewfield module

While it is simple enough to embed code directly into template files or elsewhere in the theme, the **Viewfield** module, which can be downloaded from `http://drupal.org/project/viewfield`, provides a more straightforward alternative. It exposes all available Views through a field that can be added to node type, thereby allowing a View to be embedded in a node display just like any other field.

See also

Views can also be embedded within Panels as detailed in the *Chapter 12, Rapid Layouts with Panels* recipe, *Embedding content in a Panel*.

Overriding the Views table style format

In this recipe, we will override the Views template used to render table styles. In particular, we will be overriding the standard table used to display the **Tracker** View in order to allow the spanning of rows of the same node type.

Getting ready

The Views module comes with a default View named Tracker which provides the same functionality as the Tracker module by providing a table listing nodes that the current user has either created or participated in. This View can be enabled from the Views administration page at `admin/structure/views` [**Home | Administration | Structure | Views**]. If it has already been modified, it might be best to revert the view to its default settings prior to continuing.

As we will be overriding template files in this recipe, we will be making use of the myzen theme created earlier in this book.

How to do it...

The **Tracker** View, once enabled, provides a table of pertinent content as shown in the following screenshot, which can be accessed at the URL `tracker`:

Recent posts

Type	Title	Author	Replies	Last Post ▾
Product	Product 08	Karthik		Thu, 09/08/2011 - 02:46
Product	Product 07	Karthik		Thu, 09/08/2011 - 02:46
Product	Product 06	Karthik		Thu, 09/08/2011 - 02:45
Product	Product 05	Karthik		Tue, 09/06/2011 - 13:12
Product	Product 04	Karthik		Tue, 09/06/2011 - 13:10
Product	Product 03	Karthik		Tue, 09/06/2011 - 13:10
Product	Product 02	Karthik		Tue, 09/06/2011 - 13:08
Product	Product 01	Karthik		Tue, 09/06/2011 - 13:07
Story	Hos Uxor	Anonymous	7	Thu, 08/11/2011 - 19:17
Blog entry	Caecus Lobortis Magna Saepius	Karthik	12	Thu, 08/11/2011 - 19:17
Blog entry	Elit Macto Obruo Refoveo	bar	1	Thu, 08/11/2011 - 19:17

Looking at the markup of a typical row as displayed in the following block of code, we can see that each row contains a `td` element which specifies the node type of the row. We can also see in the previous screenshot that the **Type** for multiple rows is often the same and is rather needlessly repeated.

```
<tr class="odd views-row-first">
  <td class="views-field views-field-type">Product</td>

  <td class="views-field views-field-title">
    <a href="/node/882">Product 08</a></td>
  <td class="views-field views-field-name">
    <a class="username" title="View user profile."
      href="/user/1">Karthik</a></td>
  <td class="views-field views-field-comment-count"></td>
  <td class="views-field views-field-last-comment-timestamp
    active">Thu, 09/08/2011 - 02:46</td>
</tr>
```

We are going to look at overriding the template used to display this table so that multiple rows with the same node type are replaced by a single field spanning multiple rows.

While we would normally use the Theme developer module to analyze the template structure used in rendering the table, the Views module provides a more straightforward alternative. The default template can be overridden by following these steps:

1. Browse to the Views administration page at `admin/structure/views` [**Home | Administration | Structure | Views**].

2. Locate the **Tracker** View and click on its **Edit** link.

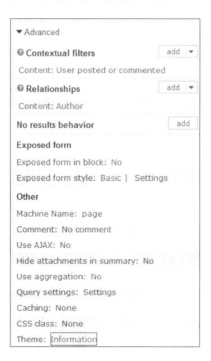

3. Within the display's **Advanced** fieldset, click on the **Theme: Information** link seen in the previous screenshot. This should display a list of templates and candidate template names used to render the View and each of its fields.

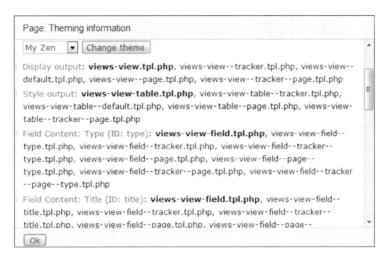

4. Click on the **Style output** link seen in the preceding screenshot to obtain the default template code for this template. It should be similar to the following:

```php
<?php
/**
 * @file views-view-table.tpl.php
 * Template to display a view as a table.
 *
 * - $title : The title of this group of rows.  May be empty.
 * - $header: An array of header labels keyed by field id.
 * - $header_classes: An array of header classes keyed by field
 * id.
 * - $fields: An array of CSS IDs to use for each field id.
 * - $class: A class or classes to apply to the table, based on
 * settings.
 * - $row_classes: An array of classes to apply to each row,
 * indexed by row.
 *   number. This matches the index in $rows.
 * - $rows: An array of row items. Each row is an array of
 * content.
 *   $rows are keyed by row number, fields within rows are keyed
 * by field ID.
 * - $field_classes: An array of classes to apply to each field,
 * indexed by
 *   field id, then row number. This matches the index in $rows.
 * @ingroup views_templates
```

```
      */
   ?>
   <table <?php if ($classes) { print 'class="'. $classes . '" '; }
     ?><?php print $attributes; ?>>
     <?php if (!empty($title)) : ?>
       <caption><?php print $title; ?></caption>
     <?php endif; ?>
     <thead>
       <tr>
         <?php foreach ($header as $field => $label): ?>
           <th <?php if ($header_classes[$field])
             { print 'class="'. $header_classes[$field] . '" '; } ?>>
             <?php print $label; ?>
           </th>
         <?php endforeach; ?>
       </tr>
     </thead>
     <tbody>
       <?php foreach ($rows as $count => $row): ?>
     <tr class="<?php print implode(' ', $row_classes[$count]); ?>">
       <?php foreach ($row as $field => $content): ?>
         <td <?php if ($field_classes[$field][$count])
           { print 'class="'. $field_classes[$field][$count] . '" ';
           } ?><?php print drupal_attributes
           ($field_attributes[$field][$count]); ?>>
           <?php print $content; ?>
         </td>
       <?php endforeach; ?>
     </tr>

       <?php endforeach; ?>
     </tbody>
   </table>
```

The code that we just saw confirms that this template is the one which is responsible for the markup used for displaying the table. The highlighted lines indicate the code that we will be looking to modify to our needs.

5. Copy the entire block of code to the clipboard.

6. Click on the **Back to Theming** information link at the top of the pop-up window to get back to the template file list.

7. Out of the available candidate template file names assigned to the **Style output** template, choose **views-view-table--tracker--page.tpl.php** which by specifically targeting the table style for the **Tracker** View is the most suitable for our case.

8. In the local filesystem, browse to the `myzen theme` folder at `sites/all/themes/myzen`.

9. Navigate into its `templates` subfolder.

10. Create a new file with the chosen candidate filename: `views-view-table--tracker--page.tpl.php`.

11. Open this file in an editor and paste the code copied earlier into it.

>
> Alternatively, we could have also copied the file `views-view-table.tpl.php` from the Views module's theme folder at `sites/all/modules/views/theme` and pasted it into the myzen theme's `templates` folder, and subsequently renamed it to `views-view-table--tracker--page.tpl.php`.

12. Amend the code as per the highlighted segments so that the file now looks similar to the following:

```php
<?php
/**
 * @file views-view-table.tpl.php
 * Template to display a view as a table.
 *
 * - $title : The title of this group of rows.  May be empty.
 * - $header: An array of header labels keyed by field id.
 * - $header_classes: An array of header classes keyed by field
 * id.
 * - $fields: An array of CSS IDs to use for each field id.
 * - $class: A class or classes to apply to the table, based on
 * settings.
 * - $row_classes: An array of classes to apply to each row,
 * indexed by row.
 *    number. This matches the index in $rows.
 * - $rows: An array of row items. Each row is an array of
 * content.
 *    $rows are keyed by row number, fields within rows are keyed
 * by field ID.
 * - $field_classes: An array of classes to apply to each field,
 * indexed by
 *    field id, then row number. This matches the index in $rows.
 * @ingroup views_templates
 */
// Calculate rowspans and store in an array.
// This code should ideally be inside a preprocess
// function.
```

```php
      foreach ($rows as $row) {
        // Initialize tracking variables.
        if (!isset($groups)) {
          $groups = array();
          $current = $row['type'];
          $count = 0;
          $total = 0;
        }

        if ($row['type'] == $current) {
          $count++;
        }
        else {
          $current = $row['type'];
          $groups[$total] = $count;
          $total += $count;
          $count = 1;
        }
      }
      $groups[$total] = $count;

?>
<table <?php if ($classes) { print 'class="'. $classes . '" '; }
  ?><?php print $attributes; ?>>
  <?php if (!empty($title)) : ?>
    <caption><?php print $title; ?></caption>
  <?php endif; ?>
  <thead>
    <tr>
      <?php foreach ($header as $field => $label): ?>
        <th <?php if ($header_classes[$field])
        { print 'class="'.$header_classes[$field] . '" '; } ?>>
          <?php print $label; ?>
        </th>
      <?php endforeach; ?>
    </tr>
  </thead>
  <tbody>
    <?php foreach ($rows as $count => $row): ?>
   <tr class="<?php print implode(' ', $row_classes[$count]); ?>">
     <?php foreach ($row as $field => $content):
        // Only group the type column.
        if ($field == 'type'):
```

```
        // Add rowspan attribute only if the current
        // row is the first of a series. If not, do not
        // display any content.
        if (isset($groups[$count])): ?>
          <td class="views-field views-field-<?php print
            $fields[$field]; ?>"
            rowspan="<?php print $groups[$count]; ?>">
            <?php print $content; ?>
          </td>
        <?php endif; ?>
      <?php else: ?>
        <td class="views-field views-field-<?php print
          $fields[$field]; ?>">
          <?php print $content; ?>
        </td>
      <?php endif; ?>
    <?php endforeach; ?>
  </tr>

    <?php endforeach; ?>
  </tbody>
</table>
```

13. Save the file and exit the editor.

14. Back in the browser, click on **Rescan template files** at the bottom of the **Theming information** section. This is the equivalent of clearing Drupal's cache which should be performed as a matter of course whenever template files are newly introduced or removed.

15. Note that **views-view-table--tracker--page.tpl.php** is now in bold next to the **Style output** link as shown in the following screenshot:

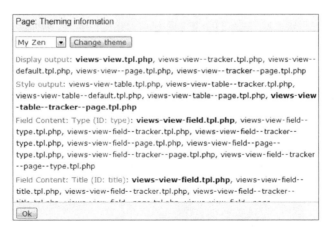

16. Click on the **OK** button.

17. Click the **Save** button to save any changes to the View.

How it works...

Refreshing the tracker page should now display a cleaner representation of its contents with node types occupying multiple rows as in the following screenshot:

Recent posts

Type	Title	Author	Replies	Last Post ▾
	Product 08	Karthik		Thu, 09/08/2011 - 02:46
	Product 07	Karthik		Thu, 09/08/2011 - 02:46
	Product 06	Karthik		Thu, 09/08/2011 - 02:45
Product	Product 05	Karthik		Tue, 09/06/2011 - 13:12
	Product 04	Karthik		Tue, 09/06/2011 - 13:10
	Product 03	Karthik		Tue, 09/06/2011 - 13:10
	Product 02	Karthik		Tue, 09/06/2011 - 13:08
	Product 01	Karthik		Tue, 09/06/2011 - 13:07
Story	Hos Uxor	Anonymous	7	Thu, 08/11/2011 - 19:17
	Caecus Lobortis Magna Saepius	Karthik	12	Thu, 08/11/2011 - 19:17
Blog entry	Elit Macto Obruo Refoveo	bar	1	Thu, 08/11/2011 - 19:17

Looking at the PHP used in the template file, we can see that we made two passes through the `$rows` array. The first iteration was expressly used to analyze the node type of each row and to create the `$groups` array which was used to keep track of contiguous blocks of identical node types. Using this information in the second iteration, we selectively displayed the type only once for each of these contiguous blocks and through the use of the `rowspan` attribute achieved our grouping effect.

See also

When none of the available styles is able to fulfill our requirements, we will have no other recourse except in *Creating a custom Views style format plugin*, the final recipe in this chapter.

Creating a custom Views style plugin

Views style plugins such as tables and lists are used to render the View in a variety of display formats. The inbuilt plugins are often all that are needed for basic displays and the ability to override their template files through the theme tends to be a straightforward answer for most customization requirements. However, more complex display scenarios, especially those that are frequently reused, necessitate a better solution – a custom style plugin.

In this recipe, we will create a custom style plugin which will render a View as an HTML definition list and use it to display a list of taxonomy terms along with their descriptions.

Getting ready

Create a View named **Definitions** to display taxonomy terms with two of their fields, the term name and the term description, and optionally also takes the vocabulary ID as an argument as shown in the following screenshot:

As shown in the previous screenshot, the display has been made accessible at the URL definitions.

We will be using the mysite module created earlier in this book to hold our custom Views style plugin.

How to do it...

Browse to the mysite module folder at sites/all/modules/mysite and perform the following steps:

1. Open the file mysite.module in an editor and add the following code which declares to the Views module that we are going to be specifying some customizations from within a folder named views:

```
/**
 * Implements hook_views_api().
 */
```

```
function mysite_views_api() {
  return array(
    'api' => 3.0,
    'path' => drupal_get_path('module', 'mysite') . '/views'
  );
}
```

2. Save the file and exit the editor.

3. Next, open `mysite.info` and add the following lines to it to ensure that our plugin files are loaded by Drupal:

```
files[] = views/mysite.views.inc
files[] = views/views_plugin_style_dlist.inc
```

4. Save the file and exit the editor.

5. Create a folder named `views`.

6. Within it, create four files named `dlist.views.theme.inc`, `mysite. views.inc`, `views_plugin_style_dlist.inc`, and `views-view-dlist .tpl.php` respectively.

 The term `dlist`—short for definition list—in the previous filenames indicates the internal name for our new plugin.

7. Add the following PHP which declares our new plugin to the file `mysite.views.inc`:

```
/**
 * Implements hook_views_plugins().
 */
function mysite_views_plugins() {
  return array(
    'style' => array(
      'dlist' => array(
        'title' => t('Definition list'),
        'type' => 'normal',
        'path' => drupal_get_path('module', 'mysite') . '/views',
        'handler' => 'views_plugin_style_dlist',
        'uses fields' => TRUE,
        'uses row plugin' => FALSE,
        'uses options' => TRUE,
        'uses grouping' => FALSE,
        'theme' => 'views_view_dlist',
        'theme path' => drupal_get_path('module', 'mysite') .
          '/views',
```

```
            'theme file' => 'dlist.views.theme.inc',
            'help' => t('Render a view as a definition list.')
          )
        )
      );
    }
```

8. Add the following PHP code which adds custom options to our plugin to the file
   `views_plugin_style_dlist.inc`:

```php
/**
 * Style plugin to render each item in a definition list.
 *
 * @ingroup views_style_plugins
 */
class views_plugin_style_dlist extends views_plugin_style {
  function options_form(&$form, &$form_state) {
    parent::options_form($form, $form_state);

    // Create an array of allowed columns.
    $field_names = $this->display->handler->get_field_labels();

    // The term field indicates the definition term.
    $form['term'] = array(
      '#type' => 'select',
      '#title' => t('Term field for the definition list
        &lt;DT&gt;'),
      '#options' => $field_names,
      '#default_value' => $this->options['ter    );

    // The definition field indicates the definition content.
    $form['definition'] = array(
      '#type' => 'select',
      '#title' => t('Definition field for the definition list
        &lt;DD&gt;'),
      '#options' => $field_names,
      '#default_value' => $this->options['definition']
    );
  }
}
```

9. Add the following PHP code which preprocesses the variables made available to the template to the file `dlist.views.theme.inc`:

```
/**
 * Make variables available to the definition list template.
 * file.
 */
function template_preprocess_views_view_dlist(&$vars) {
  template_preprocess_views_view_unformatted($vars);
  // Filter fields to only contain the term and definition.
  $vars['rows'] = $vars['view']->style_plugin->rendered_fields;
}
```

10. Add the following theme markup to the file `views-view-dlist.tpl.php`:

```
<div class="definition-list">
  <?php if (!empty($title)): ?>
    <h3><?php print $title; ?></h3>
  <?php endif; ?>
  <dl>
    <?php foreach ($rows as $id => $row): ?>
      <dt class="views-field views-field-term-<?php print $id;
        ?>">
        <?php print $row[$options['term']]; ?>
      </dt>
      <dd class="views-field views-field-definition-<?php print
        $id; ?>">
        <?php print $row[$options['definition']]; ?>
      </dd>
    <?php endforeach; ?>
  </dl>
</div>
```

This file can eventually be overridden just like any other template file.

11. Save all the files and exit their editors.

12. Rebuild the theme registry by clearing the Drupal cache.

13. Navigate to the Views management page at `admin/structure/views` [**Home | Administration | Structure | Views**].

14. Locate the custom View named **Definitions** and click on its **Edit** link.

15. Edit the displays style setting by clicking on its current style, which is by default set to **Unformatted list**:

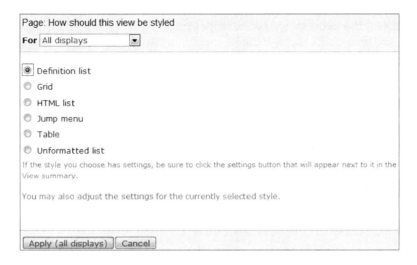

16. Set the style to the newly available **Definition list** option as in the previous screenshot.

17. Click on **Apply (all displays)** which should bring up the style's configuration page.

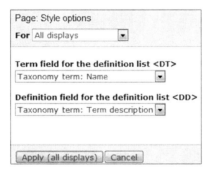

18. As shown in the previous screenshot, set the **Term field for the definition list <DT>** to **Taxonomy term: Name** and the **Definition field for the definition list <DD>** to **Taxonomy term: Term description**.

19. Click on **Apply (all displays)** again.

20. Finally, click on **Save** to save the changes to the View.

How it works...

Accessing the page display at URL `definitions/3` where `3` represents a vocabulary ID should now display the terms for said vocabulary along with their descriptions as a definition list. The following screenshot displays the View with the terms listed first and the definitions indented appropriately below:

Generally speaking, the key to constructing a custom plugin is to declare it correctly. Looking at the declaration of the `dlist` plugin in `mysite_views_plugins()`, we can see that there are a myriad options available to be set as per our requirements:

```
/**
 * Implements hook_views_plugins().
 */
function mysite_views_plugins() {
  return array(
    'style' => array(
      'dlist' => array(
        'title' => t('Definition list'),
        'type' => 'normal',
        'path' => drupal_get_path('module', 'mysite') . '/views',
        'handler' => 'views_plugin_style_dlist',
        'uses fields' => TRUE,
        'uses row plugin' => FALSE,
        'uses options' => TRUE,
        'uses grouping' => FALSE,
```

```
          'theme' => 'views_view_dlist',
          'theme path' => drupal_get_path('module', 'mysite') .
            '/views',
          'theme file' => 'dlist.views.theme.inc',
          'help' => t('Render a view as a definition list.')
        )
      )
    );
  }
```

For example, we have set the `path` and `theme path` values to point to the `views` folder within the `mysite` module as that is where we have located our files. We have also indicated that the plugin `uses fields` from the View and also `uses options` to specify the term and definition fields to be used during output.

More information on the plugin API can be gleaned from the Views documentation which can be accessed by installing the `Advanced Help` module. Furthermore, browsing through the code pertaining to the inbuilt plugins tends to be very educational as well. These files can be found within the Views module's `plugins` and `theme` subfolders.

12
Rapid Layouts with Panels

We will be covering the following recipes in this chapter:

- Using Panels to create a front-page layout
- Embedding content in a panel
- Styling a panel with rounded corners
- Creating custom styles with the Stylizer module
- Changing the layout of a panel
- Creating a custom panel layout
- Replacing the site contact page with a panel

Introduction

The Panels module is, at its heart, a visual tool for layout design. Layered on top of this core is a sometimes overwhelming myriad of features and suite of modules that give a new meaning to flexibility and ease of use. In this chapter, we will be concentrating on the layout and theming aspects of this module.

Panels are useful for everything from creating complex landing pages such as the front page of a site, to overriding system pages and replacing them with a custom layout. Besides being used to lay out the content of a page, they can just as easily be embedded within nodes or even within other panels. This enables us to design and implement intricate layouts virtually at the click of a few buttons:

The previous screenshot illustrates a typical panel layout. In this screenshot, **Top**, **Left side**, **Right side**, and **Bottom** all represent regions within the panel. Each region can contain an unlimited number of panes which are not restricted in what they can contain. For example, the **Top** region contains two panes named **Site slogan** and **Welcome message**, which as their names suggest, display the site slogan and a custom welcome message. On the other hand, the panes within the **Left side** region contain two nodes in teaser form. Lastly, the **Right side** region contains a **View** that mimics the functionality of the Tracker module.

The layout designer supports dragging and dropping panes from one region to another and within the same region. In other words, reordering or reorganizing the content within a layout becomes a painless exercise. The content itself can be chosen from a variety of sources. For example, in the previous screenshot, we have embedded site elements, nodes, custom content, and even a view.

Panels also come with style plugins which can be applied to entire regions or to individual panes. Furthermore, we can tweak region and pane properties such as their CSS classes to assist during any additional theming or for use by JavaScript.

All in all, Panels are a lot of fun as the recipes that follow will demonstrate!

The version of Panels covered in this chapter is *7.x-3.0-dev*, the latest development release after *alpha3* at the time of writing. The interface for future releases of the *7.x-3* branch should hopefully be largely unchanged.

Using Panels to create a front-page layout

Panels are useful in a variety of scenarios. But, their most common use is in implementing complex front page designs which draw input from a number of sources and attempt to display them in a coherent layout.

In this recipe, we will look at using Panels to create a basic front-page layout.

Getting ready

It is assumed that the Panels module and its dependencies, which include the Chaos tools and the Page manager modules, are installed and enabled. The Panels module controls access to its features via the Permissions page at `admin/people/permissions` [**Home | Administration | People | Permissions**]. In cases where the Panels administrator is not logged in as user ID 1, it is assumed that relevant permissions for the Panels module are assigned appropriately.

How to do it...

The following steps are performed on the Panels management page at `admin/structure/panels` [**Home | Administration | Structure | Panels**].

1. Under the **Page Wizards** heading, click on **Landing Page**.
2. In the **Landing page wizard** form, set the **Administrative title** to `Frontpage dashboard`.
3. If the title is not sufficiently indicative of the type of panel we are creating, add a description in the **Administrative description** textarea.

4. Configure the URL where the panel is to be accessible by setting the **Path** to `dashboard` as shown in the following screenshot:

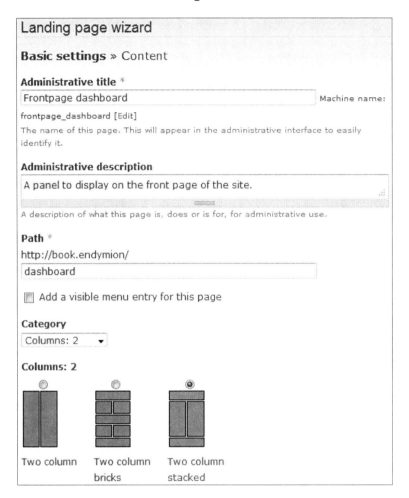

5. If need be, add a menu entry for this landing page. Front pages usually do not require this option as the Home links tend to suffice.

6. Within the layout **Category** drop down, choose **Columns: 2.**

The Builder category allows us to create our own layouts as we will see later on in this chapter. The other categories are layout groups provided either by the Panels module or by way of plugins registered by other modules or themes.

7. From the available layouts, select the one titled **Two column stacked**, which is a simpe and yet flexible layout.

8. Click on the **Continue** button.

9. On the next step, set the **Title type** to **No title** as our front page requires no title:

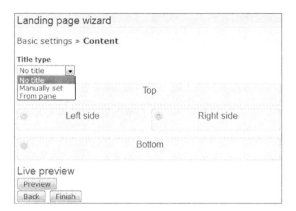

10. Click on the **Finish** button as displayed in the previous screenshot to save our changes.

11. Revisit the **Panels administration** page at `admin/structure/panels` [**Home | Administration | Structure | Panels**] and locate our newly created panel, `Frontpage dashboard`, in the **Manage Pages** table and click on its **Edit** link.

12. In the resulting interface, click on the **General** tab on the left.

13. As the next screenshot depicts, check the **Disable Drupal blocks/regions** option as we would like our front page to be devoid of any extraneous information:

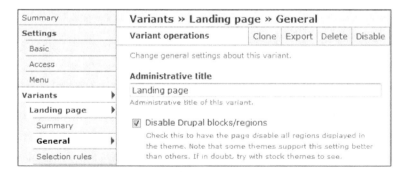

14. Click on the **Update and save** button to register our change.

15. To set our new panel up as the front page of the site, visit `admin/config/system/site-information` [**Home | Administration | Configuration | System | Site information**].

16. As shown in the next screenshot, set the value for the **Default front page** textfield to dashboard:

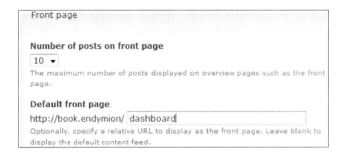

> **Front page**
>
> **Number of posts on front page**
>
> 10 ▾
>
> The maximum number of posts displayed on overview pages such as the front page.
>
> **Default front page**
>
> http://book.endymion/ dashboard
>
> Optionally, specify a relative URL to display as the front page. Leave blank to display the default content feed.

17. Click on the **Save configuration** button.

How it works...

The **Content** tab of the **Panel management** page should now look something like this:

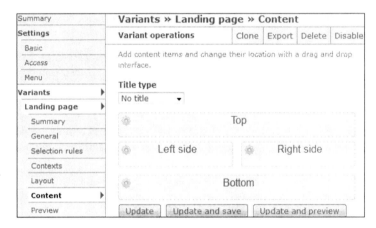

We can confirm that the regions conform to the chosen two-column stacked design. Each of **Top**, **Left side**, **Right side**, and **Bottom** are the regions of the panel layout that can each contain one or more panes added by way of the configuration icons available in the form of gears pinned to the top left of each region.

Browsing to the front page of the site or the URL dashboard should now display a valid, albeit empty page, with empty sidebars as we have chosen to hide our blocks for this layout.

See also

If we are not content with the layout chosen for a panel, we can either look at the *Changing the layout of a panel* recipe or, alternatively, at the *Creating a custom panel layout* recipe. Once we are comfortable with the layout, we can look to add content to our panel as per the next recipe, *Embedding content in a panel*.

Embedding content in a panel

Now that we have a layout ready for our front page panel, we can look into adding content to it. In this recipe, we will be embedding the site's slogan and other elements to the various regions of the `frontpage_dashboard` panel.

Getting ready

We are going to be using the `frontpage_dashboard` panel created in the previous recipe. As we will be using the site's slogan as a field, it is expected that it is filled in through the **Site information** page at `admin/config/system/site-information` [**Home | Administration | Configuration | System | Site information**].

The **Views** module interacts with **Panels** through an intermediary named **Views content panes**. If we would like to embed **Views** within our panes, then this module will also need to be enabled.

How to do it...

Visit the **Panels administration** page at `admin/structure/panels` [**Home | Administration | Structure | Panels**] and locate our newly created panel, Frontpage dashboard, in the **Pages** list and click on its **Edit** link. In the ensuing interface, perform the following steps:

1. On the **Panel management** page, click on the **Content** tab on the left.

2. The two-column stacked layout should now be visible with four regions – **Top**, **Left side**, **Right side**, and **Bottom** – each with its own configuration icon in the form of a gear. Click on the configuration icon for the top region.

3. In the context menu that appears, click on **Add content**:

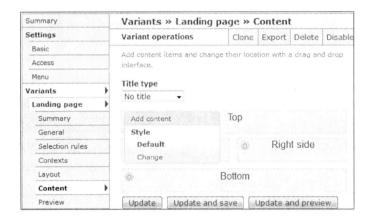

4. In the resulting pop up, select the **Page elements** tab on the left.

5. As shown in the following screenshot, click on **Site slogan** which should, predictably, add the site's slogan to the **Top** region as a pane:

6. Back in the **Content** page, click on **Update and preview** to preview our changes.

7. Once satisfied, click on the **Update and save** button to save our changes.

8. Repeat the previous steps to add other content to the other regions of this panel as necessary.

How it works...

Visiting the front page should now display the slogan of the site as content within the **Top** region. The following screenshot demonstrates the `frontpage_dashboard` panel with a number of panes added to its regions using steps similar to the ones we followed here. The site's slogan, as per this recipe, is a pane in its **Top** region, a view displaying a list of recent activity is a pane in the **Right side** region, and two nodes have been inserted as separate panes inside the **Left side** region. Additionally, the **Bottom** region contains the standard contact form provided by the Contact module:

Reorganizing the Panel

Panes within a Panel can be reorganized by dragging and dropping them at will either within or between regions.

There's more...

Just as with a Panel region, the panes within each region come with their own configuration icon that can be used to configure them further.

Editing existing content

Just like configuration icons exist for each region, each content pane can be configured by clicking on its own configuration icon which is also a gear residing on the right-hand side of the pane. Configuration options include editing CSS properties such as ID and class values of the pane, styling and performance options, and a whole lot more as shown in the following screenshot:

Views support for Panels

Views support for the Panels module can be achieved by enabling the Views content panes module which is a part of the Chaos tools suite. Once enabled, available views can be added and configured through the Panel region's configuration pop up.

If the **Views** option is unavailable even after the **Views content panes** module has been enabled, visit the **Panel modules configuration** page at admin/ structure/panels/settings [**Home | Administration | Structure | Panels | Settings**]. Under the **General** tab, ensure that the **Make all views available as panes** option is checked. Furthermore, click on the **Panel pages** tab at the top and ensure that the **New View Panes** and **New All Views** checkboxes are also enabled. Empty the Drupal cache in cases where the Views module was installed after Panels.

See also

The Panels module is commonly used in tandem with the Views module, a combination that allows developers to easily manage the presentation of our content. The Views module is covered in detail in *Chapter 11, Views Theming*.

Styling a panel with rounded corners

With our layout created and content added, we can look at using the Panel module's style plugins to pretty things up a little bit. In this recipe, we will be styling the Slogan pane created earlier in this chapter by containing it within a box with rounded corners.

Getting ready

We will be working with the frontpage_dashboard panel created earlier in this chapter and it is assumed that a Slogan pane has been added as per the previous recipe.

How to do it...

All Page panels are listed in the **Page manager** table at admin/structure/pages [**Home | Administration | Structure | Pages**]. Locate the **Frontpage dashboard** panel and click on its **Edit** link to perform the following steps:

1. In the resulting **Panel management** interface, click on the **Content** tab on the left.

2. In the **content layout** page, click on the configuration icon for the **Top** region.

3. Click on the **Change** link in the resulting context menu as shown in the following screenshot:

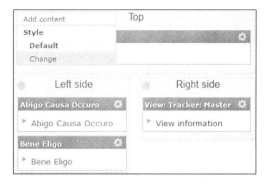

4. In the **Panel style** pop up, select **Rounded corners** from the list of available styles:

5. Click on the **Next** button.

6. In the **Box around** drop down, select **Each region** as we want the entire region to be encased in a box with rounded corners. In cases where multiple panes are contained within the region, we might need to choose **Each pane** instead:

7. Click on the **Save** button.

8. Back on the **content layout** page, click on **Update and save** to save our changes.

9. Repeat this process for each **Panel** region as necessary.

10. Refresh the site's front page in a browser to confirm that our new style settings have taken effect.

How it works...

The following screenshot demonstrates the front page panel with its regions and panes styled with the rounded corners effect:

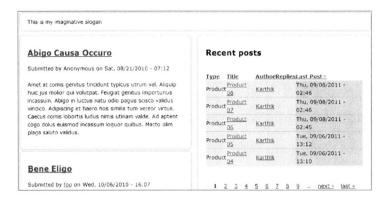

The effect is provided by a Panels style plugin which injects its own markup when the pane or region is set to be output. The plugin also includes its own CSS file and images to create the rounded corners effect.

There's more...

Just as we styled a panel region, we can also similarly style individual panes.

Styling individual panes

While we have looked at how we can apply styles to regions and all panes within a region, individual panes can also be styled similarly through their configuration screens as shown in the following screenshot:

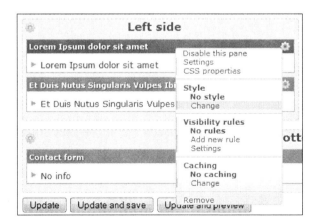

See also

In situations where the inbuilt styles do not suffice, we can choose to roll our own. The next recipe, *Creating custom styles with the Stylizer module*, explains how.

Creating custom styles with the Stylizer module

While we learned how to apply styles to panel regions and panes earlier in this chapter, this recipe will outline how we can utilize the **Stylizer** module to easily create and apply our own custom styles. We will create a style using Stylizer and apply it to the Slogan pane which is part of the Frontpage dashboard panel we have been working on thus far in this chapter.

Getting ready

Stylizer comes with the Chaos tools group of modules and is assumed to have been enabled along with its dependencies, chief among which is the Color module. The module exposes a permission named **Use the Stylizer UI** which is required to add and manage our custom styles.

While we will be using the Frontpage dashboard panel created earlier in this chapter as an example panel to implement our styles, it is not a prerequisite. This recipe can be easily adapted to work with any available pane.

How to do it...

The Stylizer module enables us to create styles particular to panel regions and panes. These styles can either be created on-the-fly from region or pane configuration screens, or as recommended in the following steps, created through the Stylizer management interface and then applied to the regions and panes as appropriate:

1. Navigate to **Stylizer management** page at `admin/structure/stylizer` [**Home | Administration | Structure | Stylizer**].
2. Click on the **Add link** at the top of the page.

3. In the resulting page give our new style a title—Prominence in this case—and description as seen in the following screenshot:

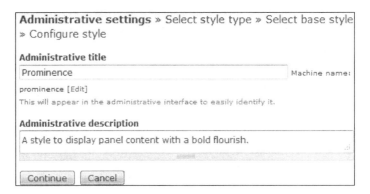

4. Click on the **Continue** button.

5. In the next step, choose **Panel pane** in the **Type** drop down as we want to apply this style to panes rather than panels.

6. Click on the **Continue** button to proceed to the next step.

7. Select the **Rounded shadow box** style as seen in the next screenshot and click on **Continue**:

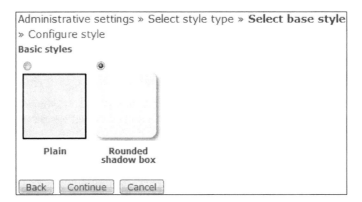

8. In the next page, use the Color module's color form to choose the scheme for the pane and the font and padding fieldsets for additional styling. The values for the Slogan pane can be seen in the following screenshot:

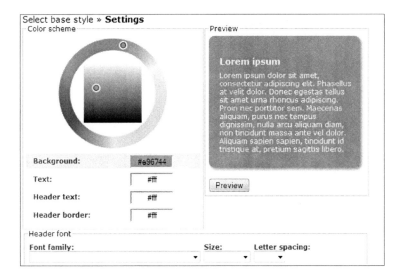

As the Slogan pane does not have a header field, these fields can be left as it is.

9. Use the **Preview** button to preview the new style using the provided sample of text.

10. Finally, click on the **Finish** button to save the style.

    Now that we have created the style, we can use it to style our panel panes.

11. Browse to our Frontpage dashboard panel's administration page and click on the **Content** tab on the left side.

12. Click on the configuration icon of the Slogan pane and in the ensuing context menu, click on **Change** under the **Style** menu as shown in the following screenshot:

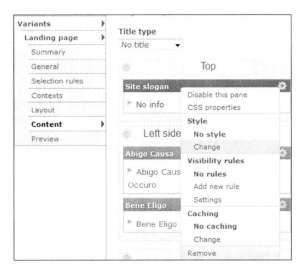

13. In the resulting pop up, select **Prominence** and click on **Next** as shown in the following screenshot:

14. Back in the **Panel management** page, click on **Update and Save** to save our changes.

15. Refresh the site's front page to confirm that the new style has taken effect.

How it works...

In this recipe, we have created and applied a pane style named **Prominence** to the Mission pane. This transforms what was a simple line of text into a block with rounded corners, a drop-shadow, modified background and foreground colors, text alignment, font styling, and if need be, a lot more. The end result is demonstrated in the following screenshot:

There's more...

The Stylizer module can be very effective when styling both regions and panes. Furthermore, updating the Stylizer preset will automatically also update the styles of associated regions and panes.

Stylizer for regions/panels and panes

The Stylizer module allows us to create specific styles for panel regions and panes. As their names suggest, region styles affect entire panel regions whereas pane styles affect individual panes. In the following screenshot, we can see the **Slogan** pane styled with the `Prominence` style situated within the `Top` region which is unstyled. Below it, we can see the `Left` region styled with a region style and two panes within which are both styled individually with pane styles:

See also

While we look at creating a custom style in this recipe, the previous recipe, *Styling a panel with rounded corners*, lists the steps required to style a panel using one of the default styles.

Changing the layout of a panel

Plans are seldom perfect and during the development of a site, there is an inevitable stage where things are chopped and changed leading to a lot of wasted time and effort. The Panels module, however, eases these concerns making nudges, tweaks, and even large-scale modifications relatively pain free.

In this recipe, we will be looking at changing the entire layout of a Panel from a Two column stacked layout to a Two column bricks layout which provides us with more regions. As we are effectively adding three more regions, we will see how the module allows us to intelligently merge the content from one set of regions to another.

Getting ready

We will be using the `frontpage_dashboard` layout created earlier in this chapter to serve as an example panel in this recipe.

How to do it...

Navigate to `admin/structure/pages` [**Home | Administration | Structure | Pages**] and locate the **Frontpage dashboard** panel. Click on its **Edit** link to perform the following steps:

1. Click on the **Layout** tab on the left:

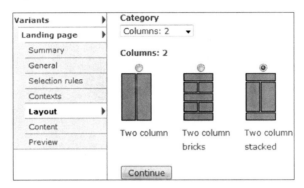

2. As shown in the preceding screenshot, change the layout from the **Two column stacked** layout to the **Two column bricks** layout.

3. Click on **Continue**.

   The next screen provides us with an opportunity to migrate content from our existing layout to the new layout which might not retain a similar structure. In this case, we are moving from a layout with four regions to one with seven regions.

4. In the following screenshot, we can see that are seven distinct destination regions namely **Top**, **Middle**, **Bottom**, **Left above**, **Right above**, **Left below**, and, **Right below**. All the content from the original **Bottom**, **Left side**, **Right side**, and **Top** regions can be mapped, migrated, and even merged into each of these regions as appropriate:

5. Click on **Update and save** to complete the migration.

6. Back in the **Panel management** page, confirm that our layout is now a **Two column bricks** layout.

How it works...

Layout migration is a painless procedure that allows us to make changes at will without losing any of the styles or customizations applied to panes. This is done by mapping old regions to new regions and simply changing their region values accordingly in the database. Panels also intelligently only offers to migrate regions that are populated with content panes.

In the next screenshot, we can see that the new Two column bricks layout has now been activated and all the panes from the four original regions have been migrated and three new empty regions are now available for use:

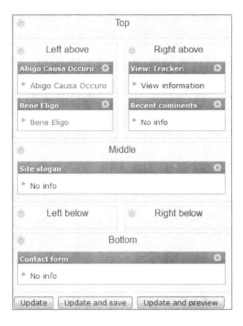

See also

The first recipe in this chapter titled *Using Panels to create a front-page layout*, details the steps required to create a panel using one of the inbuilt layouts. On the other hand, the next recipe, *Creating a custom panel layout*, explains how we can create our own layouts if the default options do not suffice.

Creating a custom panel layout

The myriad layouts that the Panels module comes packaged with are usually sufficient for most requirements. That said, themers wanting to display content using more interesting and complex layouts can also roll their own. While it used to be the case that custom panel layouts needed to be added in as a plugin, this is no longer necessary.

In this recipe, we will make use of the Panel module's Layout designer to create our own custom layout designed for a page requiring a lot of regions.

Getting ready

It is a good idea to sketch an outline of our layout either on paper or in a graphics editor to get an idea of what we want prior to fiddling with the Layout designer. For example, the layout that we are looking to create in this recipe will be based on the rudimentary sketch in the next screenshot which was created using Microsoft Paint:

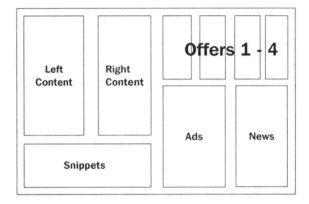

How to do it...

Create an empty Panel page named **Blurbs** with particular care taken to choose **Flexible** (which should be the default option under the **Builders** category) as its layout during creation. Once this layout has been selected, we gain access to the Layout designer and can create our layout as follows:

1. Navigate to the **Blurbs panel management** page and click on its **Content** tab.
2. Click on the **Show layout designer** button which should be visible above the region titled **Center** as in the following screenshot:

3. Click on the **Region** link which contains the **Center** region and select **Region settings**.

> Note the presence of the **Remove region** option which will come in handy while reworking the layout, if necessary.

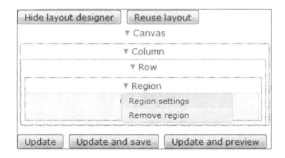

4. In the region configuration pop up, set the **Region title** to **Snippets**.

5. Optionally, add a class to enable easy access to the region from CSS or JavaScript:

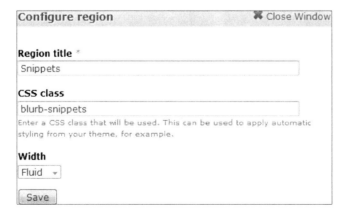

6. Click on the **Save** button to save our changes.

7. Back in the designer, click on the **Column** link and select **Add row on top**.

8. In the **Add row** pop up, select **Columns** in the **Contains** drop down and click **Save**.

9. Click on the newly created row and select **Add column**.

10. In the **Add column** pop up, set the value of the **Width** drop down to **Fluid** and click on **Save**.

11. Repeat this process to add a second column to the right which should result in our layout looking like the following screenshot:

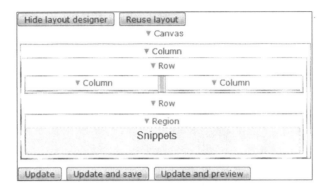

Note the presence of the resize handle between the two columns which allow us to adjust their width, if required.

12. Click on the newly created **Column** link on the left and click on **Add row**.

13. This time, however, select **Regions** in the **Add row** pop up and click on **Save**.

14. Click on the newly created row and select **Add region**.

15. In the resulting pop up, set the **Region** title to **Left content**.

16. Set the **Width** to **Fluid** and click on **Save**.

17. Similarly, add a row and a region named **Right content** to the second column as well which should result in our layout looking like the following screenshot:

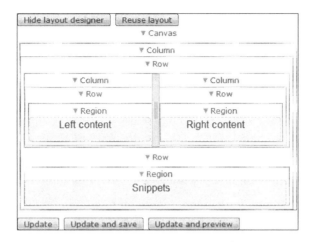

 It is a good idea to **Update and save** our progress after any significant changes have been made to the layout.

18. Now that we have the first column from our sketched layout up and running, we can create the second column by clicking on the **Canvas** link and selecting **Add column to right**.

19. In the resulting pop up, set the **Width** to **Fluid** and click on **Save**.

20. As we did earlier, add two rows to the column which are set to contain regions.

21. In the top row, add four regions named **Offers 1**, **Offers 2**, **Offers 3**, and **Offers 4** so that the layout now looks like the following screenshot:

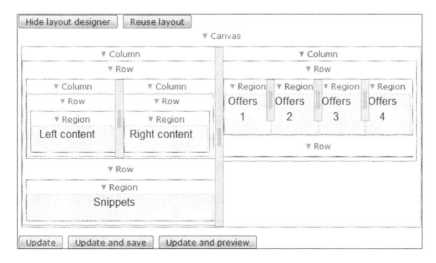

22. In the bottom row, create two regions named **Ads** and **News** respectively so that our layout now resembles the following screenshot:

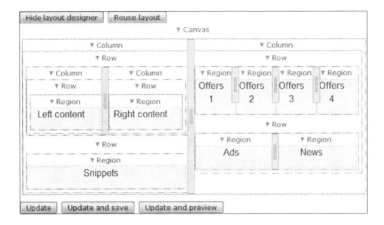

23. Finally, click on **Update and save** to create our custom layout.

How it works...

Looking at our newly created panel from the **Content** tab of the **Panel manager** with the **Layout designer** switched off results in a layout as shown in the following screenshot:

The Layout designer uses a JavaScript-based frontend to allow the user to design the layout. Once done, the specifics of the layout are saved in the Drupal database and loaded during runtime to provide us with our layout. The layouts that come with Panels are, on the other hand, stored as code.

The PHP representation of our new layout can be viewed by clicking on the **Export** link at the top of the **Panel management** page. For our more involved endeavors, it might be worth exporting our layout into a module, especially in situations where we might want to reuse the layout elsewhere.

There's more...

The Layout designer can take some getting used to and we will initially find ourselves doing a lot of chopping and changing in order to get our layout just right.

Removing regions, rows, and columns

While working with the Layout designer, it is often necessary to remove elements to rework or tweak the layout. This, however, is not always a simple process. The rule of thumb with removing elements in the Panel layout designer is that the element being removed has to be empty. As columns contain rows and rows contain regions, removing a row requires that any regions within it will need to be removed first. Similarly, removing a column requires that any rows contained within it will also need to be removed first, and consequently, all regions within said rows!

See also

While we looked at creating a custom layout in this recipe, the first entry in this chapter, titled *Using Panels to create a front-page layout*, covers the creation of a panel using one of the built-in layouts.

Replacing the site contact page with a panel

The **Contact** module's contact form is, by default, rather static and plain with no straightforward option to add new content or to reorganize it. In this recipe, we will replace the standard contact page with a panel thereby allowing us to take advantage of the power of Panels.

Getting ready

The **Contact** module is assumed to be enabled and configured with a couple of categories. We will be embedding the default contact form in one of our new panel's panes.

To demonstrate how using panels allows us to easily add new content, we will be embedding a view into one of its panes. The view is to be titled **Addresses** and should return a list of custom contact nodes containing sample contact information where the title represents the country and the body represents the contact address within the country. Other fields such as phone and e-mail can also be added.

It is assumed that the sample nodes and view have been created and are available for use by the panel.

How to do it...

The **Page manager** module allows the overriding of specific Drupal pages. These pages are listed along with custom panels on the **Page management** interface accessible at `admin/structure/pages` [**Home | Administration | Structure | Pages**]. The contact page can be overridden by following the next procedure:

1. Locate the entry for the site contact page in the table and enable it by clicking on its **Enable** link:

Type	Name	Title	Path	Storage	Operations
System	term_view	Taxonomy term template	/taxonomy/term/%taxonomy_term	In code	Enable ▼
System	contact_site	Site contact page	/contact	In code	Enable ▲ Edit
System	blog	All blogs	/blog	In code	
System	node_edit	Node add/edit form	/node/%node/edit	In code	Enable ▼
System	user_view	User profile template	/user/%user	In code	Enable ▼
System	node_view	Node template	/node/%node	In code	Enable ▼
Custom 🔒 *page-ptest*	ptest	/ptest	Normal	Enable ▼
Custom	page-frontpage_dashboard	Frontpage dashboard	/dashboard	Normal	Edit ▼
Custom	page-blurbs	Blurbs	/blurbs	Normal	Edit ▼
System	blog_user	User blog	/blog/%user	In code	Enable ▼
System	contact_user	User contact	/user/%user/contact	In code	Enable ▼

2. Once enabled, click on the same entry's **Edit** link.

3. By default, there are no panels available and Drupal uses the standard contact form. To remedy this, let us create one by clicking either on the **Add a new variant** link or the **Add variant** tab at the top.

4. Give the variant a title such as **Contact** or as shown in the next screenshot, **Contact with addresses**:

5. Click on **Create variant**.

6. In the resulting layout page, choose a suitable layout. In our case, a simple **Two column** layout will suffice.

7. Click on the **Continue** button.

8. In the **Panel settings** page, check the **Disable Drupal blocks/regions** option and again, click on the **Continue** button.

9. In the **Panel content** step, set the **Title** type to **No title**.

10. Click on the **Create variant** button.

11. Click on **Save** to complete the creation process.

12. With the variant created, click on its **Content** tab on the left.

13. Access the **Left side** region's configuration icon and choose **Add content**.

14. In the ensuing pop up, click on the **Widgets** tab on the left.

15. Choose the **Contact** form on the right:

16. Click on the **Finish** button on the next page.

17. Similarly, add content to the **Right side** column which, in this case, is the **Addresses** view which returns a list of addresses of offices around the world:

18. Finally, with the layout resembling the preceding screenshot, click on **Update and save** to save our changes.

How it works...

Browsing to the contact form at the URL contact should now display our panel as displayed in the following screenshot:

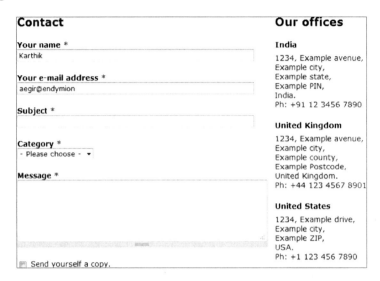

We can see that along with the standard contact form, we now have the **Addresses view** also displayed alongside. As the form as well as the view are both panes, we can now also style them at will.

Index

Thank you for buying
Drupal 7 Theming Cookbook

About Packt Publishing

Packt, pronounced 'packed', published its first book "*Mastering phpMyAdmin for Effective MySQL Management*" in April 2004 and subsequently continued to specialize in publishing highly focused books on specific technologies and solutions.

Our books and publications share the experiences of your fellow IT professionals in adapting and customizing today's systems, applications, and frameworks. Our solution based books give you the knowledge and power to customize the software and technologies you're using to get the job done. Packt books are more specific and less general than the IT books you have seen in the past. Our unique business model allows us to bring you more focused information, giving you more of what you need to know, and less of what you don't.

Packt is a modern, yet unique publishing company, which focuses on producing quality, cutting-edge books for communities of developers, administrators, and newbies alike. For more information, please visit our website: www.packtpub.com.

About Packt Open Source

In 2010, Packt launched two new brands, Packt Open Source and Packt Enterprise, in order to continue its focus on specialization. This book is part of the Packt Open Source brand, home to books published on software built around Open Source licences, and offering information to anybody from advanced developers to budding web designers. The Open Source brand also runs Packt's Open Source Royalty Scheme, by which Packt gives a royalty to each Open Source project about whose software a book is sold.

Writing for Packt

We welcome all inquiries from people who are interested in authoring. Book proposals should be sent to author@packtpub.com. If your book idea is still at an early stage and you would like to discuss it first before writing a formal book proposal, contact us; one of our commissioning editors will get in touch with you.

We're not just looking for published authors; if you have strong technical skills but no writing experience, our experienced editors can help you develop a writing career, or simply get some additional reward for your expertise.

Drupal 7 Module Development

ISBN: 978-1-84951-116-2   Paperback: 420 pages

Create your own Drupal 7 modules from scratch

1. Specifically written for Drupal 7 development

2. Write your own Drupal modules, themes, and libraries

3. Discover the powerful new tools introduced in Drupal 7

4. Learn the programming secrets of six experienced Drupal developers

Drupal 7 Themes

ISBN: 978-1-84951-276-3   Paperback: 320 pages

Create new themes for your Drupal 7 site with a clean layout and powerful CSS styling

1. Learn to create new Drupal 7 themes

2. No experience of Drupal theming required

3. Discover techniques and tools for creating and modifying themes

4. The first book to guide you through the new elements and themes available in Drupal 7

Please check **www.PacktPub.com** for information on our titles

PACKT

PUBLISHING

open source
community experience distilled

Drupal 7
Social Networking

Build a social or community website with friends lists, groups, custom user profiles, and much more

Michael Peacock

PACKT open source

Drupal 7 Social Networking

ISBN: 978-1-84951-600-6   Paperback: 328 pages

Build a social or community website with friends lists, groups, custom user profiles, and much more

1. Step-by-step instructions for putting together a social networking site with Drupal 7

2. Customize your Drupal installation with modules and themes to match the needs of almost any social networking site

3. Allow users to collaborate and interact with each other on your site

4. Requires no prior knowledge of Drupal or PHP; but even experienced Drupal users will find this book useful to modify an existing installation into a social website

Drupal 7 First Look

Learn the new features of Drupal 7, how they work and how they will impact you

Mark Noble

PACKT open source

Drupal 7 First Look

ISBN: 978-1-84951-122-3   Paperback: 288 pages

Learn the new features of Drupal 7, how they work and how they will impact you

1. Get to grips with all of the new features in Drupal 7

2. Upgrade your Drupal 6 site, themes, and modules to Drupal 7

3. Explore the new Drupal 7 administration interface and map your Drupal 6 administration interface to the new Drupal 7 structure

4. Complete coverage of the DBTNG database layer with usage examples and all API changes for both Themes and Modules

Please check **www.PacktPub.com** for information on our titles

CPSIA information can be obtained at www.ICGtesting.com
Printed in the USA
BVOW050304240412

288465BV00003B/9/P